VOCABULARY
& SPELLING SUCCESS

VOCABULARY & SPELLING SUCCESS

IN 20 MINUTES A DAY

3rd Edition

LEARNINGEXPRESS

NEW YORK

Copyright © 2002 LearningExpress, LLC.

All rights reserved under International and Pan-American Copyright Conventions.
Published in the United States by LearningExpress, LLC, New York.

Library of Congress Cataloging-in-Publication Data:
Vocabulary & spelling success.—3rd ed.
    p. cm.
  ISBN 1-57685-401-9 (pbk.)
   1. Vocabulary—Problems, exercises, etc. 2. English language—Orthography and
spelling—Problems, exercises, etc. I. Title: Vocabulary and spelling success.

PE1449 .V58 2002
428.1—dc21

                       2001038953

Printed in the United States of America
9 8 7 6 5
Third Edition

ISBN 1-57685-401-9

For more information or to place an order, contact LearningExpress at:
  55 Broadway
  8th Floor
  New York, NY 10006

Or visit us at:
  www.learnatest.com

LIST OF CONTRIBUTORS

Jessica Beckett-McWalter, a former math and social studies teacher, is currently a law student at University of California, Hastings College of the Law, where she has accepted the Tony Patino fellowship. As former Program Director of Playing to Win, a community technology center in Harlem, she not only directed the organization, she also developed curriculum for adult and youth technology classes, and taught classes. Currently, she lives in San Francisco, California.

Glenn Devine is an English and science teacher in New York. He has taught at both the middle- and high-school levels. He is a graduate of James Madison University in Virginia.

Brooke Jackson teaches high school English at the New York City Lab School. She is also an adjunct instructor and doctoral student in the English Education department at Teachers College, Columbia University.

Wendy Ratner, a freelance writer, has been an educator for the past 26 years. She has taught English from grades 6 through post-high school. She has developed a writing center, written education grants, and served on curriculum advisory councils. She has a Bachelor of Arts in English, a Master of Science in Reading, and a Professional Diploma in School District Administration. Currently, she teaches middle school English in Mastic Beach, New York.

CONTENTS

INTRODUCTION

The words we use to communicate every day are important in every aspect of our lives. From relaxing, to working, to studying, to taking tests, we use words to share with others how we feel, what we think, and why we think that way. Without words, it is difficult to express our ideas to the rest of the world. The more words we know—the larger our vocabulary—the more clearly we can communicate with others. Our vocabularies reveal our knowledge to the world; therefore, a person with a large vocabulary has the advantage of self-expression.

This book will help you learn the words you need to know to successfully express yourself in school, work, and your personal life. The words in this book have been carefully chosen to help you learn important words you need to know to pass any test—from standardized tests, to civil service tests, to college entrance exams, and professional job interviews—and continue to build your vocabulary, even after you have finished using this book.

In each chapter throughout this book, you will complete practice exercises that have been created specifically to help you understand words inside out—from pronunciation, to spelling, to context, definitions, word parts, denotation and connotation, synonyms, and antonyms. The word lists are grouped into categories, so you can associate them with like words and remember them even more easily. There is also a crossword puzzle at the beginning of each chapter to introduce you to new words before you even get down to the practice exercises. Then, you can take the Post-Test at the end of the book and gauge how much you've really learned about words and how you have improved your vocabulary.

HOW TO USE THIS BOOK

BUILD YOUR VOCABULARY

Everyone has three vocabularies in each language that we speak:

- A **speaking** vocabulary—words and expressions we use every day to communicate
- A **listening** vocabulary—words and expressions we have heard but may have never used
- A **reading** vocabulary—words and expressions we have encountered in print but have neither heard, nor used

One of the best ways to increase your vocabulary is to make a conscious effort to move words from your listening or reading vocabularies to your speaking vocabulary—the words you cannot only understand, but also use. This book is especially helpful because the exercises you complete help you *use* your new vocabulary words so you know them cold. Suddenly, you'll find yourself speaking and writing with these new words, and you will also find that reading will become much easier as you begin to recognize more and more words.

Test makers try to assess how well you have absorbed the language of your culture and how well you can use and identify the words you know to both express yourself and understand others who are trying to express themselves. Each lesson in this book will help you prove to test makers and prospective employers alike that you know how to communicate clearly and effectively, and that you understand what others are trying to communicate to you. Once you have learned the vocabulary words and completed the exercises in this book, you'll know what you need to ace your exam or job interview.

WRITE IT DOWN

If this book is yours, write in it as much as you like. Write your answers in the blanks indicated and write notes to yourself in the margins. It is meant for you to consume. Pull out important details from the surrounding text to make them more visible and accessible to you. Underline or highlight information that seems important to you. Make notes in the margins that will help you follow what's important as you practice and learn your new words.

MAKE FLASH CARDS

If you are having trouble remembering words, even after the drills and practice exercises in the book, buy some index cards and make flash cards for yourself. Write the vocabulary word on one side of the card, and then write its definition, synonyms, antonyms, or other essential information on the other side of the card. You can carry the cards with you to review when you have a free moment, on the bus, in study hall, at lunch, or whenever you have a few extra moments.

ASK FOR HELP

Enlist a friend or relative to help drill you on any word with which you are having trouble. You'll be surprised at how much more you will remember if you share what you know with someone else, and if they help you with clues to help you jog your brain.

KEEP A LIST

In addition to the words you learn in this book, make a list of flash cards for new, useful words that you encounter at work, at school, on TV, in your reading, or even at home. They will more than double the benefit you will get from using this book.

How the Book Is Set Up

Each chapter of this book that contains a word list starts with a crossword puzzle to help you get acquainted with your new words. Do your best to fill it in; if there are some words you don't recognize, you can flip to the next page, where you will find the full definition, pronunciation and part of speech of each word in the word list. Take a good look at how each word is pronounced, especially the accented syllables. You should pronounce each word aloud several times. There is a sentence below each definition that illustrates the word's meaning. You should fill in the blank inside each sentence with the correct word from the list. It is a good idea to say the entire sentence aloud.

Second, you will encounter several words from the Vocabulary List in context. If you do not remember the meaning of the words, you should circle any clues in the text that might help you figure out the meaning of these unfamiliar words.

Then, you will read and fill in the blank by selecting the best choice from the Vocabulary List on which you are working that completes the sentence. Read each sentence slowly and carefully. There are usually clues within each sentence that tell you which word from the list is the best choice.

Next, you will encounter exercises dealing with synonyms and antonyms. You will read a group of words and decide which one is not a synonym. Then, you will read a group of words and select the word from the Vocabulary List that is mostly nearly opposite in meaning from the entire group of words.

You will also complete matching, true/false, and choosing the right word exercises that will help you reinforce the meanings of each new word you have learned. Then, at the end of the book, you will take a 75-question Post-Test so that you can see how much you've really learned as you've worked your way through this book.

The Pretest that follows this Introduction will help you see how good you are at identifying unfamiliar words. Then, Chapters 3 and 4 will teach you about the basics of vocabulary. In Chapter 3 you'll learn important vocabulary terms and about language origins, and then in Chapter 4, you'll learn important spelling rules to help you become a better speller, even on those tricky or foreign words. Then, you'll get to the word lists. The 15 Vocabulary List chapters consist of helpful exercises to drill you on new words, so that by the end of each lesson, you'll know them inside out. Finally, completing the Post-Test will show you how far you've come, and how well you know your new words.

You can also check out Appendices A and B to learn important studying strategies and find out about other valuable resources.

SELF-ANALYSIS

Find out how you feel about your own vocabulary with the following self-assessment. Mark the sentences that best describe your own vocabulary habits.

_____ 1. I feel confident that I express myself clearly in speaking.

_____ 2. I sometimes feel uncomfortable when I know what I want to say but just can't think of the right word.

_____ 3. I notice unfamiliar words in print and wonder about their meanings.

_____ 4. Sometimes I come across unfamiliar words in print and feel that I should know them.

_____ 5. I remember words that I had on vocabulary quizzes and tests at school.

_____ 6. If I write down new words, I can learn them.

_____ 7. If I come across an unfamiliar word in print, I will look it up in the dictionary.

_____ 8. If I come across an unfamiliar word in print, I will ask someone to tell me the meaning.

_____ 9. If I hear an unfamiliar word in conversation or on TV, I will ask someone to tell me its meaning.

_____ 10. If I meet an unfamiliar word, I am usually embarrassed to ask for or to look up its meaning.

Your answers to the questions above should give you a good sense of how you feel about and use your vocabulary.

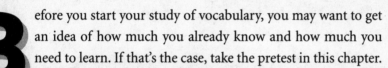

C·H·A·P·T·E·R

PRETEST

1

Before you start your study of vocabulary, you may want to get an idea of how much you already know and how much you need to learn. If that's the case, take the pretest in this chapter.

The pretest is 50 questions introducing you to many of the words you will encounter and learn as you complete the exercises in this book. Even if you get all the questions on this pretest right, it's almost guaranteed that you will find a few words in this book that you didn't already know. On the other hand, if you know hardly any of the words on the pretest, don't despair. Out of the many words in this book, you'll find a few that you are already familiar with, and that will make the going easier.

So, use this pretest just to get a general idea of how much of this book you already know. If you get a high score on this pretest, you may be able to spend less time with this book than you originally planned. If you get a lower score, you'll be amazed at how much your vocabulary will improve by completing the exercises in each chapter.

1.	ⓐ	ⓑ	ⓒ	ⓓ	18.	ⓐ	ⓑ	ⓒ	ⓓ	35.	ⓐ	ⓑ	ⓒ	ⓓ
2.	ⓐ	ⓑ	ⓒ	ⓓ	19.	ⓐ	ⓑ	ⓒ	ⓓ	36.	ⓐ	ⓑ	ⓒ	ⓓ
3.	ⓐ	ⓑ	ⓒ	ⓓ	20.	ⓐ	ⓑ	ⓒ	ⓓ	37.	ⓐ	ⓑ	ⓒ	ⓓ
4.	ⓐ	ⓑ	ⓒ	ⓓ	21.	ⓐ	ⓑ	ⓒ	ⓓ	38.	ⓐ	ⓑ	ⓒ	ⓓ
5.	ⓐ	ⓑ	ⓒ	ⓓ	22.	ⓐ	ⓑ	ⓒ	ⓓ	39.	ⓐ	ⓑ	ⓒ	ⓓ
6.	ⓐ	ⓑ	ⓒ	ⓓ	23.	ⓐ	ⓑ	ⓒ	ⓓ	40.	ⓐ	ⓑ	ⓒ	ⓓ
7.	ⓐ	ⓑ	ⓒ	ⓓ	24.	ⓐ	ⓑ	ⓒ	ⓓ	41.	ⓐ	ⓑ	ⓒ	ⓓ
8.	ⓐ	ⓑ	ⓒ	ⓓ	25.	ⓐ	ⓑ	ⓒ	ⓓ	42.	ⓐ	ⓑ	ⓒ	ⓓ
9.	ⓐ	ⓑ	ⓒ	ⓓ	26.	ⓐ	ⓑ	ⓒ	ⓓ	43.	ⓐ	ⓑ	ⓒ	ⓓ
10.	ⓐ	ⓑ	ⓒ	ⓓ	27.	ⓐ	ⓑ	ⓒ	ⓓ	44.	ⓐ	ⓑ	ⓒ	ⓓ
11.	ⓐ	ⓑ	ⓒ	ⓓ	28.	ⓐ	ⓑ	ⓒ	ⓓ	45.	ⓐ	ⓑ	ⓒ	ⓓ
12.	ⓐ	ⓑ	ⓒ	ⓓ	29.	ⓐ	ⓑ	ⓒ	ⓓ	46.	ⓐ	ⓑ	ⓒ	ⓓ
13.	ⓐ	ⓑ	ⓒ	ⓓ	30.	ⓐ	ⓑ	ⓒ	ⓓ	47.	ⓐ	ⓑ	ⓒ	ⓓ
14.	ⓐ	ⓑ	ⓒ	ⓓ	31.	ⓐ	ⓑ	ⓒ	ⓓ	48.	ⓐ	ⓑ	ⓒ	ⓓ
15.	ⓐ	ⓑ	ⓒ	ⓓ	32.	ⓐ	ⓑ	ⓒ	ⓓ	49.	ⓐ	ⓑ	ⓒ	ⓓ
16.	ⓐ	ⓑ	ⓒ	ⓓ	33.	ⓐ	ⓑ	ⓒ	ⓓ	50.	ⓐ	ⓑ	ⓒ	ⓓ
17.	ⓐ	ⓑ	ⓒ	ⓓ	34.	ⓐ	ⓑ	ⓒ	ⓓ					

PRETEST

Choose the best word to fill in the blank.

1. Because his teacher could not read his essay, the student had to rewrite the _____ paper.
   a. disinterested
   b. copious
   c. audible ✓
   d. illegible

2. The _____ data supports the belief that there has been an increase in population.
   a. nominal
   b. demographic ✓
   c. pragmatic
   d. puerile

3. The veterinarian came out and told the cat's owner that its _____ for recovery is good.
   a. prognosis ✓
   b. etymology
   c. pragmatism
   d. euphemism

4. The detective uncovered the meaning of the _____ message.
   a. chronic
   b. agoraphobic
   c. cryptic ✓
   d. incisive

5. Scientists research gene _____ in fruit flies to see how genes change from one generation to the next.
   a. remittance
   b. mutation ✓
   c. mediocre
   d. cliché

6. The newspaper tried to _____ the mistake by correcting the misprint.
   a. debut
   b. rectify ✓
   c. recapitulate
   d. exempt

7. Please turn up the volume on the radio; the song is barely _____.
   a. equity
   b. audible ✓
   c. bandwidth
   d. abrogate

8. Our club values the _____ of its members; we know we can always count on one another.
   a. perjury
   b. epigram
   c. fidelity ✓
   d. firewall

9. It is _____ by your high grade that you prepared for the test.
   a. moot
   b. prose
   c. churlish
   d. evident ✓

10. The one year the company did not break even was just a/an _____.
    a. acme
    b. facetious
    c. syllogism
    d. anomaly

Choose the word that is closest in meaning to the **bold** word.

11. purge
- a. cite
- b. purify
- c. perspective
- d. decimate

12. parity
- a. equality
- b. mimicry
- c. antipathy
- d. sympathy

13. furtive
- a. open
- b. demote
- c. secret
- d. utopia

14. vivacious
- a. lively
- b. relevant
- c. ornate
- d. flippant

15. audacious
- a. badinage
- b. guttural
- c. bold
- d. stolid

16. acme
- a. pinnacle
- b. server
- c. retrospect
- d. consortium

17. staid
- a. pallor
- b. sham
- c. sober
- d. elite

18. addle
- a. stolid
- b. empiric
- c. ruminate
- d. muddle

19. erudite
- a. genteel
- b. scholarly
- c. garrulous
- d. bequest

20. tenet
- a. belief
- b. antecedent
- c. teleology
- d. demote

Choose the word that is most nearly the OPPOSITE of the **bold** word.

21. feisty
- a. staid
- b. relevant
- c. tangential
- d. hot

22. bigotry
- a. prognosis
- b. open-mindedness
- c. badinage
- d. parity

23. agonize
 a. blasé
 b. rectify
 c. enjoy
 d. trivial

24. élan
 a. fidelity
 b. ingénue
 c. error
 d. frumpy

25. bane
 a. solace
 b. crux
 c. pun
 d. downfall

26. banal
 a. puerile
 b. trite
 c. fresh
 d. obtuse

27. dross
 a. improvise
 b. waste
 c. oblique
 d. essential

28. extricate
 a. remove
 b. entangle
 c. malaise
 d. gauche

29. avant-garde
 a. cliché
 b. vendetta
 c. original
 d. trivial

30. purloin
 a. larceny
 b. wallow
 c. return
 d. plausible

Choose the word that is spelled correctly.

31. a. percieve
 b. achieve
 c. reciept
 d. hygeine

32. a. knarled
 b. blight
 c. alite
 d. fraut

33. a. indeight
 b. indite
 c. indight
 d. indict

34. a. kerchiefs
 b. kerchievs
 c. kerchieves
 d. kerchiefs

35. a. curiculums
 b. curriculmns
 c. curriculas
 d. curricula

36. Spike was the most _____ dog you could ever wish for.
 a. peacable
 b. paeceable
 c. paecable
 d. peaceable

37. The job was a really great ____ because his boss taught him all about the business.
   a. opportunity
   b. opportuneity
   c. oportunity
   d. oportuneity

38. Al and Jane hired attorneys, and together, the ____ added up to over $10,000.
   a. lawyer's bills
   b. lawyers' bills'
   c. lawyers' bills
   d. lawyers bills

39. The county commissioners said ____ going to discuss the taxation issue at the meeting next week.
   a. they're
   b. there
   c. their
   d. thei'r

40. Superman was nearly ____, but not quite.
   a. invincible
   b. invincable
   c. invensible
   d. invinseble

Match the definition in column B to the correct word in column A.

41. consummate	a. elegant
42. copious	b. inclined
43. euphemism	c. rise and fall
44. mediocre	d. inelegant
45. urbane	e. complete
46. gauche	f. embodiment
47. fluctuate	g. abundant
48. epitome	h. average
49. mete	i. allocate
50. prone	j. inoffensive expression

ANSWERS

1. d	26. c
2. b	27. d
3. a	28. b
4. c	29. a
5. b	30. c
6. b	31. b
7. b	32. b
8. c	33. d
9. d	34. a
10. d	35. d
11. b	36. d
12. a	37. a
13. c	38. c
14. a	39. a
15. c	40. a
16. a	41. e
17. c	42. g
18. d	43. j
19. b	44. h
20. a	45. a
21. a	46. d
22. b	47. c
23. c	48. f
24. d	49. i
25. a	50. b

C·H·A·P·T·E·R

VOCABULARY TERMS AND LANGUAGE ORIGINS

CHAPTER SUMMARY

This chapter tells you about many terms associated with vocabulary.

There are three ways we learn vocabulary:

From the **sound** of words

From the **structure** of words

From the **context** of words—how words are used in communication

Therefore, when you encounter unfamiliar words, you should ask yourself:

1. Does this word sound like anything I've ever heard?
2. Does any part of the word look familiar?
3. How is this word used in the sentence I just read or heard?

Each lesson of this book presents a word list so you can try this process. As you look through each word list, you'll find that you already recognize some of the words—maybe even from your reading and listening vocabularies—and the rest you will learn as you proceed through the lesson.

WORD PARTS—PREFIXES, SUFFIXES, AND ROOTS

You use prefixes, suffixes, and word roots every day, whether you realize it or not. These parts of words make up almost all of the words we use in the English language and you will find that the meanings of many unfamiliar words become much more clear when you understand the meanings of the most common of these word parts.

PREFIXES

A prefix is the word part placed at the beginning of a word. It is usually only one syllable, but sometimes it is more. Its job is to change or add to the meaning of a word. For example, you probably use the word *review* on a regular basis. What does it mean? Let's break it down. First, we can break it down into syllables: re-view. *View* means to look at, and the prefix, *re-* adds to the meaning of the word. *Re-* means back or again, so by putting together what you already know, you can figure out that the word *review* means to look back at, or to look at again. Other common prefixes include, *in-*, *anti-*, *pre-*, *post-*, *un-*, *non-*, *con-*, and *dis-*. You will learn more about prefixes and their meanings in Chapter 4.

SUFFIXES

A suffix is a word part placed at the end of a word that signals how a word is being used in a sentence and to identify its part of speech. When you attach different suffixes onto the base of a word it changes the word's part of speech. For example, the word *sterilize* is a verb meaning *to sanitize*. As an adjective, it takes the suffix, *-ile* and becomes *sterile*. As a noun, it takes the suffix *–tion* and becomes *sterilization*. The prefix changes the word's job in a sentence, and it also helps to give you a clue as to the meaning of an unfamiliar word. You will learn more about suffixes and their meanings and jobs in Chapter 5.

ROOTS

The pieces of words that carry direct meaning are called roots. Many English words stem from ancient Greek and Latin words, and because so many English words have their source in certain recurring root words, knowing some of the most commonly used roots gives you access to many words at once. Thus, when you combine your knowledge of prefixes and suffixes with your knowledge of roots, you can figure out the meaning of many unfamiliar words. For example the word root *cogn-* means *to know*. Words that include this root are *recognize*, meaning to identify as known, *incognito*, meaning unknown, and *cognition*, meaning knowledge. You can see how knowing the base of these three words, in addition to having knowledge of prefixes and suffixes, can really help you work out the meanings of unfamiliar words. You'll learn more about roots in Chapters 6 and 7.

SYLLABLES

When you were first learning to read, you learned about syllables, the parts of words that carry separate sounds. Breaking words into syllables is one of the best strategies for seeing if a word is in your listening or reading vocabularies. It also helps you break larger words into smaller, more manageable, and often more recognizable parts. This will be especially helpful in Chapters 4, 5, 6, and 7 when you are working with Vocabulary Lists that teach you about prefixes, suffixes, and roots. By breaking words down into syllables, you will be able to identify the meanings of unfamiliar words that contain these word parts.

RULES FOR DIVIDING WORDS INTO SYLLABLES

Here are a couple of quick rules for dividing words by syllables:

1. Divide between double consonants: hammock.
2. Divide after prefixes and before suffixes: invest-ment.

If you already have some feel for how the word sounds, you can divide it according to the sound of the vowels:

3. Divide after the vowel if it has the long sound: so-lar.
4. Divide after the consonant if the vowel sound is short: pris-on.

SYNONYMS AND ANTONYMS

Questions on standardized tests and civil service exams often ask you to find the synonym or antonym of a word. Therefore, as you learn the words in this book, you should try to think of or look up synonyms and antonyms of the words in the Vocabulary Lists. You will also be asked to complete exercises in this book to help you learn even more synonyms and antonyms.

SYNONYMS

A word is a synonym of another word if it has the same, or nearly the same, meaning as the word to which it is being compared. For example, the words *conceal* and *hide* are synonyms. They both mean the same thing: to keep out of sight.

ANTONYMS

An antonym is a word that means the opposite of the word to which it is being compared. A couple of obvious examples of antonym pairs are happy and sad, good and bad, and love and hate.

DENOTATION AND CONNOTATION

The denotation of a word is its dictionary definition, while the connotation of a word has to do with the tone of the word, that is, the emotions it evokes in the reader. For example if you were to look up the word *joke* in the dictionary, you might get a definition similar to that of some of its synonyms like *quip*, or *prank*—something like "something said or done to provoke laughter"—but all three of these words have different connotations; in other words, they bring to mind different feelings, one positive, one negative, and one neutral. As you are learning the words in this book, try to think of other similar words that might be synonyms but might also have slightly different connotations, or tones.

HOMONYMS

Homonyms are words that sound the same, but aren't. They have the same pronunciation, but they are neither spelled the same way, nor do they have the same meaning. For example, *which* and *witch* are homonyms, and so are *their, there,* and *they're.* When you are listening to the words, or reading them in context, it is easy to work out their meaning; however, it is very important to know which definition corresponds to the correct spelling of the homonym. If you misspell a homonym, people will have a difficult time understanding what you are trying to communicate to them. You will learn more about homonyms in the next chapter.

CONTEXT CLUES

Context is the surrounding text in which a word is used. Most people automatically use context to help them determine the meaning of an unknown word. When you encounter a word in its surroundings, it is much easier to figure out its meaning, or at least its connotation. The best way to take meaning from context is to search the surrounding text for key words in sentences or paragraphs that convey the meaning of the unfamiliar word.

Often, restatement and contrast clues will lead you right to the meaning of unfamiliar words. For example, read the following sentence and see if you can figure out the meaning of the italicized word from closely examining the surrounding text.

> Although when Hannah joined the company she was promised *perquisites* every six months, she has been working at the company for two years and has never received any sort of bonus.

The words *although,* and *bonus* should give you a clue as to the meaning of *perquisite.* You know that Hannah has never received a bonus in two years of work for the same company, and you know that she was promised something, so the word *although* gives you the final clue because it signals a contrast. You can conclude that a *perquisite* is a synonym for *bonus.*

> She was *exempt* from duty that day. She was excused because she had been injured.

In this sentence, the meaning of *exempt* is restated for you. *Exempt* is a synonym for *excused.*

You will get plenty of practice identifying the meanings of unfamiliar words in context throughout the rest of this book.

Good communication skills—including vocabulary and spelling—are essential. A good vocabulary increases your ability to understand reading material and to express yourself in speaking and in writing. Without a broad vocabulary, your ability to learn is limited. The good news is that vocabulary skills can be developed with practice, which is exactly what this book gives you.

C·H·A·P·T·E·R

SPELLING RULES

3

CHAPTER SUMMARY

This chapter is designed to help you refresh your spelling skills by teaching you the rules you need to know to spell your best. You'll learn strategies to help you spell words with tricky letter combinations, unusual plurals, prefixes, suffixes, hyphenated and compound words, apostrophes, and abbreviations.

In the English language, if you simply wrote words the way they sound, you'd come up with some very peculiar spellings. If you tried to sound out every word and pronounce it exactly the way it's written, you'd come up with some pretty odd pronunciations too.

Here are some general multisensory tips for studying spelling:

- Use your eyes.
  - ✓ Look at words carefully. With a marker or pen, highlight the part of the word that is hard to remember.
  - ✓ Visualize the word with your eyes closed.
- Use your ears.
  - ✓ Listen for the sound of words you hear in conversation or on the radio or television.
  - ✓ Listen to the sound of the spelling of words: Ask someone to dictate the words and their spelling, and listen as the word is spelled out.

- Use your hands.
  - ✓ Write the word several times, spelling it in your head as you write.

There are two main stumbling blocks to spelling by sight and sound. One we have already identified—the fact that English is both phonetically inconsistent and visually confusing. Here are four strategies that can guide your way through a difficult system and give you some ways to make good spelling a part of your life.

1. Learn the rules, but expect some exceptions. The lessons that follow point out both spelling rules and their exceptions.

2. Use mnemonics (memory tricks) to help you remember how to spell unfamiliar or confusing words. The most common type of mnemonic is the *acronym*. An acronym is a word created from the first letters in a series of words. Another type of mnemonic is a silly sentence or phrase, known as an *acrostic*, which is made out of words that each begin with the letter or letters that start each item in a series that you want to remember.

3. Write it down. This book provides you with helpful exercises that require you to write your vocabulary words in a blank space. This act will help your hand and eye remember how to spell the word. Making sure to spell the word correctly as you go along so you don't have to relearn the word's spelling later on. After you are done with this book, you can teach yourself to spell new words in the same way. The simple act of writing it down several times will help you cement word spellings in your brain.

4. Referring to a pronunciation chart in any dictionary will help guide you through pronouncing the words in our book and also familiarize you with pronouncing other new words you encounter in everyday life. You can also access pronunciation charts online. The following is a list of a few online resources:
   - WWWebster Dictionary: www.m-w.com/aschart.htm
   - The Newbury House Online Dictionary: nhd.heinle.com/pronounce.html
   - American Heritage Dictionary of the English Language Online at Bartleby.com: www.bartleby.com/61/12.html

There are many other online dictionaries such as www.dictionary.com; just type online dictionary into any search engine, and get ready to pronounce.

VOWELS

WHEN TO USE *IE* AND *EI*

You probably learned this saying years ago in school:

> i before e except after c and when sounding like "ay" as in neighbor and weigh.

This saying should help you remember the basic principle of when to use *ie* and *ei* when spelling words. The following sections outline the specifics of when to spell a word with *ie* and when to spell a word with *ei* and their exceptions.

THE *IE* RULE

Here are some examples of words that use *ie* to make the long *e* sound:

achieve	niece
belief	piece
cashier	retrieve
chief	series
fierce	wield

EXCEPTIONS

Sometimes, the *ie* combination has other sounds:

- It can sound like short *e*, as in *friend*
- It can sound like long *i*, as in *piety, fiery, quiet, notoriety, society, science*
- The only time the *ie* combination comes after *c* is when it sounds like *sh*, as in *ancient, deficient, conscience*.

THE *EI* RULE

Here are some examples of words in which *ei* makes the long *a* sound:

deign	reign
eight	sleigh
feign	surveillance
freight	vein
heinous	weight

EXCEPTIONS

Sometimes you will simply have to memorize words that use the *ei* combination because they don't follow the rule.

- In some words, *ei* is used even though it sounds like *ee*: *either, seize, weird, sheik, seizure, leisure*
- Sometimes *ei* sounds like long *i*: *height, sleight, stein, seismology*
- Sometimes *ei* sounds like short *e*: *heifer, their, foreign, forfeit*
- As you learned in the saying above, after *c* you use *ei*, even if it sounds like *ee*: *ceiling, deceit, conceited, receive, receipt*.

SPELLING PRACTICE 1

Circle the word in the parentheses that is spelled correctly. Check your answers at the end of the lesson.

1. She took her (**niece/neice**) to the zoo on Saturday.

2. The agents were allowed to (**sieze/seize**) the narcotics at the border.

3. The doctor checked the baby's (**hieght/height**) and (**weight/wieght**).

4. He was very (**relieved/releived**) when the ordeal was over.

5. The (**riegn/reign**) of the new Miss America began that night.

6. They gave the (**cashier/casheir**) the money for the bill.

7. They had the criminal under (**surviellance/surveillance**) for over six months.

8. The (**frieze/freize**) at the Parthenon in Greece is one of the most famous works of art known to man.

9. The (**chief/cheif**) of police was under investigation for corruption while in office.

10. She believed him to be the (**fiend/feind**) who had stolen the old woman's inheritance.

MORE VOWEL COMBINATIONS

When two vowels are together, the first one is usually long, or says its own name, and the second one is silent. For example, in the word *reach,* you hear long *e,* but not the short *a.* Similarly, if you know how to pronounce the word *caffeine,* you stand a chance at spelling it correctly because you hear that the *e* sound comes first. If you know what sound you hear, that sound is likely to be the first of two vowels working together.

Here are some examples of words using *ai, ui,* and *ea* combinations in which the vowel you hear is the one that comes first.

Words with *ai*	Words with *ea*	Words with *ui*
abstain	cheap	juice
acquaint	conceal	nuisance
chaise	gear	ruin
paisley	heal	suit
prevail	lead	
refrain	reveal	
traipse	steal	

THE EXCEPTIONS

There are several exceptions to this rule, which you will simply have to recognize by sight rather than by sound.

Exceptions
porcelain
beauty
healthy
hearse
hearty

The following are some tips to help you remember these exceptions. Remember the word *heart* is in *hearty.* Think of it like this, "A hearty person is good hearted." Some people put ice in juice. You can think, "Juice is cooler if you add ice." And, the word *heal* appears in *healthy.* Think of it like this, "The doctor will heal you and help you stay healthy."

WORDS WITH *AI* OR *IA*

When the vowel pair has one sound and says "uh" (e.g. *captain*), it uses *ai.* When the vowel pair has separate sounds (e.g. *genial*), it uses *ia.* However, there is an exception: When words combine *t* or *c* with *ia,* they make a "*shuh*" sound, for example *martial, beneficial, glacial.* The following are some examples of words that follow the *ai* and *ia* rules:

Words with *ai*	Words with *ia*
Britain	alleviate
captain	brilliant
certain	civilian
chieftain	familiar
curtain	guardian
fountain	median
villain	menial

CONSONANTS

SILENT CONSONANTS

Many English words include silent consonants, ones that are written but not pronounced. Unfortunately, there is no rule governing silent consonants; you simply have to learn the words by sight. The following list includes some common examples, with the silent consonants highlighted.

answer	gnaw	pseudonym
autumn	indict	psychology
blight	kneel	rhetorical
calm	knight	subtle
debt	knowledge	through
ghost	psalm	write

MEMORY TRICKS

Use sound cues or sight cues, depending on which works better for you—or use both to reinforce your learning.

- Pronounce the silent consonants in your mind as you write them. Say **subtle**, **often**, and so on.
- Write the words on index cards and highlight the missing consonant sounds with a marker.

SPELLING PRACTICE 2

Fill in the missing (silent) letters in the words below.

11. __night

12. ans__er

13. de__t

14. __narled

15. indi__t

16. __salm

17. su__tle

18. g__ost

19. of__en

20. autum__

DOUBLING CONSONANTS

Most of the time a final consonant is doubled when you add an ending. For example, *drop* becomes *dropping*, *mop* becomes *mopping*, *stab* becomes *stabbing*. But what about *look/looking, rest/resting, counsel/counseled*?

THE RULES

There are two sets of rules: one for when you're adding an ending that begins with a vowel (such as *-ed, -ing,* *-ance, -ence, -ant*) and another set for when the ending begins with a consonant (such as *-ness* or *-ly*).

1. When the ending begins with a vowel:

- Double the last consonant in a one-syllable word that ends with one vowel and one consonant. For example, *flip* becomes *flipper* or *flipping, quit* becomes *quitter* or *quitting,* and *clap* becomes *clapper* or *clapping.*
- Double the final consonant when the last syllable is accented and there is only one consonant in the accented syllable. For example, *acquit* becomes *acquitting, refer* becomes *referring,* and *commit* becomes *committing.*

You can remember a shorter version of the rules about doubling before an ending that begins with a vowel; one syllable or accented last syllable doubles the single consonant.

2. When the ending begins with a consonant:

- Keep a final *n* when you add *-ness.* You end up with a double *n: keenn*ess, leann*ess.*
- Keep a final *l* when you add *-ly.* You end up with a double *l: formall*y, regall*y, legall*y.

In other cases, then, you don't double the consonant.

THE EXCEPTIONS

There are exceptions to the above rules, but not many. Here are a few of them:

- *Bus* becomes *buses*
- *Chagrin* becomes *chagrined*
- *Draw* becomes *drawing*

SPELLING PRACTICE 3

This exercise focuses on double consonants. Choose an appropriate ending for each word: *-ed, -ing, -ness,* or *-ly.* Rewrite the word on the line that follows it, doubling the consonant if necessary.

21. final _____

22. submit _____

23. think _____

24. roam _____

25. control _____

26. plain _____

27. rebel (v) _____

28. throb _____

29. legal _____

30. rain _____

THE SPECIAL CHALLENGES OF C AND G

The letters *c* and *g* can sound either soft or hard. When *c* is soft, it sounds like *s;* when it's hard, it sounds like *k.* When *g* is soft, it sounds like *j;* when it's hard, it sounds like *g* as in guess. But the difference isn't as confusing as it seems at first. The letters *c* and *g* are soft when followed by *e, i,* or *y.* Otherwise, they are hard. Thus, *c* sounds like *s* when it is followed by *e, i,* or *y,* as in *central, circle, cycle.* It sounds like *k* when followed by other vowels: *case, cousin, current.* The same rule also applies to the letter *g: g* sounds like *j* when followed by *e, i,* or *y,* as in *genius, giant, gym.* When followed by other vowels, *g* is hard: *gamble, go, gun.*

The following are examples of words in which *e, i* or *y* makes a soft *c* or *g.*

centimeter	general
centrifuge	generous
circulate	genteel
circus	germ
cyclical	giraffe
cymbal	gyrate

One more thing to remember is that a *k* is added to a final *c* before an ending that begins with *e, i,* or *y.* If you didn't add the *k,* the *c* would become soft and sound like *s.* So in order to add *-ing* to panic, for example, you have to put a *k* first: *panicking.*

The following words are examples of words that have had a *k* added to *c* before an ending beginning with *e, i,* or *y.*

mimicking	picnicked
panicky	trafficking

There are virtually no exceptions to the rules about using *c* and *g.* Listen to the words as you spell them and let the rule guide your choice: *c, s,* or *k; g* or *j.*

SPELLING PRACTICE 4

Using the list above, add the missing letters to the words below:

31. The crashing of the c__mbal made them all pay attention.

32. He was a g__nerous man who gave willingly of what he had.

33. He was arrested for traffic__ing in drugs.

34. The g__neral ordered the troops into battle.

35. The fan helped to c__rculate the air.

HOMONYMS

Homonyms are words that sound the same, but are spelled differently. Many of these words have just one change in the vowel or vowel combination. There's no rule about these words so you'll simply have to memorize them. Here are some examples of word pairs that can be troublesome. Sometimes it helps to learn each word in terms of the job it will do in a sentence. Often the two words in a homophone pair are a different part of speech. Take a look at the following examples:

affect/effect	led/lead
altar/alter	minor/miner
bare/bear	passed/past
bloc/block	peal/peel
cite/site	piece/peace
cord/chord	sheer/shear
coarse/course	stationery/stationary
descent/dissent	weak/week
dual/duel	which/witch
heal/heel	write/right

Since the meanings of these homonyms are different, context is probably the best way to differentiate between these words.

Examples in Context
- He led a **dual** (*adjective*) life as a spy.
  He fought a **duel** (*noun*) with his great enemy.
- He had to **alter** (*verb*) his clothes after he lost weight.
  The bride smiled as she walked toward the **altar** (*noun*).
- His words had a great **effect** (*noun*) on me.
  The test score will not **affect** (*verb*) your final grade.

  Try the following exercise to practice identifying the correct homonym in context.

SPELLING PRACTICE 5
Circle the word that fits correctly into the sentence. Check your answers at the end of the lesson.

36. He felt (**week/weak**) after losing so much blood.

37. I can't (**bare/bear**) to leave the house looking like this.

38. He couldn't drink alcohol because he was a (**miner/minor**).

39. He had to (**peel/peal**) five pounds of potatoes for dinner.

40. There were (**shear/sheer**) curtains hanging on the window.

41. They built the new building on a prime (**cite/site**).

42. There is a controversy over the (**right/write**) to bear arms granted in the Constitution.

43. I tripped over the a telephone (**cord/chord**) on my way to the kitchen.

44. I've met him before, sometime in the (**passed/past**).

45. We watched the airplane's (**dissent/descent**) waiting for my uncle at the airport.

ENDINGS

WHEN TO DROP A FINAL *E*
It's hard to remember when to drop letters and when to keep them. This lesson will nail down some simple rules to help you with those decisions.

RULE 1

Drop the final *e* when you add an ending that begins with a vowel

- With *-ing*
  change + *-ing* = changing
- With *-able*
  argue + *-able* = arguable
- With *-ous*
  virtue + *-ous* = virtuous
- With *-ity*
  opportune + *-ity* = opportunity

THE EXCEPTIONS

- Keep the final *e* after soft *c* or soft *g* in order to keep the soft sound.
  peace + -able = peaceable
  courage + -ous = courageous
- Keep the final *e* in other cases when you need to protect pronunciation.
  shoe + *-ing* = shoeing (not shoing)
  guarantee + *-ing* = guaranteeing (not guaranteeing)

RULE 2

Keep the final *e* before endings that begin with consonants. Here are some examples of words that use this rule:

- With *-ment*
  advertise + *-ment* = advertisement
- With *-ness*
  appropriate + *-ness* = appropriateness
- With *-less*
  care + *-less* = careless
- With *-ful*
  grace + *-ful* = graceful

THE EXCEPTION

There's one important exception to the rule about keeping the final *e* when you add an ending that begins with a consonant:

- Drop the final *e* when it occurs after the letters *u* or *w*.
  argue + *-ment* = argument
  awe + *-ful* = awful
  true + *-ly* = truly

SPELLING PRACTICE 6

Write the following combinations in the blanks provided, keeping or omitting the final e as necessary.

46. It was a (surprise + *-ing*)
_____ ending.

47. The real estate agent said that the property would be very (desire + *-able*)
_____ on the market.

48. The astronauts were remarkably (courage + *-ous*) _____ men and women.

49. The storm brought a (scarce + *-ity*) _____ of fresh food and electricity.

50. The Quakers are a (peace + *-able*) _____ people.

51. He read a great (advertise + *-ment*) _____ in the paper today.

52. He had to learn not to be so (care + *-less*) _____ with his wallet.

53. He was known for his (polite + *-ness*) _____ and good manners.

54. They had an (argue + -*ment*)

_____ on the phone.

55. He left the room in a (disgrace + -*ful*)

_____ condition.

WHEN TO KEEP A FINAL *Y* OR CHANGE IT TO *I*

When you add a suffix to a word ending in *y*, keep the *y* if it follows a vowel. This time it doesn't matter whether the suffix begins with a vowel or a consonant. Always keep the *y* if it comes immediately after a vowel. The following are some examples.

- With -*s*
  attorney + -*s* = attorneys
- With -*ed*
  play + -*ed* = played
- With -*ing*
  relay + -*ing* = relaying
- With -*ance*
  annoy + -*ance* = annoyance
- With -*able*
  enjoy + -*able* = enjoyable

THE EXCEPTIONS

Some words break this rule and change the *y* to *i*.

- *day* becomes *daily*
- *pay* becomes *paid*
- *say* becomes *said*

When you add a suffix to a word ending in *y*, change the *y* to *i* if it follows a consonant. Again, it doesn't matter whether the suffix begins with a vowel or a consonant. Here are some examples:

- With *ful*
  beauty + -*ful* = beautiful
- With -*ness*
  lonely + -*ness* = loneliness
- With -*ly*
  angry + -*ly* = angrily
- With -*es*
  salary + -*es* = salaries

THE EXCEPTION

There's one group of exceptions to the above rule:

- When you add -*ing*, keep the final *y*.
  study + -*ing* = *studying*

SPELLING PRACTICE 7

Rewrite the words with their suffixes in the blanks below.

56. We hired two (attorney + -*s*)

_____ to handle the case.

57. She insisted on (relay + -*ing*)

_____ the message to her father.

58. I found the movie very (enjoy + -*able*)

_____.

59. The children were (play + -*ing*)

_____ outdoors.

60. The mosquitoes were a serious (annoy + -*ance*) _____.

61. He always (hurry + -*es*)

_____ to get to school early.

62. The lumberjack ate (hearty + -*ly*)

_____ through a stack of pancakes.

63. She spent all her spare time (study + -ing) _____ for the exam.

64. He (angry + -ly) _____ slammed the door.

65. There was a (plenty + -ful) _____ supply of fish in the lake.

PLURALS

One of the difficulties of spelling in English is the making of plurals. Unfortunately, you can't always simply add the letter -s to the end of the word to signal more than one.

WHEN TO USE -S OR -ES TO FORM PLURALS

There are two simple rules that govern most plurals.

> Most nouns add -s to make plurals.
> If a noun ends in a sibilant sound (s, ss, z, ch, x, sh), add -es.

The following are some examples of plurals:

cars	faxes	dresses
computers	indexes	churches
books	lunches	guesses
skills	dishes	buzzes

THE EXCEPTION

Remember from the last lesson that when a word ends in a y preceded by a consonant, the y changes to i when you add -es.

Singular	Plural
fly	flies
rally	rallies

PLURALS FOR WORDS THAT END IN O

THE RULE

There's just one quick rule that governs a few words ending in o.

> If a final o follows another vowel, it takes -s.

Here are some examples:

patios	radios
studios	videos

THE EXCEPTIONS

When the final o follows a consonant rather than a vowel, there's no rule to guide you in choosing -s or -es. You just have to learn the individual words.

The following words form a plural with -s alone:

albinos	pianos
altos	silos
banjos	sopranos
logos	broncos

The following words take –es

heroes	tomatoes
potatoes	vetoes

When in doubt about whether to add -s or -es, look it up in the dictionary.

SPELLING PRACTICE 8

Add -s or -es to the words in the sentences below.

66. He sent me two fax_____ last night.

67. There were flash_____ of lightning in the dark sky.

68. He struck several match_____ before one finally caught fire.

69. You have two guess_____ at the correct answer.

70. Spelling is one of the most helpful skill_____ you can develop.

71. He peeled so many potato_____ in the army that he wouldn't eat french fries for a year.

72. The two soprano_____ gave a wonderful performance.

73. He wished there were more hero_____ in the world today.

74. The piano_____ were out of tune.

75. The farmers harvest their tomato_____ in the summer months.

PLURALS FOR WORDS THAT END IN -F

Some words that end in f or fe just take -s to form the plural. Others change the f to v and add -es or -s. Unfortunately, there are no rules that can apply to this category of plurals; you just have to memorize them.

The following are some of the words that keep the final f and add -s:

beliefs	gulfs
chiefs	kerchiefs
cuffs	proofs

Here are some of the words that change the final f to v and take -es:

elves	loaves	thieves
knives	selves	wives
leaves	shelves	wolves

PLURALS THAT DON'T USE -S OR -ES

There are many words that don't simply use -s or -es to form plurals. These are usually words that still observe the rules of the languages from which they were adopted. Most of these plurals are part of your reading, speaking, and listening vocabularies. You can see that there are patterns that will help you. For instance, in Latin words, -um becomes -a, -us becomes –i, and in Greek words, -sis becomes -ses. A good way to remember these plurals is by saying the words aloud, because for the most part they do change form and you may remember them more easily if you listen to the sound of the spelling.

Singular	Plural	Singular	Plural
child	children	fungus	fungi
deer	deer	medium	media
goose	geese	stratum	strata
man	men	analysis	analyses
mouse	mice	axis	axes
ox	oxen	basis	bases
woman	women	oasis	oases
alumnus	alumni	parenthesis	parentheses
curriculum	curricula	thesis	theses
datum	data		

PUTTING WORDS TOGETHER

PREFIXES

Generally, when you add a prefix to a root word, neither the root nor the prefix changes spelling:

un- + prepared = unprepared

mal- + nutrition = malnutrition

sub- + traction = subtraction

mis- + informed = misinformed

This rule applies even when the root word begins with the same letter as the prefix. Generally you use both consonants, but let your eye be your guide. If it looks funny, it's probably not spelled correctly. The following are some examples:

dissatisfied	irreverent
disservice	misspelled

illegible   misstep

irrational   unnatural

SPELLING PRACTICE 9

Circle the correctly spelled word in each of the following sentences.

76. The argument seemed (**ilogical/illogical**) to me.

77. He was busy (**collating/colating**) all the pages.

78. She was (**irreverent/ireverent**) in church today.

79. The (**comentator/commentator**) on TV summarized the news of the day.

80. They (**colaborated/collaborated**) on the project for school.

HYPHENS

When you put words and word parts together, it's difficult to know when to leave the words separate, when to hyphenate, and when to put the words or word parts together into one new word. Do you write co-dependent or codependent? Do I have a son in law or a son-in-law? There are several rules for using hyphens to join words. Often these words are joined so they can perform a new function in the sentence.

- Combine words with a hyphen to form an adjective when the adjective appears before a noun.
  - a well-heeled man
  - a first-rate hotel
  - a well-known actor
- When the combination of words that makes an adjective appears after the noun, the combination is not hyphenated.

It's a job ill suited to his talents.

She is well regarded in the community.

The hotel is first rate.

- Combine words with a hyphen when the words are used together as one part of speech. This includes family relationships.
  - editor-in-chief
  - jack-of-all-trades
  - maid-of-all-work
  - mother-in-law
  - runner-up
  - sister-in-law
- Use a hyphen before *elect* and after *vice, ex,* or *self.*
  - ex-President
  - ex-teacher
  - self-styled
  - Senator-elect
  - Vice-Admiral
- Use a hyphen when joining a prefix to a capitalized word.
  - mid-Atlantic
  - pan-European
  - post-Civil War
  - trans-Siberian
  - un-American
- Use a hyphen to make compound numbers or fractions.
  - thirty-nine years
  - one and two-thirds cups of broth
  - one-half of the country
  - three-fourths of the electorate
- Also use a hyphen when you combine numbers with nouns.
  - a class of six-year-olds
  - a two-year term
  - a twenty-five-cent fare

- Use a hyphen to form ethnic designations.
  an African-American woman
  the Sino-Russian War
  the Austro-Hungarian Railroad

Except for the cases noted above, prefixes are also joined directly to root words. The best rule of thumb is this: If the phrase acts like an adjective, it probably needs a hyphen. If you want to put two words together and they don't seem to fit into any of these rules, the best strategy is to consult a dictionary.

APOSTROPHES AND ABBREVIATIONS

Apostrophes are often misused, and knowing when to use them and when not to can be confusing. Of all the punctuation marks, the apostrophe is the one most likely to be abused and confused. Fortunately, there are a few simple rules; if you follow them, you won't go wrong with apostrophes.

THE RULES

1. Use an apostrophe to show possession: Jack's book.

2. Use an apostrophe to make a contraction: We don't like broccoli.

3. Do not use an apostrophe to make a plural: I have two apples (not apple's).

POSSESSIVES

The following rules show you how to use apostrophes to show possession.

- Singular noun: add 's
  the child's cap

- Singular noun ending in *ss*: add '
  the hostess' home

- Plural noun ending in *s*: add '
  the lawyers' bills

- Plural noun not ending in *s*: add 's
  The Children's Museum, the men's clothes

- Proper noun (name): add 's
  Jenny's watch, Chris's car, the Jones's house

- Singular indefinite pronoun: add 's
  one's only hope

- Plural indefinite pronoun: add '
  all the others' votes

- Compound noun: add ' or 's after the final word
  the men-at-arms' task, my mother-in-law's house

- Joint possession: add 's to the final name
  Jim and Fred's coffee house

- Separate possession: add 's after both names
  Betty's and Ching's menus

CONTRACTIONS

A contraction is formed by putting two words together and omitting one or more letters. The idea is that you add an apostrophe to show that letters have been left out. For example, "We have decided to move to Alaska" becomes, "We've decided to move to Alaska."

Here's a list of some of the most common contractions:

he will = he'll
I will = I'll
we will = we'll
it is = it's
she is = she's
you are = you're
they are = they're
we are = we're
cannot = can't
do not = don't

does not = doesn't
have not = haven't
should not = shouldn't
will not = won't

There are other ways in which an apostrophe can represent missing letters:

- In dialect: "I'm goin' down to the swimmin' hole," said the boy.
- When the letter *o* represents of: "Top o' the morning" or Mr. O'Reilly.

SPELLING PRACTICE 10

Practice using apostrophes by correcting the following sentences.

81. Mrs. Clarks' store had been built in the 1970s.

82. Everyones lawn chair's were stored in John and Marys backyard.

83. They had gone to the ladies room to powder their nose's.

84. Wed rather have dinner at my mother-in-laws house next door.

85. Shouldnt he pick up his fax's before he goes home?

ABBREVIATIONS

Many words and expressions in English are shortened by means of abbreviations. Though certain abbreviations are not usually used in formal writing, such as abbreviations for days of the week, they can be useful in less formal situations. Abbreviations are usually followed by periods.

THE EXCEPTIONS

- Don't use periods with the two-letter postal code abbreviations for states: CA, FL, IL, NJ, NY, TX, and so on.
- Don't use periods for initials representing a company or agency: FBI, CBS, NFL.
- Don't use periods after the letters in acronyms.

Common Abbreviations

Type	Examples
Names of days	Sun., Mon., Tues., Wed., etc.
Names of months	Jan., Feb., Mar., Apr., etc.
Titles and degrees	Mr., Mrs., Ms., Esq., Dr., Hon., M.D., Ph.D., Ed.D.
Rank	Sgt., Capt., Maj., Col., Gen.
Business terms	C.O.D. (collect on delivery), Mfg. (Manufacturing), Inc. (Incorporated), Assn. (Association), Ltd. (Limited)

SPELLING PRACTICE 11

Circle the correct bold term in each sentence below.

86. I will have two (**week's/weeks'**) vacation in (**N.O.V./Nov.**) this year.

87. Gen. (**Jone's/Jones's**) order was to leave on (**Sun./Sund.**)

88. My letter to my professor was addressed, "Mary Stevens, (**PHD./Ph.D.**)"

89. (**Les's and Larry's/Les and Larry's**) mopeds were parked outside.

90. The ancient Greeks worshiped at the (**goddess'/goddess's**) shrine every spring.

ANSWERS

SPELLING PRACTICE 1

1. niece
2. seize
3. height, weight
4. relieved
5. reign
6. cashier
7. surveillance
8. frieze
9. chief
10. fiend

SPELLING PRACTICE 2

11. knight
12. answer
13. debt
14. gnarled
15. indict
16. psalm
17. subtle
18. ghost
19. often
20. autumn

SPELLING PRACTICE 3

21. finally
22. submitting, submitted
23. thinking
24. roaming, roamed
25. controlling, controlled
26. plainness
27. rebelling, rebelled
28. throbbing, throbbed
29. legally
30. raining, rained

SPELLING PRACTICE 4

31. cymbal
32. generous
33. trafficking
34. general
35. circulate

SPELLING PRACTICE 5

36. weak
37. bear
38. minor
39. peel
40. sheer
41. site
42. right
43. cord
44. past
45. descent

SPELLING PRACTICE 6

46. surprising
47. desirable
48. courageous
49. scarcity
50. peaceable
51. advertisement
52. careless
53. politeness
54. argument
55. disgraceful

SPELLING PRACTICE 7

56. attorneys
57. relaying
58. enjoyable

59. playing
60. annoyance
61. hurries
62. heartily
63. studying
64. angrily
65. plentiful

SPELLING PRACTICE 8
6. faxes
67. flashes
68. matches
69. guesses
70. skills
71. potatoes
72. sopranos
73. heroes
74. pianos
75. tomatoes

SPELLING PRACTICE 9
76. illogical
77. collating
78. irreverent
79. commentator
80. collaborated

SPELLING PRACTICE 10
81. Clark's
82. Everyone's, chairs, Mary's
83. ladies', noses
84. We'd, mother-in-law's
85. Shouldn't, faxes

SPELLING PRACTICE 11
86. Weeks', Nov.
87. Jones's, Sun.
88. Ph.D
89. Les's and Larry's
90. Goddess'

C·H·A·P·T·E·R 4
VOCABULARY LIST 1: PREFIXES

CHAPTER SUMMARY

When actors analyze a character, they break the person's characteristics down into personality, mannerisms, and appearance in order to see what makes them tick. You do much the same thing when you analyze a word. Breaking a new word down into its parts can help you understand its meaning.

I n order to be able to unlock the meaning of many words in our language, it is useful for you to understand what a prefix is. A prefix is a word part at the beginning of a word that changes or adds to the meaning of the root word in some way. By learning some common prefixes, you will learn to recognize many unfamiliar words. After you have completed the exercises in this chapter, you will become acquainted with the meanings suggested by some of the more common prefixes, which will improve your reading, speaking, and listening vocabularies.

Choose the word from the Vocabulary List that best fits into the crossword puzzle. You can check your answers at the end of the chapter following the answers to the questions.

Vocabulary List 1: Prefixes

antecedent
antipathy
circumvent
consensus
controversy
decimate
demote
disinterested
euphemism
exorbitant
illegible
intermittent
malevolent
precursor
prognosis
retrospect
subordinate
synthesis
transcend
trivial

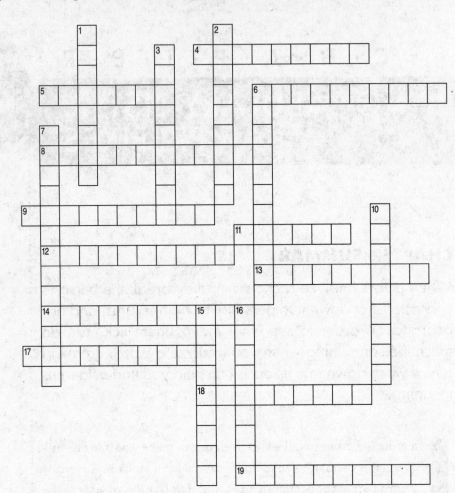

Across

4 medical "forecast"
5 unimportant
6 avoid, elude
8 occasional
9 preexistent, previous
11 the opposite of promote
12 excessive
13 integration
14 inferior
17 hindsight
18 predecessor
19 sinister, venomous

Down

1 destroy
2 to exceed
3 unreadable
6 dispute, argument
7 neutral, unprejudiced
10 general agreement
15 aversion, loathing
16 an expression for

antecedent   (an·ti·ˈsēd·ənt)

prefix: **ante** means before

(*adj.*)

going before in time

The event was _____ to the Civil War.

antipathy   (an·ˈtip·ə·thē)

prefix: **anti** means against

(*noun*)

revulsion, any object of strong dislike

The child had an _____ toward snakes.

circumvent   (sər·kəm·ˈvent)

prefix: **circum** and **circ** mean around

(*verb*)

to go around; to catch in a trap; to gain superiority
     over; to prevent from happening

Police tried to _____ the riot by moving the
     crowd along.

consensus   (kən·ˈsen·səs)

prefix: **con** means with, together

(*noun*)

agreement, especially in opinion

The committee reached _____ about gun
     control.

controversy   (ˈkon·trə·ver·sē)

prefix: **contr** means against

(*noun*)

a discussion of a question in which opposing views
     clash

There is a _____ about building nuclear power
     plants.

decimate   (ˈdes·i·māt)

prefix: **dec** means ten

(*verb*)

to destroy or kill a large portion of something, to
     take or destroy a tenth part of something

Caterpillars can _____ trees.

demote   (di·ˈmōt)

prefix: **de** means down, away from

(*verb*)

to lower in grade or position

Upper ranked officers can _____ a lower ranked
     person.

disinterested   (dis·ˈin·tər·est·ed)

prefix: **dis** means not, opposite of

(*adj.*)

not motivated by personal interest or selfish motives

A loyal citizen is _____.

euphemism   (ˈu·fə·mizm)

prefix: **eu** means good, well

(*noun*)

the use of a word or phrase that is considered less
     distasteful or offensive than another

"She is at rest" is a _____ for "she is dead."

exorbitant   (ek·ˈzor·bi·tənt)

prefix: **ex** means out of, away from

(*adj.*)

going beyond what is reasonable and proper

The colonists rebelled against _____ taxes.

illegible   (i·ˈlej·ə·bəl)

prefix: **il** means not, opposite

(*adj.*)

not able to be read

The student had to rewrite the _____ paper.

intermittent   (in·tər·'mit·ənt)
prefix: **inter** means between
(*adj.*)
stopping and starting again at intervals
The weather forecaster predicted _____
    showers.

malevolent   (mə·'lev·ə·lent)
prefix: **mal** means bad
(*adj.*)
having an evil disposition toward others
A _____ person rejoices in the misfortune of
    others.

precursor   (pre·'kər·sər)
prefix: **pre** means before
(*noun*)
a forerunner, a harbinger, one who or that which
    goes before
Calmness is usually a _____ to a storm.

prognosis   (prog·'nō·sis)
prefix: **pro** means before
(*noun*)
a forecast; especially in medicine
The injured animal's _____ for recovery is
    good.

retrospect   ('ret·rō·spekt)
prefix: **retro** means back, again
(*verb*)
to think about the past
(*noun*)
looking back on or thinking about things past
In _____, the world leader wished he had acted
    differently.

subordinate   (sub·'or·din·it)
prefix: **sub** means under
(*adj.*)
inferior to or placed below another in rank, power,
    or importance
(*noun*)   (sub·'or·din·it)
a person or thing of lesser power or importance than
    another
(*verb*)   (sub·'or·din·āt)
to treat as inferior or less important
The wise president treated her _____ with
    respect.

synthesis   ('sin·thə·sis)
prefix: **syn, sym** means with or together
(*noun*)
putting of two or more things together to form a
    whole
In chemistry, the process of making a compound by
    joining elements together is called _____.

transcend   (tran·'send)
prefix: **trans** means across
(*verb*)
to go beyond the limits of; to overstep; to exceed
A seeing eye dog enables blind people to _____
    their disability.

trivial   ('triv·ē·əl)
prefix: **tri** means three
(*adj.*)
of little worth or importance
The research scientist did not have time for
    _____ pursuits because he was so busy
    conducting important experiments.

WORDS IN CONTEXT

The following exercise will help you figure out the meaning of some words from Vocabulary List 1 by looking at context clues. After you have read and understood the paragraph, explain the context clues that helped you with the meaning of the vocabulary word. Check the answer section at the end of this chapter for an example.

> In our country, the use of nuclear power as a viable source of energy has been an ongoing *controversy*. During the gas and oil shortages of the 1970s, energy prices were *exorbitant*. The federal government supported nuclear power as a new energy source that would be cost effective. Now, the President's National Energy Policy Report lists nuclear power as a safe and affordable alternative. Today, as in the past, many people have voiced their *antipathy* toward nuclear power plants, especially in the wake of the 1979 partial meltdown of the Three Mile Island nuclear power plant. At that time, scientists scrambled to *circumvent* a total meltdown in a facility that was designed to be fail-safe. There was great fear that the meltdown would be complete and *decimate* the area. Now, the federal government is once again promoting this alternative energy source.

SENTENCE COMPLETION

Insert the correct word from Vocabulary List 1 into the following sentences.

1. World leaders and anti-globalization protesters are at odds in the continuing _____ about how to assist sluggish world economies.

2. At the Cradle of Aviation Museum, a _____ of man's first trip to the moon in 1969 will include a restored lunar module.

3. Soon after the war began in Bosnia in April 1992, the damaged, dynamited, and burned homes reduced the country to ruins and _____ the landscape.

4. Scientists have discovered what could be the closest _____ to man, an upright walking ape-like creature.

5. The stock market has generally declined over the past year, with _____ periods of growth.

6. Oprah Winfrey was able to _____ her humble roots to become one of the nation's most respected, wealthy, and powerful women.

7. The police department's crime stopper's unit placed a drawing and description of the _____ kidnapper in the newspaper.

8. Errors caused by physicians' _____ handwriting have sparked proposals to add handwriting courses to medical school curricula.

9. After the implantation of a heart pacemaker, the patient's _____ was good.

10. "Downsizing a company" is a _____ for letting go or firing employees.

11. Different ethnic groups' _____ toward each other has resulted in many wars throughout the world.

12. Because of the _____ price and gas consumption of the sports utility vehicle, the

first-time buyer selected a small, energy-efficient sedan.

13. After the _____ successfully increased the company's sales and production, the chief executive officer promoted her to regional sales manager.

14. Environmentalists and energy analysts have not reached _____ about how best to meet America's growing energy needs in a safe and financially sound manner.

15. Due to his mistreatment of fellow officers, the captain was _____ to the rank of sergeant.

16. The famous actor seemed _____ in fame and the constant media attention he received; he continued to live his life in the same way as before his rise to fame.

17. A patchwork quilt is the result of the _____ of many smaller pieces sewn together to make a unique design.

18. In order to _____ the impending storm, the pilot changed his flight plan to avoid turbulence and lightning.

19. My _____ were some of the first colonial activists in the United States; they took part in the Boston tea party.

20. What some may consider _____ or unimportant ideas sometimes blossom into good business ventures.

SYNONYMS

The following exercise lists vocabulary words from this chapter. Each word is followed by five answer choices. Four of them are synonyms of the vocabulary word in bold. Your task is to choose the one that does **not** fit.

21. controversy
a. dispute
b. quarrel
c. consensus
d. debate
e. disputation

22. disinterested
a. selfish
b. impartial
c. neutral
d. objective
e. unbiased

23. antipathy
a. aversion
b. dislike
c. hatred
d. sympathy
e. abhorrence

24. exorbitant
a. reasonable
b. excessive
c. overpriced
d. inflated
e. steep

25. intermittent
a. sporadic
b. alternating
c. recurring
d. occasional
e. continual

26. malevolent
   a. malicious
   b. spiteful
   c. nasty
   d. disinterested
   e. wicked

27. transcend
   a. exceed
   b. descend
   c. excel
   d. surpass
   e. outdo

28. precursor
   a. successor
   b. forerunner
   c. ancestor
   d. antecedent
   e. predecessor

29. synthesis
   a. mixture
   b. fusion
   c. separation
   d. amalgamation
   e. blend

30. decimate
   a. demolish
   b. annihilate
   c. build
   d. slaughter
   e. kill

ANTONYMS

Choose the word from Vocabulary List 1 that means the opposite, or most nearly the opposite of the following groups of words.

31. descendant, successor, progeny, heir _____

32. readable, decipherable, comprehensible, clear _____

33. direct, face, aim, confront _____

34. disagreement, wrangle, conflict, dissent _____

35. promote, encourage, sponsor, support _____

36. benevolent, caring, compassionate, kindly _____

37. leading, chief, primary, foremost _____

38. trail, follow, tail, drag _____

39. significant, major, important, noteworthy _____

40. continuous, constant , nonstop, incessant _____

MATCHING

Match the word in the first column with the corresponding word in the second column.

41. circumvent   **a.** dispute

42. retrospect   **b.** combination

43. euphemism   **c.** excessive

44. precursor   **d.** destroy

45. synthesis   **e.** skirt

46. antipathy   **f.** predecessor

47. disinterested   **g.** hindsight

48. exorbitant   **h.** pleasant substitute words

49. controversy   **i.** hatred

50. decimate   **j.** neutral

PRACTICE ACTIVITIES

Write ten words that begin with the same prefixes as the words in this unit. Write your definition of each word based on what you already know about each prefix. Be sure to check your answers with a dictionary definition of each word.

Example: *preactivity* means a warm-up activity that comes before the main activity.

Create a personal "pictionary" prefix book. List common prefixes along with their definitions and create drawings that remind you of their meanings.

Example:

Prefix	Definition	Illustration
anti	against	(draw a no smoking sign)
		🚭 to show you are **against** smoking

ANSWERS

WORDS IN CONTEXT

We learn that nuclear energy has its supporters and opponents who continually debate each other; therefore, *controversy* means a public dispute. We read that, energy prices were *exorbitant* and the government began to promote nuclear power as a *financially reasonable alternative.* The implication is that *exorbitant* is excessive. After reading what has gone wrong with one particular power plant, we can infer that *antipathy* refers to the *negative feelings* of a significant portion of the population who oppose and intensely *dislike the idea* of nuclear power plants. After the disaster, we learn that scientists tried to *circumvent,* or *prevent,* a total meltdown. Finally, it was necessary for the scientists to stop a complete meltdown because it would *decimate,* or totally destroy, the area. The partial meltdown of the reactor was disastrous enough, so the result of a total meltdown would be unimaginable destruction.

SENTENCE COMPLETION

1. *controversy.* If you got this question wrong, refer back to the word's definition.
2. *retrospect.* If you got this question wrong, refer back to the word's definition.
3. *decimated.* If you got this question wrong, refer back to the word's definition.
4. *precursor.* If you got this question wrong, refer back to the word's definition.
5. *intermittent.* If you got this question wrong, refer back to the word's definition.
6. *transcend.* If you got this question wrong, refer back to the word's definition.
7. *malevolent.* If you got this question wrong, refer back to the word's definition.

8. *illegible.* If you got this question wrong, refer back to the word's definition.
9. *prognosis.* If you got this question wrong, refer back to the word's definition.
10. *euphemism.* If you got this question wrong, refer back to the word's definition.
11. *antipathy.* If you got this question wrong, refer back to the word's definition.
12. *exorbitant.* If you got this question wrong, refer back to the word's definition.
13. *subordinate.* If you got this question wrong, refer back to the word's definition.
14. *consensus.* If you got this question wrong, refer back to the word's definition.
15. *demoted.* If you got this question wrong, refer back to the word's definition.
16. *disinterested.* If you got this question wrong, refer back to the word's definition.
17. *synthesis.* If you got this question wrong, refer back to the word's definition.
18. *circumvent.* If you got this question wrong, refer back to the word's definition.
19. *antecedents.* If you got this question wrong, refer back to the word's definition.
20. *trivial.* If you got this question wrong, refer back to the word's definition.

SYNONYMS

21. c. *consensus.* Controversy is a discussion where opposing views clash. Therefore, consensus would not be a synonym of the word because it means to come to an agreement.
22. a. *selfish.* Disinterested means not motivated by personal interest. Therefore, selfish would not be a synonym of the word because it means to have a personal interest.

23. d. *sympathy.* Antipathy means to have a feeling of hatred toward someone or something. Since sympathy means to have feelings of compassion for someone or something, it cannot be a synonym of the word.

24. a. *reasonable.* Exorbitant means excessive; thus, reasonable is the opposite in meaning and cannot be a synonym.

25. e. *continual.* Intermittent means to happen at regular intervals whereas continual means without stopping; therefore, it cannot be the synonym of the word.

26. d. *disinterested.* Malevolent means to have evil feelings and intentions toward someone or something. Disinterested means to be neutral about someone or something; thus, it cannot be the synonym of the word.

27. b. *descend.* Transcend means to go beyond whereas descend means to go below and cannot be a synonym of the word.

28. a. *successor.* A precursor is something that comes before. Successor cannot be a synonym because it means something that comes after.

29. c. *separation.* A synthesis is a blending together of things to form something; therefore, separation cannot be a synonym of the word.

30. c. *build.* Decimate means to destroy; therefore, build cannot be a synonym of the word.

ANTONYMS

31. *antecedent.* Antecedent means ancestors, the opposite of the meaning of the words in the group.

32. *illegible.* Illegible means unreadable, the opposite of the words in the group.

33. *circumvent.* Circumvent means to go around, the opposite of the words in the group.

34. *consensus.* Consensus means agreement, the opposite of the words in the group.

35. *demote.* Demote means to downgrade, the opposite of the meaning of the words in the group.

36. *malevolent.* Malevolent means evil, the opposite of the meaning of the words in the group.

37. *subordinate.* Subordinate means secondary, the opposite of the meaning of the words group.

38. *transcend.* Transcend means exceed, the opposite of the meaning of the words in the group.

39. *trivial.* Trivial means unimportant, the opposite of the meaning of the words in the group.

40. *intermittent.* Intermittent means interrupted, the opposite of the meaning of the words in the group.

MATCHING

41. e
42. g
43. h
44. f
45. b
46. i
47. k
48. c
49. a
50. d

Across

4 prognosis
5 trivial
6 circumvent
8 intermittent
9 antecedent
11 demote
12 exorbitant
13 synthesis
14 subordinate
17 retrospect
18 precursor
19 malevolent

Down

1 decimate
2 transcend
3 illegible
6 controversy
7 disinterested
10 consensus
15 antipathy
16 euphemism

C·H·A·P·T·E·R

VOCABULARY LIST 2: SUFFIXES

5

CHAPTER SUMMARY

Just as a movie director must check each part of a movie set in order to make sure it's functioning correctly, readers must check each part of a word in order to analyze its meaning. Just as the end of a movie is as important as its beginning, a word ending plays an important role in determining the part of speech of a word.

Word endings that are added to the main part, or root, of words are called suffixes. Suffixes are word parts that signal how a word is being used in a sentence. You will note that each word in the list is a particular part of speech (*noun, verb, adjective,* or *adverb*). Suffixes often change the part of speech of a word.

For example, take the word *deferment* from the following vocabulary list. A *deferment* is a noun that means a postponement. If the suffix (word ending -*ment*) is removed, the word becomes *defer,* and it is used as a verb meaning to postpone.

As a *verb* it appears as *defer*:

I will *defer* the payment until next month.

As a *noun* it appears as it is:

The bank gave him a *deferment.*

Choose the word from the Vocabulary List that best fits into the crossword puzzle. You will use 17 of the words from the Vocabulary List to solve the puzzle. You can check your answers at the end of the chapter following the answers to the questions.

Vocabulary List 2: Suffixes

bigotry
consummate
copious
cryptic
deferment
etymology
furtive
laudable
mutation
obsolescence
parity
pragmatism
protagonist
provocative
puerile
rectify
relentless
satirize
venerate

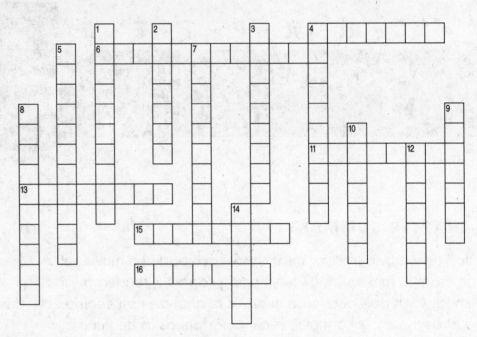

Across

4 to correct, make right
6 uselessness
11 praiseworthy
13 change, variation
15 to honor
16 obscure, secret

Down

1 perfect, complete, accomplished
2 bountiful
3 delay
4 unceasing
5 irritating, stirring into action
7 to make worse
8 practicality
9 childish
10 stealthy
12 prejudice, intolerance
14 equality

As an *adjective* it appears as *deferred*:

The *deferred* payment is due in one month.

The following table shows suffixes used in this Vocabulary List. They are divided into the parts of speech, or the "jobs" they suggest for the words. Other words that contain those suffixes are listed. In the last column add at least one other word that uses the suffix, besides the one in today's Vocabulary List.

NOUN ENDINGS

Suffix	Meaning	Examples
-tion	act or state of	retraction, contraction
-ment	quality	deportment, impediment
-ist	one who	anarchist, feminist
-ism	state or doctrine of	barbarism, materialism
-ity	state of being	futility, civility
-ology	study of	biology
-escence	state of	adolescent
-y, -ry	state of	mimicry, trickery

ADJECTIVE ENDINGS

Suffix	Meaning	Examples
-able	capable	perishable, flammable
-ic	causing, making	nostalgic, fatalistic
-ian	one who is or does	tactician, patrician
-ile	pertaining to	senile, servile
-ious	having the quality of	religious, glorious
-ive	having the nature of	sensitive, divisive
-less	without	guileless, reckless

VERB ENDINGS

Suffix	Meaning	Examples
-ize	to bring about	colonize, plagiarize
-ate	to make	decimate, tolerate
-ify	to make	beautify, electrify

agrarian   (ə·'grer·ē·ən)
suffix: -**ian** means one who is or does
(*adj.*)
having to do with agriculture or farming
The farmer loved his _____ life.

antagonist   (an·'ta·gə·nist)
suffix: -**ist** means one who
(*noun*)
one that contends with or opposes another
In the movie *Batman*, the Joker is Batman's

_____ .

bigotry   ('big·ə·trē)
suffix: -**ry** means state of
(*noun*)
unreasonable zeal in favor of a party, sect, or
    opinion; excessive prejudice _____ can
    lead to malevolent actions.

consummate   ('kon·səm·māt)
suffix: -**ate** means to make
(*verb*)
to complete, to carry to the utmost degree
The business woman needed to _____ the deal
    quickly.

copious   ('cōp·ē·əs)
suffix: -**ious** means having the quality of
(adj.)
abundant; plentiful; in great quantities
A _____ amount of sunshine is predicted for
    the summer.

cryptic   ('krip·tik)
suffix: -**ic** means causing
(*adj.*)
hidden; secret; having a hidden or ambiguous
    meaning
The detective uncovered the meaning of the
    _____ message.

deferment   (di·'fər·mənt)
suffix: -**ment** means quality of
(*noun*)
the act of putting off or delaying; postponement
The bank offered the struggling college graduate a
    _____ on his student loan payment.

furtive   ('fər·tiv)
suffix: -**ive** means having the nature of
(*adj.*)
done in a stealthy manner; sly and underhanded
The two criminals who were in cahoots gave each
    other _____ looks behind the detective's
    back.

laudable   ('law·də·bəl)
suffix: -**able** means capable of
(*adj.*)
praiseworthy
Her dedication and ability to rehabilitate the injured
    is _____ .

geology   (jē·'ä·lə·jē)
suffix: -**ology** means study of
(*noun*)
the study of the history of the earth and its life,
    especially as recorded in rocks
The _____ major traveled to Mt. Etna to
    examine the effects of the volcano's most recent
    eruption.

minimize   ('mi·nə·mīz)
suffix: -**ize** means to subject to an action
(*verb*)
to play down; to keep to a minimum
The President tried to _____ his involvement in
    the trial so that he would not be implicated in
    the scandal.

mutation (mū·ʹtā·shən)

suffix: -**tion** means action of, state of

(*noun*)

the act or process of changing

Scientists research gene _____ in fruit flies to see how genes change from one generation to the next.

obsolescence (äb·sə·ʹles·ens)

suffix: -**escence** means state of

(*noun*)

the state of being outdated

With the advent of the personal computer, the typewriter has been in _____ for many years.

parity (ʹpar·i·tē)

suffix: -**ity** means state of being

(*noun*)

the state or condition of being the same in power, value or rank; equality

Women and minorities continue to fight for _____ in the workplace.

pragmatism (ʹprag·mə·tizm)

suffix: -**ism** means state or doctrine of

(*noun*)

faith in the practical approach

The man's _____ enabled him to run a successful business.

provocative (prō·ʹvok·ə·tiv)

suffix: -**ive** means having the nature of

(*adj.*)

something that stirs up an action

The _____ words of the environmental activist inspired many to volunteer for the community clean-up day.

puerile (ʹpyoor·əl)

suffix: -**ile** means pertaining to

(*adj.*)

childish, silly, immature

The teen's _____ actions at the party couldn't be ignored.

rectify (ʹrek·ti·fī)

suffix: -**ify** means to make

(*verb*)

to make right; to correct

The newspaper tried to _____ the mistake by correcting the misprint

relentless (re·ʹl·ənt·les)

suffix: -**less** means without

(*adj.*)

harsh; unmoved by pity; unstoppable

She was _____ in her search for knowledge; she read everything she could get her hands on.

venerate (ʹven·ə·rāt)

suffix: -**ate** means to make

(*verb*)

to look upon with deep respect and reverence

Some cultures _____ their elders.

WORDS IN CONTEXT

The following exercise will help you figure out the meaning of some words from Vocabulary List 2 by looking at context clues. After you have read and understood the paragraph, explain the context clues that helped you with the meaning of the vocabulary word. Check the answer section at the end of this chapter for an example.

The latest remake of *Planet of the Apes* develops the theme of *bigotry* in a world where apes are the dominant culture and humans are enslaved. *Parity* between the two species is unthinkable because the simians regard humans as inferior creatures. Leo, the central character, is the story's protagonist. He is a human astronaut who lands on a strange planet where apes *venerate* their own kind by offering praise and promotions for negative actions taken against humans. Leo's *antagonist*, General Thade is the leader of the apes in this bizarre culture, and encourages the mistreatment of humans by apes. In General Thade's opinion, extermination of the humans is a *laudable* cause and he mounts a full-scale campaign to exterminate humans from the planet.

SENTENCE COMPLETION

Insert the word from Vocabulary List 2 that best completes the sentences.

1. Pulitzer Prize-winning novelist Eudora Welty was _____ in her obituary.

2. You would never accuse Mark of _____; he's the most open-minded person I know.

3. It took several months to _____ the merger, but after tough negotiation, the two companies became one.

4. His removal from the little league game was due to the young boy's _____ behavior of throwing the bat when he was angry.

5. Rainforests are known for their _____ amounts of rainfall that supply the fauna with many nutrients.

6. During WWII, Native Americans worked to develop a _____ code that could not be deciphered by the enemy.

7. Because of the family's _____ search, they were quickly reunited with their lost dog.

8. My little brother is the _____ in the family; he constantly provokes fights with my sister and me.

9. Wear these protective goggles to _____ your chances of injury to your eyes.

10. Due to the _____ of the budget director's financial policies, the economy grew stronger.

11. In order to _____ the wrongdoing of the internment of innocent Japanese Americans during WWII, the U.S. government has agreed to pay reparations to victims.

12. A _____ in certain strains of powerful bacteria has turned them into drug-resistant menaces.

13. The actions of a few skittish animals _____ the majority of horses to stampede.

14. Union officials continuously fight for _____ in pay and safe working conditions.

15. The horse and buggy had reached its _____ in the early 1900s with the production of the automobile.

16. In order to entice the consumer, companies will offer a short-term _____ on payments for buying merchandise.

17. I loved studying _____ because I enjoyed looking at interesting rocks and how they came to be on Earth.

18. The young teen's heroic effort to save the family from the sinking car was _____.

19. The spy's disguise and _____ actions were undetected by foreign government officials.

20. The haying season is my favorite part of _____ life.

SYNONYMS

The following exercise lists vocabulary words from this chapter. Each word is followed by five answer choices. Four of them are synonyms of vocabulary word in bold. Your task is choose the one that does **not** fit.

21. relentless
   a. unstoppable
   b. persistent
   c. unyielding
   d. capitulate
   e. inexorable

22. laudable
   a. praiseworthy
   b. worthy
   c. commendable
   d. creditable
   e. furtive

23. parity
   a. equity
   b. inequality
   c. par
   d. fairness
   e. evenhandedness

24. venerate
   a. respect
   b. honor
   c. minimize
   d. revere
   e. worship

25. puerile
   a. childish
   b. juvenile
   c. mature
   d. infantile
   e. babyish

26. furtive
   a. stealthy
   b. secret
   c. sly
   d. honest
   e. surreptitious

27. copious
   a. scarce
   b. abundant
   c. numerous
   d. plentiful
   e. profuse

28. cryptic
   a. mysterious
   b. enigmatic
   c. puzzling
   d. obvious
   e. secret

29. provocative
   a. challenging
   b. inciting
   c. stimulating
   d. confrontational
   e. conciliatory

30. mutation
   a. static
   b. changing
   c. transformation
   d. metamorphosis
   e. alteration

ANTONYMS

Choose the word from Vocabulary List 2 that means the opposite, or most nearly the opposite of the following groups of words.

31. curtail, shorten, curb, limit _____

32. tolerance, broadmindedness, open-mindedness, acceptance _____

33. impracticality, uselessness, fruitlessness, pointlessness _____

34. straightforward, forthright, candid, up-front _____

35. scarce, limited, inadequate, scant _____

36. protagonist, leader, hero, supporter _____

37. inequality, inequity, discrimination, disparity _____

38. urban, city, metropolitan, cosmopolitan _____

39. despise, loathe, scorn, hate _____

40. magnify, intensify, enhance, overplay _____

CHOOSING THE RIGHT WORD

Circle the word in bold that best completes the sentence.

41. Since I grew up on a ranch in Montana, I appreciate the constant struggle of the (**antagonist, agrarian**) lifestyle.

42. She filled an entire notebook with the (**copious, laudable**) notes that she took during the class.

43. The car salesman wanted to (**consummate, rectify**) the car deal before the customers changed their minds.

44. Her (**cryptic, puerile**) behavior made her seem childish and immature.

45. The automotive industry builds a certain amount of (**pragmatism, obsolescence**) into cars so that they will need to be replaced in few years.

46. Language interpreters can even decipher (**provocative, cryptic**) phrases that most people wouldn't understand.

47. In order to eliminate (**bigotry, geology**) many schools have included programs to reduce hatred of others and increase tolerance.

48. The Coast Guard's (**relentless, furtive**), search for any survivors of the airplane crash lasted three weeks.

49. In some cultures, people (**minimize, venerate**) their elders by seeking their wisdom.

50. Scientists can monitor the (**mutation, deferment**) of certain bacteria by watching them change form over time.

PRACTICE ACTIVITIES

List all the words in this chapter and try changing the part of speech of each word by changing its suffix. For instance, change *deferment* to *deferred* or *defer*. Be sure to check the definition of the altered word.

> Example: **Venerate** changed to **veneration** means a feeling of deep respect.

Find words in the newspaper that have the same suffixes as the words in this unit. Write them next to the chapter words and take a guess at their meanings. Check your definition with a dictionary definition.

For example, one of the suffixes in the vocabulary list is *"tion"* which means state of or action of. The word found in the newspaper is *evolution* meaning the act of changing over a period of time.

ANSWERS

WORDS IN CONTEXT

After reading the paragraph, we learn that the movie Planet of the Apes is an upside-down world where apes rule over humans and believe them to be inferior creatures whose only use are to be slaves; thus, we may conclude that *bigotry* means intolerance. Since the humans are slaves, their ape owners would **not** want them to achieve *parity*; therefore, the inference is that **parity** means equality. Leo, the central character, is the protagonist. Therefore, we know that *antagonist* must mean someone who is opposing him, because Thade mounts an attempt to exterminate humans and we know that Leo is a human. The story shows the *antipathy*, the hatred, between apes and humans. The apes *venerate*, show respect, and honor their leaders. They respect their species and reward *laudable* deeds such as capturing escaped humans. We can infer that *laudable* means praiseworthy.

SENTENCE COMPLETION

1. *venerated.* If you got this question wrong, refer back to the word's definition.
2. *bigotry.* If you got this question wrong, refer back to the word's definition.
3. *consummate.* If you got this question wrong, refer back to the word's definition.
4. *puerile.* If you got this question wrong, refer back to the word's definition.
5. *copious.* If you got this question wrong, refer back to the word's definition.
6. *cryptic.* If you got this question wrong, refer back to the word's definition.
7. *relentless.* If you got this question wrong, refer back to the word's definition.
8. *antagonist.* If you got this question wrong, refer back to the word's definition.
9. *minimize.* If you got this question wrong, refer back to the word's definition.
10. *pragmatism.* If you got this question wrong, refer back to the word's definition.
11. *rectify.* If you got this question wrong, refer back to the word's definition.
12. *mutation.* If you got this question wrong, refer back to the word's definition.
13. *provoked.* If you got this question wrong, refer back to the word's definition.
14. *parity.* If you got this question wrong, refer back to the word's definition.
15. *obsolescence.* If you got this question wrong, refer back to the word's definition.
16. *deferment.* If you got this question wrong, refer back to the word's definition.
17. *geology.* If you got this question wrong, refer back to the word's definition.
18. *laudable.* If you got this question wrong, refer back to the word's definition.
19. *furtive.* If you got this question wrong, refer back to the word's definition.
20. *agrarian.* If you got this question wrong, refer back to the word's definition.

SYNONYMS

21. d. *capitulate.* Relentless means to never give up, so capitulate would not be a synonym of the word, since it means to surrender.
22. e. *furtive.* Laudable means worthy of praise, so furtive would not be a synonym of the word, since it means sneaky.
23. b. *inequality.* Parity means equality, thus inequality would not be a synonym of the word because it means to not be equal.

24. c. *minimize.* Venerate means to hold in the highest regard, so minimize would not be a synonym of the word, since it means to play down or keep to a minimum.

25. c. *mature.* Puerile means childish, so mature would not be a synonym of the word, since it means grown-up.

26. d. *honest.* Furtive means sneaky and underhanded, so honest would not be a synonym of the word, since it means open.

27. a. *scarce.* Copious means plentiful, so scarce would not be a synonym of the word, since it means in short supply.

28. d. *obvious.* Cryptic means hidden, so obvious would not be a synonym of the word, since it means clear.

29. e. *conciliatory.* Provocative means inciting to action, so conciliatory would not be a synonym of the word, since it means appeasing.

30. a. *static.* Mutation means to change in form, so static would not be a synonym of the word since it means unchanging.

ANTONYMS

31. *consummate.* Consummate means to complete, the opposite of the meaning of the words in the group.

32. *bigotry.* Bigotry means narrow-mindedness, the opposite of the meaning of the words in the group.

33. *pragmatism.* Pragmatism means common sense, the opposite of the meaning of the words in the group.

34. *furtive.* Furtive means secretive, the opposite of the meaning of the words in the group.

35. *copious.* Copious means plentiful, the opposite of the meaning of the words in the group.

36. *antagonist.* An antagonist is opposition or an adversary, the opposite of the meaning of the words in the group.

37. *parity.* Parity means equality, the opposite of the meaning of the words in the group.

38. *agrarian.* Agrarian means having to do with farming and agriculture, the opposite of the words in the group.

39. *venerate.* Venerate means to honor, the opposite of the meaning of the words in the group.

40. *minimize.* Minimize means to play down or keep to a minimum, the opposite of the meaning of the words in the group.

CHOOSING THE RIGHT WORD

41. *agrarian.* Context clue is the ranch in Montana; life on a ranch would have to do with agriculture and farming.

42. *copious.* Context clue is that she filled a notebook with her notes.

43. *consummate.* Context clue is that the car salesman wanted the customers to finish the transaction by buying a car.

44. *puerile.* Context clue is that her behavior appeared childish and immature.

45. *obsolescence.* Context clue is that the car industry makes cars that eventually must be replaced.

46. *cryptic.* Context clue is that most people wouldn't understand the phrase.

47. *bigotry.* Context clue is that many schools have programs to reduce hatred.

48. *relentless.* Context clue is that the Coast Guard searched for three weeks.

49. *venerate.* Context clue is that people in some cultures seek their elder's wisdom.

50. *mutation.* Context clue is that the bacteria change over time.

Across

4 rectify
6 obsolescence
11 laudable
13 mutation
15 venerate
16 cryptic

Down

1 consummate
2 copious
3 deferment
4 relentless
5 provocative
7 exacerbate
8 pragmatism
9 puerile
10 furtive
12 bigotry
14 parity

VOCABULARY LIST 3: LEARNING ROOTS

6

...ARY

...e Greek and Latin roots will help you
...y by helping you recognize words.

...lener builds a lovely garden by having its plants
...healthy roots, you will see your vocabulary grow
...mmon roots. Although it is the main part of a
...t necessarily a complete word. It is the base for
...fix might be added.
...vill become familiar with twenty common roots.
...are various suffixes that you have already become
...ter 5. You are on your way toward building a
...king the connections between these word parts
...anings.

Handwritten note: Convey = to deliver or make understood / Ex:

Choose the word from the Vocabulary List that best fits into the crossword puzzle. You can check your answers at the end of the chapter following the answers to the questions.

Vocabulary List 3:
Learning Roots

agonize
audible
belligerent
chronic
demographic
fidelity
fluctuate
genocide
incognito
inducement
interrogate
loquacious
nominal
pathos
protracted
rejected
sophisticated
tenacious
verify
vivacious

Across

3 confirm
5 incentive
9 able to be heard
10 undercover
13 intentional destruction of an entire group of people
14 small amount
17 experienced and aware
18 change often
19 constant, continuous
20 drawn out

Down

1 persistent
2 discarded
4 to provoke
6 question, investigate
7 talkative, garrulous
8 statistical characteristics of human populations
11 hostile, aggressive
12 pathetic quality
15 faithfulness
16 lively, ebullient

agonize   (ˈa·gə·nīz)
root: **agon** means struggle, contest
(*verb*)
to suffer intense pain, to struggle over something
I _____ over every decision I make; I can never
   decide what I want.

audible   (ˈô·də·bəl)
root: **aud** means hear
(*adj.*)
able to heard
Please turn up the volume on the radio; the song is
   barely _____ .

belligerent   (bəl·ˈlij·ər·ənt)
root: **bell** means war
(*adj.*)
warlike, hostile
The opposition's _____ attitude made matters
   worse.

chronic   (ˈkron·ik)
root: **chron** means time
(*adj.*)
constant, habitual
Children's _____ ear infections must be treated
   with antibiotics.

demographic   (dem·ə·ˈgraf·ik)
root: **dem** means people
(*noun*)
statistical characteristics of human population, such
   as age or income
The Internet has access to many _____ statistics
   about your city.

fidelity   (fi·ˈdel·i·tē)
root: **fid** means faith
(*noun*)
faithfulness
Our club values the _____ of its members; we
   know we can always count on one another.

fluctuate   (ˈflək·chu·āt)
root: **flux, flu** means to flow
(*verb*)
to move up and down, constantly changing
Bring along several changes of clothing because the
   weather report said that the temperature will
   _____ .

genocide   (ˈjen·ə·sīd)
root: **gen** means race or kind
(*noun*)
the deliberate extermination of an entire group of
   people
They fled their country because of rumors of
   terrorists committing _____ .

incognito   (in·kog·ˈnē·tō)
root: **cog, gno** means to know
(*noun*)
disguised, unrecognizable
As part of the Witness Protection Program, he had to
   travel _____ .

inducement   (in·ˈdüs·mənt)
root: **duc** means lead
(*noun*)
motive, leading to an action, incentive
As an _____ to come to the fair, free admission
   was offered to anyone who arrived before noon.

interrogate   (in·'ter·rə·gāt)
root: **rog** means to ask
(*verb*)
to question
Customs agents have the right to _____
    passengers.

loquacious   (lō·'kwā·shəs)
root: **loq** means speak
(*adj.*)
talkative
The _____ guest monopolized the conversation.

nominal   ('nom·ən·əl)
root: **nom** means name
(*adj.*)
in name only, small amount
She expended only _____ energy during the
    heat wave so that she wouldn't collapse.

pathos   ('pā·thōs)
root: **path** means feelings
(*noun*)
suffering; feeling of sympathy or pity
Children who are raised to feel _____ are not
    usually bullies.

protracted   (prō·'trak·ted)
root: **tract** means draw; pull
(*adj.*)
drawn out in time, prolonged
The union and the city could not agree on
    contractual terms, which led to a _____
    settlement.

rejected   (ri·'jek·ted)
root: **ject** means to throw or send
(*verb*)
sent back, refused, discarded
She _____ his offer of marriage, so he took the
    ring back to the jeweler.

sophisticated   (sə·'fis·ti·kā·ted)
root: **soph** means wisdom
(*adj.*)
knowledgeable; refined, experienced, and aware
The dance couple mastered the _____ jazz step.

tenacious   (tə·'nā·shəs)
root: **ten** means hold
(*adj.*)
unwilling to let go, stubborn
The _____ grip of the pit bull is what makes it
    so dangerous.

verify   ('ver·ə·fī)
root: **ver** means truth
(*verb*)
to establish as truth, confirm
Scientists have not been able to _____ the
    existence of UFOs.

vivacious   (vi·'vā·shəs)
root: **viv** means life
(*adj.*)
lively in manner
The _____ teen became captain of the
    cheerleading team.

WORDS IN CONTEXT

The following exercise will help you figure out the meaning of some words from Vocabulary List 3 by looking at context clues. After you have read and understood the paragraph, explain the context clues that helped you with the meaning of the vocabulary word. Check the answer section at the end of this chapter for an example.

Medical researchers can now *verify* that college freshman living in dormitories are at a greater risk of contracting meningitis than other college students. Meningococcal meningitis is a *tenacious* bacterial infection of membranes around the brain and spinal chord that if left untreated could be fatal. Symptoms include fever, neck stiffness, and constant pain from a *chronic* headache. College officials are using this information as an *inducement* for vaccinating incoming freshman. Many universities are now offering this vaccine either free or for a *nominal* fee. The vaccination's *protracted* effectiveness is three to five years.

SENTENCE COMPLETION

Insert the correct word from Vocabulary List 3 into the following sentences.

1. Cambodian government officials are preparing to prosecute those leaders most responsible for the Khmer Rouge _____ of one fifth of the total population of the country.

2. Almost every area of our lives will be affected by our country's _____ changes as the baby boomers age.

3. Some infomercials promise rock-hard abdominals as a/an _____ to buy a variety of exercise machines.

4. Janice is awfully quiet and pale tonight; it's such a contrast to her normally _____ personality.

5. Because of the _____ they feel for people, studies show that dogs in hospitals treat human patients with unconditional love.

6. During the annual San Fermin running of the bulls festival, spectators try to avoid the path of _____ bulls.

7. After the car collision, the passenger suffered from _____ back pain for the rest of his life.

8. Health fitness experts now _____ that walking ranks as America's most popular activity.

9. Temperatures in the desert can _____ greatly from brutally hot during the day to freezing temperatures at night.

10. Because of their known _____ toward their human companions, over one thousand dogs were sent overseas to protect American soldiers during the Vietnam War.

11. It's hard for my grandfather not to _____ over having to go into a retirement home; he wants to remain independent as long as possible, and is very concerned with losing his independence.

12. Famous sports and movie personalities often travel _____ in order to avoid being hounded by the media.

13. In order to _____ the alleged thief, proper police procedures must be followed.

14. The celebrity guest was known for his exciting story telling; the talk-show host asked her _____ guest to tell the story of his youth.

15. After placing their home for sale, the homeowners _____ their first offer for their house because it was too low.

16. Even after being treated with strong antibiotics, the _____ ear infection would not ease its grip on its victim.

17. The new stereo system made every sound, no matter how minute, clearly _____.

18. The _____ dispute between management and the team players lasted several years.

19. Since there was only a _____ fee to enter the bike race, even the poorest cyclists could enter the race.

20. Animal cloning begins with a _____ procedure where scientists remove the DNA-containing nucleus of a female animal's egg and replace it with the genetic material from a body cell of an adult animal's donor.

SYNONYMS

The following exercise lists vocabulary words from this chapter. Each word is followed by five answer choices. Four of them are synonyms of the vocabulary word in bold. Your task is to choose the one that does **not** fit.

21. vivacious
   a. cheerful
   b. bubbly
   c. animated
   d. tenacious
   e. spirited

22. interrogate
   a. grill
   b. verify
   c. ask
   d. cross-examine
   e. interview

23. fidelity
   a. betrayal
   b. devotion
   c. faithfulness
   d. reliability
   e. trustworthiness

24. chronic
   a. continuing
   b. constant
   c. intermittent
   d. unceasing
   e. never-ending

25. incognito
   a. disguised
   b. undercover
   c. anonymously
   d. secretly
   e. open

26. illegible
   a.   indecipherable
   b.   scrawled
   c.   scribbled
   d.   audible
   e.   unreadable

27. fluctuate
   a.   vary
   b.   steady
   c.   up and down
   d.   oscillate
   e.   ebb and flow

28. agonize
   a.   struggle
   b.   torment
   c.   contend
   d.   upset
   e.   endure

29. nominal
   a.   supposed
   b.   small amount
   c.   actual
   d.   in name only
   e.   so-called

30. pathos
   a.   sorrow
   b.   joy
   c.   suffering
   d.   pity
   e.   grief

ANTONYMS

Choose the word from Vocabulary List 3 that means the opposite, or most nearly the opposite of the following groups of words.

31. passive, peaceful, nonviolent, diplomatic _____

32. silent, reserved, reticent, taciturn _____

33. disloyalty, betrayal, unfaithfulness, treachery _____

34. accepted, agreed to, assented, wanted _____

35. primitive, unrefined, uncultured, naïve _____

36. agreeable, amenable, easygoing, flexible _____

37. disprove, refute, invalidate, contradict _____

38. candidly, openly, honestly, frankly _____

39. languid, unenergetic, unhurried, lethargic _____

40. brief, concise, short-lived, pithy _____

MATCHING

Match the word in the first column with the corresponding word in the second column.

41. genocide   a. sent back

42. audible   b. sympathy

43. verify   c. destruction of a race

44. tenacious   d. disguised

45. rejected   e. talkative

46. fidelity   f. to suffer anguish

47. loquacious   g. can be heard

48. agonize   h. loyalty

49. incognito   i. stubborn

50. pathos   j. prove

PRACTICE ACTIVITIES

The following are words that have the same roots as the words in this chapter. Divide each word into its parts: prefix, root, suffix. See if you can recognize the meaning of the new words and check your answers using a dictionary.

agony, audit, antebellum, chronicle, democracy, infidel, influx, progeny, diagnosis, surrogate, soliloquy, anonymous, apathy, distracted, interjected, philosopher, tenable, voracious, vivid

Select any five words from the above list and create your own sentences.

ANSWERS

WORDS IN CONTEXT

Answer: After reading the paragraph we learn that a study has been done that shows that college freshmen living in dormitories have a higher risk of getting meningitis; therefore, we can conclude that *verify* means confirm. Because this disease could be fatal, we can understand that once contracted, this disease is not easily wiped out; thus, we can infer that *tenacious* means persistent and not easily stopped. Since the symptoms include constant pain from a headache, we can deduce that *chronic* means continual. It makes sense that college officials are concerned about the possible outbreak of such a disease on campus and would take measures to prevent its occurrence, so we can infer that *inducement* means encouragement. Students would be encouraged to take the vaccine if it were free or inexpensive; therefore, we can see that *nominal* means a small amount. Finally, we can gather that *protracted* means drawn out by the mention that the vaccine will last from three to five years.

SENTENCE COMPLETION

1. *genocide.* If you got this question wrong, refer back to the word's definition.
2. *demographic.* If you got this question wrong, refer back to the word's definition.
3. *inducement.* If you got this question wrong, refer back to the word's definition.
4. *vivacious.* If you got this question wrong, refer back to the word's definition.
5. *pathos.* If you got this question wrong, refer back to the word's definition.
6. *belligerent.* If you got this question wrong, refer back to the word's definition.
7. *chronic.* If you got this question wrong, refer back to the word's definition.
8. *verify.* If you got this question wrong, refer back to the word's definition.
9. *fluctuate.* If you got this question wrong, refer back to the word's definition.
10. *fidelity.* If you got this question wrong, refer back to the word's definition.
11. *agonize.* If you got this question wrong, refer back to the word's definition.
12. *incognito.* If you got this question wrong, refer back to the word's definition.
13. *interrogate.* If you got this question wrong, refer back to the word's definition.
14. *loquacious.* If you got this question wrong, refer back to the word's definition.
15. *rejected.* If you got this question wrong, refer back to the word's definition.
16. *tenacious.* If you got this question wrong, refer back to the word's definition.
17. *audible.* If you got this question wrong, refer back to the word's definition.
18. *protracted.* If you got this question wrong, refer back to the word's definition.
19. *nominal.* If you got this question wrong, refer back to the word's definition.
20. *sophisticated.* If you got this question wrong, refer back to the word's definition.

SYNONYMS

21. d. *tenacious.* Vivacious means lively, so tenacious would not be a synonym of the word, since it means stubborn.
22. b. *verify.* Interrogate means to question, so verify would not be a synonym of the word, since it means confirm.

23. a. *betrayal.* Fidelity means loyalty, so betrayal would not be synonym of the word, since it means disloyal.

24. c. *intermittent.* Chronic means recurring, so intermittent would not be a synonym of the word, since it means alternating.

25. e. *open.* Incognito means in disguise, so open would not be synonym of the word, since it means visible.

26. d. *audible.* Illegible means hard to read, so audible would not be a synonym of the word, since it means easy to hear.

27. b. *steady.* Fluctuate means to change, so steady would not be a synonym of the word, since it means unchanging.

28. e. *endure.* Agonize means to struggle, so endure would not be a synonym of the word, since it means to bear, or to accept.

29. c. *actual.* Nominal means supposed, so actual would not be a synonym of the word, since it means real.

30. b. *joy.* Pathos means sadness, so joy would not be a synonym of the word, since it means delight.

ANTONYMS

31. *belligerent.* Belligerent means aggressive, the opposite of the meaning of the words in the group.

32. *loquacious.* Loquacious means talkative, the opposite of the meaning of the words in the group.

33. *fidelity.* Fidelity means loyalty, the opposite of the meaning of the words in the group.

34. *rejected.* Rejected means not wanted, the opposite of the meaning of the words in the group.

35. *sophisticated.* Sophisticated means urbane, the opposite of the meaning of the words in the group.

36. *tenacious.* Tenacious means stubborn, the opposite of the meaning of the words in the group.

37. *verify.* Verify means to prove, the opposite of the meaning of the words in the group.

38. *incognito.* Incognito means in disguise, the opposite of the meaning of the words in the group.

39. *vivacious.* Vivacious means energetic, the opposite of the meaning of the words in the group.

40. *protracted.* Protracted means long, drawn-out, the opposite of the meaning of the words in the group.

MATCHING

41. c
42. g
43. j
44. i
45. a
46. h
47. e
48. f
49. d
50. b

Across

3 verify
5 inducement
9 audible
10 incognito
13 genocide
14 normal
17 sophisticated
18 fluctuate
19 chronic
20 protracted

Down

1 tenacious
2 rejected
4 antagonize
6 interrogate
7 loquacious
8 demographic
11 belligerent
12 pathos
15 fidelity
16 vivacious

C·H·A·P·T·E·R 7

VOCABULARY LIST 4: MORE ROOTS

CHAPTER SUMMARY

The more roots you can recognize, the stronger your vocabulary will be. Just as many people in our culture have their roots in other countries, roots of English words have their beginnings from many other languages. The words of our language have actually been borrowed from other languages over the course of history. The history of a word is called its etymology. Many of the roots in Chapter 6 come from Greek and Latin languages. We have included 20 more words with important roots in this chapter because the more roots and origins you are familiar with, the more you will be able to recognize related words.

or example, in this chapter you will be introduced to the root *phobe* which means fear. You can then guess that any word that contains this root has to do with the fear of something. For instance, claustrophobia means abnormal fear of small spaces.

Choose the word from the Vocabulary List that best fits into the crossword puzzle. You can check your answers at the end of the chapter following the answers to the questions.

Vocabulary List 4:
More Roots

agoraphobic
assimilate
attribute
benevolent
biodegradable
conspicious
contradiction
credence
evident
gregarious
impediment
incisive
inference
mediocre
philanthropy
precedent
recapitulate
remittance
tangential
urbane

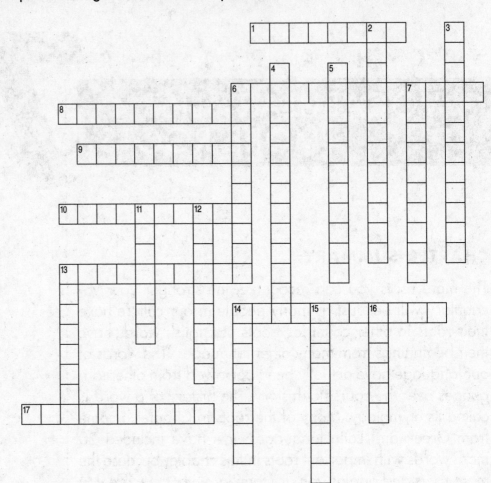

Across

1 average
6 able to be broken down by living things
8 payment
9 to credit
10 relating to
13 hindrance
14 easily noticed
17 social

Down

2 summarize
2 goodwill towards men
4 denial
5 fear of open or public spaces
6 bighearted, good
7 to fit in
11 obvious
12 deduction
13 clear cut
14 belief
15 preceding
16 suave

agoraphobic   (ag·ə·rə·ˈfō·bik)

root: **phobe** means fear

(*adj.*)

fear of open or public spaces

The _____ person refused to leave his home.

assimilate   (əs·ˈsim·ə·lāt)

root: **simul** means copy

(*verb*)

to fit in

The college freshman had to _____ to college
   life.

attribute   (ˈat·tri·būt)

root: **trib** means to give

(*noun*)

a special quality

(*verb*)   at·trib·ˈūt

to credit

He had the most important _____ for a
   business partner, loyalty.

benevolent   (bə·ˈnev·ə·lent)

root: **ben** means good

(*adj.*)

kind, having goodwill

The _____ family volunteered their time to help
   others.

biodegradable   (bī·ō·dē·ˈgrād·ə·bəl)

root: **bio** means life

(*adj.*)

able to be broken down by living things

As consumers become more aware of how we will
   dispose of our waste, more _____
   products are available in stores.

conspicuous   (con·ˈspic·ū·əs)

root: **spic, spec** mean see

(*adj.*)

highly visible

The sailor admired the _____ 100-foot yacht.

contradiction   (con·trə·ˈdik·shən)

root: **contra** means against, **dict** means say

(*noun*)

the act or state of disagreeing

Since times has changed, Congress created a law in
   the year 2001 that was a direct _____ of an
   older law written in 1959.

credence   (ˈkrē·dəns)

root: **cred** means believe

(*noun*)

belief, believability

The large hole in the ozone layer gives _____ to
   the global warming theory.

evident   (ˈev·i·dent)

root: **vid** means see

(*adj.*)

obvious

It is _____ by your high grade that you
   prepared for the test.

gregarious   (gre·ˈgair·ē·əs)

root: **greg** means crowd

(*adj.*)

sociable

The _____ hostess was the life of the party.

impediment   (im·ˈped·ə·mənt)

root: **ped, pod** means foot, **ped** means child

(*noun*)

a barrier or hindrance

She overcame her speech _____ and became an
   excellent public speaker.

incisive   (in·ˈsī·siv)
root: **cis, cid** mean to cut
(*adj.*)
penetrating, clear cut
The news reporter was known for his _____
    accounts of world events.

inference   (ˈin·fər·ens)
root: **fer** means bear or carry
(*noun*)
guess or surmise
Mathematicians use the results of equations to make
    _____ about patterns in the world.

mediocre   (mēd·ē·ˈō·kər)
root: **med** means middle
(*adj.*)
of medium quality, neither good nor bad, average
The actress was not selected for the part because of
    her _____ audition.

philanthropy   (fi·ˈlan·thrə·pē)
root: **phil** means love
(*noun*)
giving generously to worthy causes
Because of the community's _____, the cultural
    arts center was built.

precedent   (ˈpres·i·dənt)
root: **ced** means go
(*noun*)
a prior ruling or experience
Lawyers found a _____ that would help their
    client's case.

recapitulate   (rē·ka·ˈpitch·ū·lāt)
root: **cap** means head
(*verb*)
to review in detail
The professor _____ key details before the
    exam.

remittance   (re·ˈmit·əns)
root: **mit, mis** means to send
(*noun*)
payment, transmittal of money
Please enclose your _____ along with the
    coupon for the merchandise.

tangential   (tan·ˈjen·shəl)
root: **tang, tac, tig** mean touch
(*adj.*)
touching slightly, relating to
According to restaurant goers, a food's nutritional
    value is _____ to its taste.

urbane   (ər·ˈbān)
root: **urb** means city
(*adj.*)
polished, sophisticated
The company looks for hard-working, _____
    people as representatives.

WORDS USED IN CONTEXT

The following exercise will help you figure out the
meaning of some words from Vocabulary List 4 by
looking at context clues. After you have read and understood the paragraph, explain the context clues that
helped you with the meaning of the vocabulary word.
Check the answer section at the end of this chapter for
an example.

Scientists at New York Aquarium in Brook-
lyn have discovered that bottle nosed
dolphins may have self-awareness. They

attribute this belief to the result of experiments by Dr. Diane Reiss at the Osborn Lab of Marine Science. She and her team gave further *credence* to this notion by marking dolphins' noses with an *x* and an *o*. Sometimes the mark was done with just water, sometimes with colored waterproof dye. Each time a dolphin was marked, it would check itself in the mirror. If it had a *conspicuous* colored mark, it would swim to the side of the pool and try to rub it off. As a result of these experiments, scientists made an *inference* that because these dolphins recognized their image in a mirror, they were self-aware. Before these experiments, gorillas set the *precedent* of being the only other mammals other than humans who could recognize their images.

SENTENCE COMPLETION

Insert the correct word from Vocabulary List 4 into the following sentences.

1. Reaching heights of 310 feet, the Millennium Force roller coaster is the most _____ ride at the Cedar Point Amusement Park.

2. In one generation, the immigrant family was able to _____ to its new surroundings.

3. Recent ocean-floor discoveries have made it _____ that the huge part of our planet hidden underwater still holds surprises that are waiting to be uncovered.

4. Some pest control companies guarantee that their _____ products will not leave any traces in either air or soil.

5. The _____ couple founded *Out of Africa* rehabilitation and learning center for abandoned or injured wild cats.

6. In order to become more _____ the shy young woman enrolled in a public speaking course.

7. The largest _____ to advancing in society is a lack of education.

8. Despite recent attacks, it is no _____ that humans are much more dangerous to sharks than sharks are to humans.

9. In order for the brain to function at an optimum rather than a _____ level, it needs proper nutrition, sleep, oxygen, caring, and laughter.

10. Lance Armstrong's recovery from cancer and comeback as world champion cyclist gives _____ to his positive attitude and perseverance.

11. As a result of the administration's tax rebate policy, most U.S. taxpayers will receive a _____ of $300–600 this year.

12. The multimillion dollar cultural arts center was built due to the _____ of wealthy patrons.

13. Scientists made _____ predictions about the damage from Europe's most active volcano, Mount Etna in Sicily.

14. In her warm and funny short stories, Eudora Welty preferred to talk about simple, humble characters rather than _____ high-society people.

15. Her local association was _____ to the world-wide environmental organization.

16. The writer _____ from his publisher's e-mail message that his book was approved.

17. The elderly woman became increasingly _____ and refused to leave her apartment.

18. He used the first chapter of his novel to _____ the historical background of the special air force unit in WWII.

19. Research has shown that as adults, even twins who are separated at birth have similar _____.

20. Before Sandra Day O'Connor's appointment, there was no _____ set for a federally appointed female Supreme Court Justice.

SYNONYMS

The following exercise lists vocabulary words from this chapter. Each word is followed by five answer choices. Four of them are synonyms of the vocabulary word in bold. Your task is to choose the one that does **not** fit.

21. benevolent
   a. compassionate
   b. caring
   c. malevolent
   d. kind
   e. generous

22. recapitulate
   a. repeat
   b. summarize
   c. reiterate
   d. decimate
   e. review

23. urbane
   a. sophisticated
   b. advanced
   c. complicated
   d. polished
   e. puerile

24. conspicuous
   a. cryptic
   b. evident
   c. visible
   d. prominent
   e. noticeable

25. incisive
   a. keen
   b. insightful
   c. unclear
   d. intuitive
   e. penetrating

26. gregarious
   a. sociable
   b. companionable
   c. outgoing
   d. extroverted
   e. shy

27. assimilate
   a. incorporate
   b. reject
   c. absorb
   d. digest
   e. understand

28. impediment
   a. hindrance
   b. obstacle
   c. obstruction
   d. aid
   e. barrier

29. inference
  a. deduction
  b. assumption
  c. obsolescence
  d. suggestion
  e. supposition

30. credence
  a. authority
  b. unbelievable
  c. credibility
  d. belief
  e. acceptance

ANTONYMS

Choose the word from Vocabulary List 4 that means the opposite, or most nearly the opposite, of the following groups of words.

31. aid, assistance, support, backing   _____

32. bill, cost, charge   _____

33. central, vital, innermost, crucial   _____

34. nastiness, greed, selfishness, gluttony   _____

35. unsophisticated, simple, crude, unrefined   _____

36. disbelief, incredulity, doubt, mistrust   _____

37. agreement, consensus, accord, harmony   _____

38. hidden, obscure, cryptic, concealed   _____

39. outstanding, exceptional, superior, first-rate   _____

40. unclear, murky, indistinct, doubtful   _____

CHOOSING THE RIGHT WORD

Circle the word in bold that best completes the sentence.

41. Because she was fearful of wide-open spaces, she was diagnosed as being (**agoraphobic, gregarious**).

42. During the scavenger hunt, the easily seen clue was left under a (**conspicuous, incisive**) rock.

43. The quickly dissolving fertilizer was (**mediocre, biodegradable**).

44. (**Benevolent, urbane**) Peace Corps volunteers selflessly devote their time to help others in need.

45. In order to receive high marks, Olympic ice skaters' performances cannot be (**conspicuous, mediocre**)

46. His blindness did not stop him from becoming a Grammy winner, nor was it an (**impediment, precedent**) to him becoming a singing sensation.

47. In the Preamble of the Constitution it clearly states, "We hold these truths to be self (**evident, benevolent**) that all men are created equal."

48. To sum up the important events, the producer had the narrator (**attribute, recapitulate**) those events at the movie's finale.

49. It's always a good idea to send your (**inference, remittance**) to the phone company immediately after you receive your bill.

50. Because of their clarity and logic, no one questioned the (**incisive, mediocre**) orders of the captain.

PRACTICE ACTIVITIES

The following is a list of words that contain the same roots as the words in this chapter. See if you can determine the word meanings. Check your definitions with the dictionary definitions.

xenophobia, facsimile, contribution, beneficiary, bionic, introspection, dictate, credulous, video, egregious, pedestrian, precise, interfere, media, bibliophile, intercede, commission, contiguous, suburban

Select any five words from the above list and create your own sentences.

ANSWERS

WORDS IN CONTEXT

After reading the paragraph, we learn that scientists have made a discovery about bottle-nosed dolphins. Because of their experiments using mirrors, they believe that the dolphins can recognize themselves in a reflection. Therefore they credit these experiments with proving this to be true. We can deduce that *attribute* means giving credit to the results that support this finding. The next word we see is *credence*. Further experiments of placing marks on the noses of these dolphins cause them to seek out their reflection to check their noses for marks that they try to wipe off. We can presume that *credence* means it makes these findings more believable. Because the dolphins tried to rub off *conspicuous* colored marks on their noses, we can imply that *conspicuous* marks were highly visible. Because of the results of these experiments, the scientists *inferred* that dolphins could recognize their own images. We can tell that the *inference* was their conclusion. The last vocabulary word we see is *precedent*. Since there have been no other examples of mammals being aware of their own image, other than gorillas setting a *precedent*, we can infer that the discovery of gorillas' self-awareness came before the dolphin discovery.

SENTENCE COMPLETION

1. *conspicuous.* If you got this question wrong, refer back to the word's definition.
2. *assimilate.* If you got this question wrong, refer back to the word's definition.
3. *evident.* If you got this question wrong, refer back to the word's definition.
4. *biodegradable.* If you got this question wrong, refer back to the word's definition.
5. *benevolent.* If you got this question wrong, refer back to the word's definition.
6. *gregarious.* If you got this question wrong, refer back to the word's definition.
7. *impediment.* If you got this question wrong, refer back to the word's definition.
8. *contradiction.* If you got this question wrong, refer back to the word's definition.
9. *mediocre.* If you got this question wrong, refer back to the word's definition.
10. *credence.* If you got this question wrong, refer back to the word's definition.
11. *remittance.* If you got this question wrong, refer back to the word's definition.
12. *philanthropy.* If you got this question wrong, refer back to the word's definition.
13. *incisive.* If you got this question wrong, refer back to the word's definition.
14. *urbane.* If you got this question wrong, refer back to the word's definition.
15. *tangential.* If you got this question wrong, refer back to the word's definition.
16. *inferred.* If you got this question wrong, refer back to the word's definition.
17. *agoraphobic.* If you got this question wrong, refer back to the word's definition.
18. *recapitulate.* If you got this question wrong, refer back to the word's definition.
19. *attributes.* If you got this question wrong, refer back to the word's definition.
20. *precedent.* If you got this question wrong, refer back to the word's definition.

SYNONYMS

21. c. *malevolent.* Benevolent means giving and kind, so malevolent would not be a synonym of the word since it means evil.

22. d. *decimate.* Recapitulate means to recap, so decimate would not be a synonym of the word since it means destroy.

23. e. *puerile.* Urbane means refined, so puerile would not be a synonym of the word because it means childish.

24. a. *cryptic.* Conspicuous means obvious, so cryptic would not be a synonym of the word because it means hidden.

25. c. *unclear.* Incisive means perceptive, so unclear would not be the synonym of the word because it means wishy-washy.

26. e. *shy.* Gregarious means outgoing, so shy would not be a synonym of the word.

27. b. *reject.* Assimilate means to take in, so reject would not be a synonym of the word because it means to discard or throw out.

28. d. *aid.* Impediment means an obstacle, so aid would not be a synonym of the word because it means to help.

29. c. *obsolescence.* Inference means a presumption, so obsolescence would not synonym of the word because it means outdated.

30. b. *unbelievable.* Credence means belief or trust, so unbelievable would not be a synonym since it means the opposite of the rest of the words in the list.

ANTONYMS

31. *impediment.* Impediment means hindrance, the opposite meaning of the words in the group.

32. *remittance.* Remittance means payment, opposite of the meaning of the words in the group.

33. *tangential.* Tangential means secondary or unimportant, the opposite of the meaning of the words in the group.

34. *philanthropy.* Philanthropy means generosity, the opposite of the meaning of the words in the group.

35. *urbane.* Urbane means sophisticated and cultured, the opposite of the meaning of the words in the group.

36. *credence.* Credence means belief, the opposite of the meaning of the words in the group.

37. *contradiction.* Contradiction means disagreement, the opposite of the words in the group.

38. *conspicuous.* Conspicuous means noticeable, the opposite of the words in the groups.

39. *mediocre.* Mediocre means commonplace, the opposite of the words in the group.

40. *evident.* Evident means obvious, the opposite of the meaning of the words in the group.

CHOOSING THE RIGHT WORD

41. *agoraphobic.* Context clue is that she was fearful of wide-open spaces.

42. *conspicuous.* Context clue is the easily seen clue.

43. *biodegradable.* Context clue is quickly dissolving fertilizer.

44. *benevolent.* Context clue is volunteers selflessly devote their time.

45. *mediocre.* Context clue is that Olympic skaters *cannot receive high marks.*

46. *impediment.* Context clue is the man's blindness did not stop him from becoming a Grammy winner.

47. *evident.* Context clue is *the Constitution clearly states.*

48. *recapitulate.* Context clue is that the important events were summarized.

49. *remittance.* Context clue is that the customers found the remittance to be too costly.

50. *incisive.* Context clue is that the captain's orders had clarity and logic.

Across

1 mediocre
6 biodegradable
8 remittance
9 attribute
10 tangential
13 impediment
14 conspicuous
17 gregarious

Down

2 recapitulate
3 philanthropy
4 contradiction
5 agoraphobic
6 benevolent
7 assimilate
11 evident
12 inference
13 incisive
14 credence
15 precedent
16 urbane

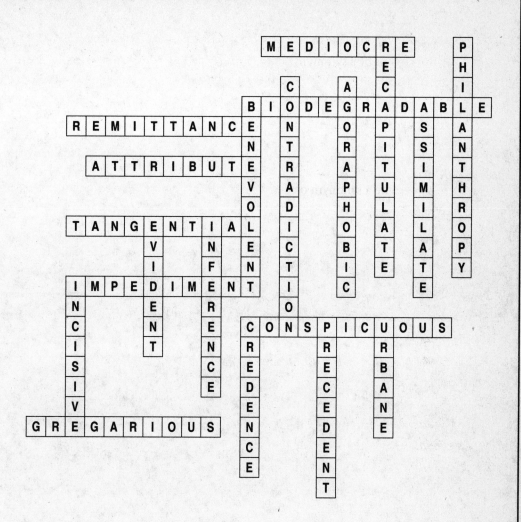

VOCABULARY LIST 5: FOREIGN LANGUAGE TERMS USED IN ENGLISH

CHAPTER SUMMARY

In this chapter you will learn words from other languages, such as French and Italian, that are used in English everyday. Many of these words have been adopted into the English language because there is not an English word that means exactly the same thing. For example, the word *naïve* is used frequently to describe someone who is young, innocent, simple, and sometimes gullible. In English we would have to use three or four words to say the same thing that the word *naïve* means. Some of these words are used frequently in articles about the arts. Other words are used in writing about history or politics. All of these words are used frequently in everyday speech and writing so it is important to be familiar with them.

I n this chapter you will practice using these words and learn the meaning and spelling of each word by completing the exercises. You may recognize many of these words when you hear them, but they may appear foreign to you when you see them written. This is because the pronunciation of each word follows the rules of the original language it is from and not necessarily traditional English pronunciation. Practice saying each word out loud as you read through the list.

Choose the word from the Vocabulary List that best fits into the crossword puzzle. You can check your answers at the end of the chapter following the answers to the questions.

Vocabulary List 5:
Foreign Language Terms
Used In English

aficionado
avant-garde
blasé
bourgeois
cliché
debut
élan
entrepeneur
epitome
fait accompli
gauche
imbroglio
ingénue
laissez faire
malaise
naïve
non sequitur
rendezvous
vendetta
vignette

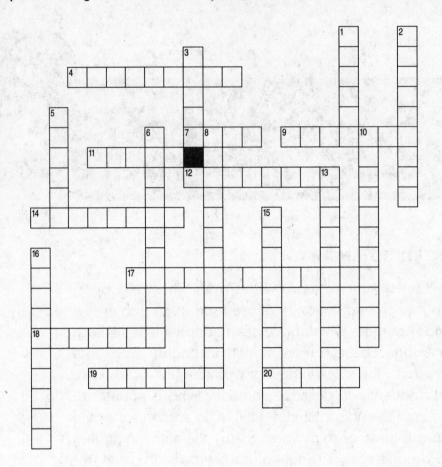

Across

4 a complicated or embarrassing situation
7 animation, spirit, life
9 a naïve young woman
11 unsophisticated and gullible
12 a short, descriptive piece of writing
14 grudge, feud
17 something finished and irreversible
18 quintessence
19 vague feeling of illness
20 first appearance

Down

1 an overly familiar, overused phrase
2 middle class
3 apathetic, uninterested
5 bumbling, crude
6 cutting edge
8 hands-off
10 a statement that has no connection to the previous statement or idea
13 someone who takes on a new business challenge or risk
15 a buff or devotee
16 to meet at an appointed place and time

aficionado   (ə·fi·shē·ˈnä·dō)

(*noun*)

a person who likes, knows about and is devoted to a
   particular activity or thing

She was a tennis _____; she loved the game and
   watched every tournament on television.

avant-garde   (ˈa·vänt·ˈgärd)

(*noun*)

a group of people who develop innovative and
   experimental concepts, especially in the arts

(*adj.*)

relating to a group of people who develop innovative
   and experimental concepts, especially in the
   arts

As a member of the _____, his paintings were
   very abstract and dealt with controversial
   topics.

His art teacher told him his painting was _____
   because he used his materials in a very creative
   and experimental way.

blasé   (blä·ˈzā)

(*adj.*)

apathetic to pleasure or excitement as a result of
   excessive indulgence in something

After going to her tenth live NBA game in a row, she
   became _____ about going to games
   because she felt like they were no longer
   exciting or fun.

bourgeois   (ˈbu̇rzh·wä)

(*adj.*)

having the attributes and beliefs of the middle class,
   marked by materialistic concerns

The rise of the middle class has made _____
   values paramount in most of American society.

cliché   (klē·ˈshā)

(*noun*)

a phrase or saying which has been overused and as a
   result has little significance or meaning

The news writer came to rely on journalistic
   _____ that weakened the vivid language
   on which his reputation rested.

debut   (ˈdā·byü)

(*noun*)

a first appearance

The young musician was very nervous at her musical
   _____ because she had never played in
   front of a crowd before.

élan   (ā·län)

(*noun*)

spirit, enthusiasm, or excitement

The freshman on the soccer team showed great
   _____ for the game by working really hard
   in every practice and cheering her teammates
   on from the sidelines when she wasn't playing.

entrepreneur   (ann·trə·prə·ˈnər)

(*noun*)

a person who takes on the challenge and risk of
   starting his or her own business

The young _____ was very excited about
   running his own restaurant, but spent many
   nights worrying about whether he would make
   a profit during his first few months of business.

epitome   (i·ˈpi·tə·mē)

(*noun*)

an exact example of something; someone or
   something that embodies the essence of a
   concept or type

He looked like the _____ of a college professor
   in his tweed jacket and horn-rimmed glasses.

fait accompli   (ˈfā·tə·käm·ˈplē)

(*noun*)

something that is complete and seemingly
    irreversible

When she signed the one-year lease for her new
    apartment it was a _____.

gauche   (ˈgōsh)

(*adj.*)

lacking social graces or sophistication

The teenager felt _____ in the company of a
    more sophisticated crowd.

imbroglio   (im·ˈbrōl·yō)

(*noun*)

a complicated or embarrassing situation due to a
    misunderstanding

When David thought that Sally was my girlfriend
    instead of my sister it created an _____
    until I cleared up the misunderstanding.

ingénue   (ˈan·jə·nü)

(*noun*)

a young girl or woman, an actress playing such a role

She was an _____; she was young and innocent.

laissez-faire   (le·sā·ˈfar)

(*noun*)

a doctrine opposing government control of
    economic matters except in the case of
    maintaining peace and the concept of property

He believed in a _____ policy because he
    thought that the government should not
    interfere with economic matters.

malaise   (mə·ˈlāz)

(*noun*)

the vague feeling of illness

She went to the doctor because she felt a general
    _____ and thought she was coming down
    with something.

naïve   (nä·ˈēv)

(*adj.*)

innocent, simple, lacking knowledge of the world

I told him he was _____ to think that his
    landlord would offer to fix his sink without a
    written or verbal request.

non sequitur   (ˈnän·ˈse·kwə·tər)

(*noun*)

a statement that has no connection to the previous
    statement or idea

My grandmother made such a _____ yesterday.
    She was telling me about her wedding and then
    in the next breath said her car needed to be
    fixed.

rendezvous   (ˈrän·dā·vü)

(*noun*)

a meeting place

(*verb*)

to meet at a meeting place

They decided the school would be their _____,
    and then they would go to the park.

vendetta   (ven·ˈde·tə)

(*noun*)

a grudge or feud characterized by acts of retaliation

He had a _____ against the man who killed his
    father and vowed he would seek revenge.

vignette   (vin·ˈyet)

(*noun*)

a short descriptive written piece

The teacher asked the class to write a _____
    about their home so they could practice writing
    short but clear descriptive pieces.

WORDS IN CONTEXT

The following exercise will help you figure out the meaning of some words from Vocabulary List 5 by looking at context clues. After you have read and understood the paragraph, explain the context clues that helped you with the meaning of the vocabulary word. Check the answer section at the end of this chapter for an example.

At the party, I watched as a young man introduced himself as an *entrepreneur* to a very *naïve* young girl, and then continued to brag about the business he recently opened. The young woman was so innocent that she didn't even realize that the man was flirting with her. For the sake of the girl, I joined the conversation rather abruptly by making a political comment about our government's *laissez faire* policy regarding economic regulation. I explained that it was ridiculous that our government did not see itself as responsible for regulating economic relations in our country because many poor people suffered as a result. The young entrepreneur seemed confused at first by my apparent *non sequitur* because it had absolutely nothing to do with his previous statement regarding his business. Yet he did not want to appear *gauche* in front of the young girl so he smiled and politely asked me to explain my view on laissez faire policies. At that point, the young girl excused herself and said that she was feeling a slight *malaise* and thought she should go home to rest. The young entrepreneur quickly suggested that they *rendezvous* at the park the following day, but the young girl politely declined.

SENTENCE COMPLETION EXERCISE

Insert the correct word from Vocabulary List 5 into the following sentences.

1. After riding the roller coaster eight times, Sally felt a feeling of _____ and thought she should probably take a break from the rides to avoid becoming ill.

2. After her older sister told on her, the young girl had a _____ against her sister and vowed that she would retaliate.

3. The young man was so _____; he honestly believed that government officials were never corrupt and did not lie.

4. Her first sentence was about her plans for college, but her next sentence was a total _____; she said she really wanted to get a dog.

5. On their first date, the young couple decided to _____ at the restaurant.

6. On the first day of class, he wrote a _____ about his house to practice his descriptive writing.

7. The young actress hated playing a(n) _____, but she always got those parts because she was young and attractive.

8. She went to dinner with some friends at a very fancy restaurant and felt so _____ because she didn't know which fork to use for her salad; when she asked her friends, they made fun of her.

9. My dad always speaks in _____ when he gives me advice. For example, the other day he told me not to count my chickens before they hatch.

10. My mother is a car _____; she knows everything there is to know about cars and loves to test drive different models.

11. Her art teacher said her sculpture was _____ because she used both metal and plastic in a way he had never seen done before.

12. When Kathy asked Sylvia if she wanted to go to the World Series with her, she was surprised that Sylvia was _____ about it, but Sylvia explained that she had been to the World Series five years in a row, and it was starting to get boring.

13. The young musician showed such _____ when he played the guitar; he played very difficult pieces without missing a note and seemed to enjoy himself immensely.

14. The _____ was very proud when he opened the doors of his new pet supply store on the first day of business.

15. She had just graduated from law school, but she looked like the _____ of a lawyer with her all-business expression, her briefcase and her professional suit.

16. The politician argued against the _____ policy because she felt that if economic matters were not regulated in our country, large companies would take advantage of consumers.

17. The plot of many TV sitcoms seems to revolve around a(n) _____; there is some big misunderstanding which results in an embarrassing situation, but it is usually resolved by the end of the show.

18. When she graduated from high school it was a _____; she had completed all of the requirements.

19. At the ballet, the young dancer made her _____ in the second act.

20. Most advertisements seem to include _____ values because middle class people are able to buy the items being advertised.

SYNONYMS QUESTIONS

The following exercise lists vocabulary words from this chapter. Each word is followed by five answer choices. Four of them are synonyms of the vocabulary word is bold. Your task is to choose the one that does **not** fit.

21. blasé
   a. bored
   b. enthusiastic
   c. apathetic
   d. neutral

22. avant-garde
   a. creative
   b. cutting edge
   c. conventional
   d. innovative

23. naïve
   a. innocent
   b. simple
   c. knowledgeable
   d. trusting

24. élan
   a. disinterest
   b. excitement
   c. spirit
   d. enthusiasm

25. aficionado
- a. fan
- b. novice
- c. devotee
- d. expert

26. non sequitur
- a. unrelated
- b. disconnected
- c. clear line of thought
- d. disjointed

27. vendetta
- a. grudge
- b. feud
- c. fight
- d. truce

28. vignette
- a. novel
- b. short piece
- c. description
- d. literary piece

29. cliché
- a. truism
- b. commonplace
- c. original statement
- d. familiar

30. malaise
- a. sickness
- b. illness
- c. healthy
- d. not well

ANTONYMS

Choose the word from Vocabulary List 5 that means the opposite, or most nearly the opposite, of the following groups of words.

31. sophisticated, graceful, classy, worldly _____

32. wise, mature, complicated, sophisticated _____

33. poor, not materialistic, working class _____

34. incomplete, reversible, disputable _____

35. old, wise, masculine _____

36. boredom, disinterest, despondent _____

37. clear, comfortable, easily understand situation _____

38. excitement, enthusiasm, wide-eyed, naïve _____

39. friendship, peaceful relationship, reconciliation _____

40. retirement, seclusion, final appearance _____

MATCHING

Match the word in the first column with the corresponding word in the second column.

41. debut   **a.** a young girl

42. aficionado   **b.** lacking social graces

43. avant-garde   **c.** a meeting place

44. élan   **d.** apathetic

45. gauche   **e.** spirit

46. naïve   **f.** a complicated misunderstanding

47. vendetta   **g.** a statement that does not relate to the previous statement

48. vignette   **h.** a completed fact

49. cliché   **i.** a feeling of sickness

50. malaise   **j.** an overused statement

51. entrepreneur   **k.** a short descriptive piece

52. epitome   **l.** a feud characterized by acts of retaliation

53. fait accompli   **m.** a fan or devotee

54. rendezvous   **n.** artistically innovative

55. ingénue   **o.** having middle class values

56. laissez faire   **p.** first appearance

57. imbroglio   **q.** one who starts his/her own business

58. bourgeois   **r.** an example or the embodiment of something

59. non sequitur   **s.** a political doctrine, which supports government deregulation of economic matters.

60. blasé   **t.** innocent, simple

PRACTICE ACTIVITIES

Many or these words are used in articles about art, politics, and history. Read a newspaper or magazine article about art or architecture, and an article about contemporary or historical politics and write down all of the foreign words you come across. How do you know if a word is a foreign word? How is it being used in the article? Add these words to your vocabulary list and look up the definition.

Now that you know these words, make a note when and where you see them. Think about the following questions: When do people use these words? What effect does it have on the piece of writing you are reading? Why have these particular words become such a regular part of our vocabulary?

ANSWERS

WORDS IN CONTEXT

In the first sentence we learn that the young man is an *entrepreneur* and that he is talking about a business he started, so we can conclude that being an *entrepreneur* has something to do with starting one's own business. The young girl is described as *naïve* and then in the next sentence described as very innocent. The narrator also explains that she enters this conversation "for the sake of the girl" so we can conclude that naïve means young and innocent and possibly in need of help. The next word we encounter is *laissez faire,* which is used to describe our government's economic policy so we know that it refers to something political and relates to economics. In the next sentence it becomes clearer that the narrator is using the word to mean that our government is not regulating economic matters. *Non sequitur* is used to refer to the narrator's comment and the fact that it was completely unrelated to the entrepreneur's previous statement so we can deduce that *non sequitur* means an unrelated statement. The entrepreneur does not want to appear *gauche* so he is polite even though he is confused by the comment. We can conclude that gauche must mean impolite or lacking social graces. We can deduce that *malaise* must mean feeling ill or tired because the girl needs to go home and rest. Finally, the entrepreneur asks the girl to "*rendezvous* at the park the next day" so we can conclude that *rendezvous* must mean meet.

SENTENCE COMPLETION

1. *malaise.* If you got this question wrong, refer back to the word's definition.
2. *vendetta.* If you got this question wrong, refer back to the word's definition.
3. *naïve.* If you got this question wrong, refer back to the word's definition.
4. *non sequitur.* If you got this question wrong, refer back to the word's definition.
5. *rendezvous.* If you got this question wrong, refer back to the word's definition.
6. *vignette.* If you got this question wrong, refer back to the word's definition.
7. *ingénue.* If you got this question wrong, refer back to the word's definition.
8. *gauche.* If you got this question wrong, refer back to the word's definition.
9. *clichés.* If you got this question wrong, refer back to the word's definition.
10. *aficionado.* If you got this question wrong, refer back to the word's definition.
11. *avant-garde.* If you got this question wrong, refer back to the word's definition.
12. *blasé.* If you got this question wrong, refer back to the word's definition.
13. *élan.* If you got this question wrong, refer back to the word's definition.
14. *entrepreneur.* If you got this question wrong, refer back to the word's definition.
15. *epitome.* If you got this question wrong, refer back to the word's definition.
16. *laissez faire.* If you got this question wrong, refer back to the word's definition.
17. *imbroglio.* If you got this question wrong, refer back to the word's definition.
18. *fait accompli.* If you got this question wrong, refer back to the word's definition.
19. *debut.* If you got this question wrong, refer back to the word's definition.
20. *bourgeois.* If you got this question wrong, refer back to the word's definition.

SYNONYMS

21. b. *enthusiastic. Blasé* means apathetic about something due to over indulgence. *Enthusiastic* would not be a synonym because it means to be excited about something.

22. c. *conventional. Avant-garde* means original and creative so *conventional* is not a synonym because it means lacking originality.

23. c. *knowledgeable. Naïve* means simple and innocent so *knowledgeable* is not a synonym because it means having knowledge.

24. a. *disinterest. élan* means spirit or enthusiasm so *disinterest* is not a synonym because it means lacking interest.

25. b. *novice.* An *aficionado* is an expert or devotee to something. A *novice* is someone who is new to something so it is not a synonym.

26. c. *clear line of thought.* A *non sequitur* is a statement that is not connected to the previous statement. A *clear line of thought* refers to several statements that follow each other so it is not a synonym.

27. d. *truce.* A *vendetta* is grudge or feud characterized by acts of retaliation. A *truce* is not a synonym because it means to settle or end a fight or disagreement.

28. a. *novel.* A *vignette* is a short descriptive piece but a *novel* is a long written story so it is not a synonym.

29. c. *original statement.* A *cliché* is a statement or saying that has been so overused that it lacks meaning. An *original statement* is not a synonym because it means a statement that is new and has not been used before.

30. c. *healthy. Malaise* means a feeling of sickness but *healthy* means to feel well so it is not a synonym.

ANTONYMS

31. *gauche. Gauche* means lacking social grace or sophistication, the opposite of the meaning of the words in the group.

32. *naïve. Naïve* means simple and innocent, the opposite of the meaning of the words in the group.

33. *bourgeois. Bourgeois* means characteristics of the middle class and materialistic, the opposite of the words in the group.

34. *fait accompli. Fait accompli* means a completed fact that is irreversible, the opposite of the words in the group.

35. *ingénue.* An *ingénue* is a young naãve girl, the opposite of the words in the group.

36. *élan. Élan* means spirit, enthusiasm, the opposite of the words in the list.

37. *imbroglio.* An *imbroglio* is a complicated situation or an embarrassing misunderstanding, the opposite of the words listed.

38. *blasé. Blasé* means apathetic due to over indulgence in something, the opposite of the words listed.

39. *vendetta. Vendetta* means a feud or grudge characterized by retaliation.

40. *debut. Debut* means first appearance, usually relating to one's entrance into society, the opposite of the words in the list.

MATCHING

41. p	**51.** q
42. m	**52.** r
43. n	**53.** h
44. e	**54.** c
45. b	**55.** a
46. t	**56.** s
47. l	**57.** f
48. k	**58.** o
49. j	**59.** g
50. i	**60.** d

Across

4 imbroglio
7 élan
9 ingénue
11 naïve
12 vignette
14 vendetta
17 fait-accompli
18 epitome
19 malaise
20 debut

Down

1 cliché
2 bourgeois
3 blasé
5 gauche
6 avant-garde
8 laissez-faire
10 nonsequitur
13 entrepreneur
15 aficionado
16 rendezvous

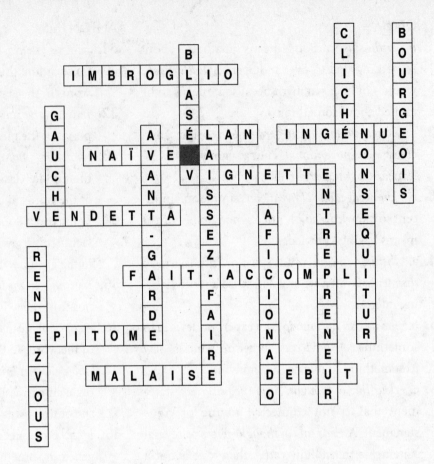

VOCABULARY LIST 6: BUSINESS TERMS

CHAPTER SUMMARY

In this chapter you will learn words frequently used in business. Many of the words in this chapter may be familiar to you, but it is very useful to become comfortable with using these words in your day-to-day life. You will see these words in articles about business and economic matters, as well as in the written policies and procedures found in most work environments. You may also see some of the words on your tax return and on other work-related forms. Think about when and where you have seen these words before and how they were used. Once you know these words, you will find that many business-related articles and policies that you encounter at work or in your day-to-day life are not only easier to understand, but are beneficial to you as an employee and a citizen. As you go through the list, say each word aloud to yourself and practice spelling it. This will help you gain more comfort with using each word. Think about other words you know that may have similar prefixes, suffixes, or roots and see if you can use this knowledge to help you remember the meaning of the new words found in this chapter.

Choose the word from the Vocabulary List that best fits into the crossword puzzle. You can check your answers at the end of the chapter following the answers to the questions.

Vocabulary List 6:
Business Terms

arbitrage
arbitration
beneficiary
capital
collusion
consortium
deduction
discrimination
entitlement
equity
exempt
fiscal
franchise
harassment
jargon
nepotism
perquisite
prospectus
subsidy
tenure

Across

4 someone who benefits from something
5 annoy or irritate persistently
6 a joining of two or more businesses for a specific purpose
8 conspiracy
11 special privilege or benefit
15 the process by which disputes are settled by a third party
16 accumulated wealth
17 fairness of treatment
18 the state or period of holding a particular position, or a guarantee of employment to teachers who have particular standards move from a grave
19 a grant

Down

1 prejudiced actions or treatment
2 favoring relatives
3 terminology
7 a business that is owned by a parent company but run by independent operators under rules set by the parent company
9 the subtraction of a cost from income
10 buying stocks, bonds, and securities to resell for a quick profit
12 bonus
13 a published report of a business and its plans
14 pertaining to money
17 excused

arbitrage   (ˈär·bə·träzh)

(*verb*)

the buying of "paper"—stocks, bonds, and
  securities—to resell for a quick profit

_____, the buying of bonds and other securities
  to sell at a higher price, is a risky business.

arbitration   (är·bə·ˈtrā·shən)

(*noun*)

the process by which disputes are settled by a third
  party

They decided to resolve the matter through
  _____; that is, they gave the decision-
  making power to an independent person.

beneficiary   (ben·nə·fi·shē·er·ē)

(*noun*)

one who will benefit from something

He is the sole _____ of her estate. He will be
  given all the property when the old woman
  dies.

capital   (ˈka·pə·təl)

(*noun*)

accumulated wealth, used to gain more wealth

She put some money in the bank and would only
  spend the interest she earned on the initial
  investment or _____.

collusion   (kə·ˈlü·zhen)

(*noun*)

a secret agreement for a deceitful or fraudulent
  purpose, conspiracy

At the poker game, Sarah and Tom made a
  _____ to cheat together so Sarah would
  win the game and then they could share the
  winnings.

consortium   (kən·ˈsor·shē·em)

(*noun*)

a joining of two or more businesses for a specific
  purpose

The joining of the three companies into one made
  for a powerful _____ that would dominate
  the industry.

deduction   (di·ˈdək·shən)

(*noun*)

the subtraction of a cost from income

He took his children as a tax _____ so that he
  could subtract the cost of their care from his
  taxes.

discrimination   (dis·kri·mə·ˈnā·shən)

(*noun*)

the act of making distinctions, the act of
  distinguishing between one group of people
  and another and treating people differently as a
  result, prejudiced actions or treatment

Many workers still face _____ in workplaces
  that choose not to hire or promote employees
  based on their sex, skin color, or ethnic
  background.

entitlement   (in·ˈtī·təl·mənt)

(*noun*)

special privilege or benefit allowed to a group of
  people

In our society, the elderly have an _____ to
  healthcare and money for food and shelter.

equity   (ˈe-kwə·tē)

(*noun*)

fairness or evenness of treatment, or the value of
  property after all claims have been made
  against it

Though she was accused of being unfair in her
  demands, she claimed she only wanted
  _____ in what was owed her.

exempt   (ig·'zem(p)t)
(*adj.*)
excused from some rule or job
She was _____ from duty that day; she was
     excused because she had been injured.

fiscal   ('fis·kəl)
(*adj.*)
pertaining to money or finance
At the end of a company's _____, or financial,
     year, the company usually announces the
     amount it earned in that year.

franchise   ('fran·chīz)
(*noun*)
a business that is owned by a parent company but
     run by independent operators under rules set
     by the parent company
Restaurants like McDonald's and Burger King are
     _____ because they are independently
     owned, but still operate under rules set out by
     the parent company.

harassment   (hə·'ras·mənt)
(*noun*)
the act of harassing someone, annoy or irritate
     persistently;
sexual harassment
(*noun*)
unwelcome physical or verbal conduct directed at an
     employee because of his or her sex
There are many laws today that protect workers from
     sexual _____ by their employer.

jargon   ('jär·gən)
(*noun*)
the specialized vocabulary of an industry or interest
     group
Learning the _____, or language, of a particular
     interest or job is an important part of learning
     about the workplace.

nepotism   ('ne·pə·ti·zəm)
(*noun*)
the employment or promotion of friends and family
     members
Many public employment arenas have been accused
     of _____, because workers related to
     persons in authority are given preference in
     hiring.

perquisite   ('pər·kwə·zet)
(*noun*)
a privilege or bonus given in addition to regular
     salary
Many companies give stock options as a _____
     in addition to an employee's salary.

prospectus   (prə·'spek·təs)
(*noun*)
a published report of a business and its plans for a
     program or offering
The company published a _____ to offer details
     of its plan for expansion. This plan offers
     potential investors pertinent information about
     the plan and the company.

subsidy   ('səb·sə·dē)
(*noun*)
a grant of money for a particular purpose
The state gave several school districts a _____
     for the purpose of rebuilding the schools in
     that district.

tenure   ('ten·yər)
(*noun*)
the state or period of holding a particular position,
     or a guarantee of employment to teachers who
     have met particular standards
Even faculty with _____ at colleges and
     universities are losing the security promised by
     their guarantee of permanent employment.

WORDS IN CONTEXT

The following exercise will help you figure out the meaning of some words from Vocabulary List 6 by looking at context clues. After you have read and understood the paragraph, explain the context clues that helped you with the meaning of the vocabulary word. Check the answer section at the end of this chapter for an example.

When she took the job as the manager of a Wendy's *franchise,* Sarah quickly learned many things about the business world. On her first day of work, she read the *discrimination* policy that stated that Wendy's does not discriminate against race, ethnicity, gender, sexual preference, or people with disabilities when hiring employees. Then she read Wendy's policy on sexual *harassment* and was glad to see that they were very strict about creating a comfortable working environment for all of the employees. Her boss explained that flirting of any kind was not tolerated at work. Next she was asked to fill out a bunch of forms including a life insurance policy. She had to pick someone to be the *beneficiary* on the policy in the event of her death so she picked her son, Michael. After she was done with all of the paperwork, Sarah followed her boss into the back room and he showed her the various systems they used and began to teach her the *jargon* used in the fast food industry. It was important to understand these terms because many vendors and members of the Wendy's company used these shorthand terms. Sarah mentioned that her sister really wanted to work at Wendy's as well, but her boss cautioned her against committing an act of *nepotism.* He

explained that it was important that every potential employee had a fair chance of employment and that as store manager it was her responsibility to ensure that she did not give preferential treatment to her family members. At the end of the meeting, her boss told her that as a *perquisite* in addition to her salary, she and her family were allowed one free meal a week at Wendy's.

SENTENCE COMPLETION

Insert the correct word from Vocabulary List 6 into the following sentences.

1. The two young men made a _____ to work together to embezzle money from their company.

2. In _____, disputes are settled by a disinterested third party.

3. Most businesses need a sum of money or _____ to get started.

4. _____ transactions are financial in nature.

5. When you learn the language of a particular workplace, you are learning its _____.

6. If you manage a store according to the rules of a parent company, you own a _____.

7. We would all like to be _____ from paying too many taxes.

8. Promotions often bring _____, or other special privileges.

9. When a teacher is given a guarantee of permanent employment, he has _____.

10. When you want to subtract certain expenses from your taxes, you want a _____.

11. If you want information about a new offering by a company, you should read the _____.

12. If a boss subjects an employee to inappropriate pressure, the boss is guilty of _____.

13. The person who stands to gain from a bequest in a will is the _____.

14. Hiring or promoting relatives in a business is called _____.

15. A group of companies might join together to create a _____.

16. Social Security is an example of an _____ that the elderly enjoy in our society.

17. My sister works in _____; she buys stocks and bonds and then quickly sells them in another market to make a profit.

18. All employees should be treated with _____, regardless of their status in the company or their education.

19. The state government gave the development company a _____ to rebuild the buildings in the public park.

20. He accused his employer of _____; he stated that he was fired because of his race.

SYNONYMS

The following exercise lists vocabulary words from this chapter. Each word is followed by five answer choices. Four of them are synonyms of the vocabulary word in bold. Your task is to choose the one that does **not** fit.

21. deduction
   a.   subtraction
   b.   to take away
   c.   addition
   d.   the cost of children on your tax forms

22. perquisite
   a.   privilege
   b.   bonus
   c.   reward
   d.   punishment

23. tenure
   a.   termination of employment
   b.   guarantee of employment
   c.   length of employment
   d.   period of employment

24. exempt
   a.   excused
   b.   forced
   c.   pardoned
   d.   set apart

25. equity
   a.   fairness
   b.   evenness
   c.   value of property
   d.   special privilege

26. beneficiary
    a. one who gives
    b. heir
    c. one who benefits
    d. one who inherits

27. collusion
    a. agreement
    b. fraudulent
    c. merger
    d. conspiracy

28. discrimination
    a. discernment
    b. the act of making distinctions
    c. prejudiced treatment
    d. fair

29. subsidy
    a. tax
    b. money
    c. gift of money
    d. grant

30. fiscal
    a. financial
    b. economic
    c. monetary
    d. franchise

ANTONYMS

Choose the word that means the opposite, or most nearly the opposite of the following groups of words.

31. addition, income, give   _____

32. favoritism, prejudiced, unfair, unjust   _____

33. punishment, harm, disadvantage, penalty   _____

34. debt, poverty, insufficient resources   _____

35. forced, duty-bound, liable   _____

36. fairness, unprejudiced, equity   _____

37. friendly, unthreatening, not provocative   _____

38. unemployed, fired, lack of job security   _____

39. separation, liquidation, singular company   _____

40. slang, proper English, clichés   _____

MATCHING QUESTIONS

Match the word in the first column with the corresponding word in the second column.

41. beneficiary   a. privilege in addition to salary

42. deduction   b. grant of money

43. arbitrage   c. period of holding a job

44. fiscal   d. published report

45. jargon   e. pertaining to money

46. exempt   f. fairness or evenness of treatment

47. franchise   g. the buying of stocks to resell for profit

48. consortium   h. one who benefits

49. discrimination   i. special privilege enjoyed by a group

50. equity   j. accumulated wealth

51. tenure   k. the employment of friends or family

52. arbitration   l. terms used in an industry

53. perquisite   m. the subtraction of cost from income

54. collusion   n. annoying persistently

55. capital   o. a deceitful agreement

56. entitlement   p. process of a dispute settled by third party

57. prospectus   q. independently run business owned by parent company

58. subsidy   r. excused from duty or job

59. nepotism   s. joining of two or more companies

60. harassment   t. the act of distinguishing between two groups of people

PRACTICE ACTIVITIES

Find a copy of a work-related memo, letter, or policy from a work environment and see if the words you have learned in this chapter are used in the piece of writing. See if you can find five more business-related words that you can add to your vocabulary list.

Find an article in the business section of the paper or a magazine dedicated to business and see how many of these words are used in the publication. What are the articles about? Are there other words you can add to your vocabulary list? Try to figure out the definition of the new words from the context of the article and then check the definition in your dictionary.

ANSWERS

WORDS IN CONTEXT

The first word we encounter is *franchise* and we know from the context that it must be a Wendy's restaurant, so franchise could refer to the individual store or restaurant in a chain. Sarah reads the *discrimination* policy that explains that Wendy's does not discriminate against people in their hiring practices, so *discrimination* must mean judging or treating someone differently. The sexual *harassment* policy does not allow flirting at work, so harassment must mean bothering someone or pressuring someone. Sarah makes her son the *beneficiary* of her life insurance policy, so we can conclude that her son will receive the money, or be the one to benefit from the policy if Sarah were to pass away. Her boss teaches her the *jargon* of the industry because she must know the terms used in the fast food industry, so *jargon* must mean language used in a particular industry. Sarah is cautioned against an act of *nepotism* and in the next sentence we can deduce that *nepotism* must mean giving your family preferential treatment. Finally, we see the word *perquisite* used to explain an extra benefit Sarah receives in addition to her salary.

SENTENCE COMPLETION

1. *collusion.* If you got this question wrong, refer back to the word's definition.
2. *arbitration.* If you got this question wrong, refer back to the word's definition.
3. *capital.* If you got this question wrong, refer back to the word's definition.
4. *fiscal.* If you got this question wrong, refer back to the word's definition.
5. *jargon.* If you got this question wrong, refer back to the word's definition.
6. *franchise.* If you got this question wrong, refer back to the word's definition.

7. *exempt.* If you got this question wrong, refer back to the word's definition.
8. *perquisites.* If you got this question wrong, refer back to the word's definition.
9. *tenure.* If you got this question wrong, refer back to the word's definition.
10. *deduction.* If you got this question wrong, refer back to the word's definition.
11. *prospectus.* If you got this question wrong, refer back to the word's definition.
12. *harassment.* If you got this question wrong, refer back to the word's definition.
13. *beneficiary.* If you got this question wrong, refer back to the word's definition.
14. *nepotism.* If you got this question wrong, refer back to the word's definition.
15. *consortium.* If you got this question wrong, refer back to the word's definition.
16. *entitlement.* If you got this question wrong, refer back to the word's definition.
17. *arbitrage.* If you got this question wrong, refer back to the word's definition.
18. *equity.* If you got this question wrong, refer back to the word's definition.
19. *subsidy.* If you got this question wrong, refer back to the word's definition.
20. *discrimination.* If you got this question wrong, refer back to the word's definition.

SYNONYMS

21. c. *addition.* *Deduction* means the act of subtracting; since c is addition, it is not a synonym.
22. d. *punishment.* *Perquisite* means a bonus or privilege given in addition to salary; since *punishment* means a penalty it is not a synonym.
23. a. *termination of employment.* *Tenure* means the state of holding a particular job or the guarantee

of employment. *Termination of employment* is not a synonym because it means the end of one's employment.

24. **b.** *force. Exempt* means to be excused from some rule or job; since *force* means to make someone do something, it is not a synonym.

25. **d.** *special privilege. Equity* means fairness or evenness of treatment, or the value of property after all claims have been have been made against it. *Special privilege* is not a synonym because it is not an even or fair arrangement. If you got this one wrong, you may have confused *equity* with *entitlement.*

26. **a.** *one who gives. Beneficiary* means one who will benefit from receiving something. Since *one who gives* is a person who gives something it is not a synonym.

27. **c.** *merger. Collusion* means a deceitful agreement for fraudulent purposes. *Merger* is not a synonym because *merger* means the combining of two companies.

28. **d.** *fair. Discrimination* means the act of making distinctions and it is often used to refer to making distinctions between different groups of people in an unfair way. Since *fair* means even or just, it is not a synonym.

29. **a.** *tax. Subsidy* means a grant of money for a particular purpose. *Tax* is money paid to the government by citizens so it is not a synonym.

30. **d.** *franchise. Fiscal* means pertaining to money or finance, since *franchise* means a business owned by a parent company but run independently, it is not a synonym.

ANTONYMS

31. *deduction. Deduction* means the subtraction of cost from income, the opposite of the words in the list.

32. *equity. Equity* means fairness or evenness of treatment, the opposite of the words in the list.

33. *entitlement. Entitlement* means a special privilege or benefit enjoyed by a group of people, the opposite of the words in the list.

34. *capital. Capital* means accumulated wealth used to earn more money, the opposite of the words in the list.

35. *exempt. Exempt* means excused from a duty or job, the opposite of the words in the list.

36. *discrimination. Discrimination* means the act of making distinctions in treatment of people, the opposite of the words in the list.

37. *harassment. Harassment* means to harass or bother someone persistently in a threatening way, the opposite of the words in the list.

38. *tenure. Tenure* means a period of holding a job or a guarantee of employment, the opposite of the words in the list.

39. *consortium. Consortium* means a joining together of two or more businesses for a specific purpose, the opposite of the words in the list.

40. *jargon. Jargon* means the language used in a particular industry, the opposite of the words in the list.

MATCHING QUESTIONS

41. h
42. m
43. g
44. e
45. l
46. r
47. q
48. s
49. t
50. f

51. c
52. p
53. a
54. o
55. j
56. i
57. d
58. b
59. k
60. n

Across

4 beneficiary
5 harassment
6 consortium
8 collusion
11 entitlement
15 arbitration
16 capital
17 equity
18 tenure
19 subsidy

Down

1 discrimination
2 nepotism
3 jargon
7 franchise
9 deduction
10 arbitrage
12 perquisite
13 prospectus
14 fiscal
17 exempt

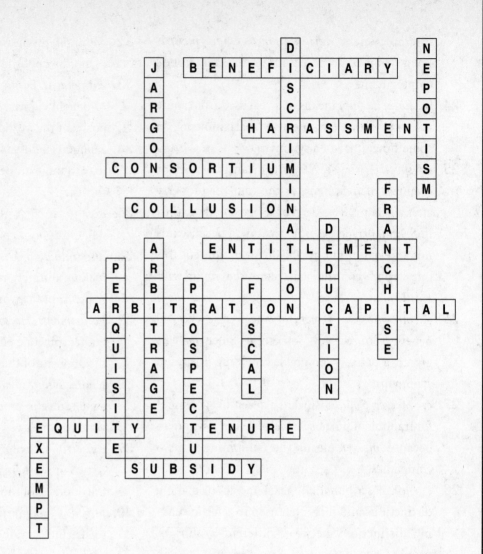

VOCABULARY LIST 7: TECHNOLOGY TERMS

CHAPTER SUMMARY

The technology terms found in this chapter are words commonly used by both technology experts and people learning how to use a computer for the first time. No matter what your computer knowledge is, learning these words will be extremely useful because they are used so frequently in advertisements, newspaper articles, computer manuals, and in many work environments. Technology is such a huge part of our daily lives that it is important to feel comfortable with the terminology or *jargon* (see Vocabulary List 6 if you are unfamiliar with this word) used in this industry. Technology jargon can be intimidating because many of the words, such as *cookie,* have other meanings or seem odd or even silly. Have fun with these words and think about what they mean and how the definition of each word influenced how the word was constructed.

Many of these words were coined very recently and are intentionally similar to other commonly used words. For instance, a *motherboard* is the main circuit board of the computer. Why do you think it is called a motherboard instead of a sisterboard or brotherboard? As you read through these words and their definitions, underline parts of the words that may serve as useful

Choose the word from the Vocabulary List that best fits into the crossword puzzle. You will use 19 words from the vocabulary list to solve the puzzle. You can check your answers at the end of the chapter following the answers to the questions.

Vocabulary List 7: Technology Terms

application
bandwidth
bitmap
cache
cookie
cursor
database
download
encryption
Ethernet
firewall
information technology
keyword
motherboard
network
plug-in
search engine
server
upload
workstation

Across

3 high-speed computer storage to help you access frequently accessed information locally
7 any computer connected to a local area network (LAN)
9 blinking line that shows where your mouse is on a computer screen
10 the main circuit board of a computer
11 transfer capacity in bits per second
14 translation of information into a secret code
15 allows a Web browser to run multimedia files
16 software program
17 information stored and organized so that a computer can quickly retrieve selected pieces of information

Down

1 a representative word that specifies a particular record or file

2 a network that allows a wide variety of computers to communicate
4 to transmit documents from your computer to a network or an online source
5 a message given to a Web browser by a Web server that is stored in the browser and sent back to the server every time the browser contacts the server for a Web page
6 a system to prevent unauthorized access to and from a private network
8 a program that searches documents for a keyword and then provides a list of those documents
12 a group of two or more computers linked together
13 to copy a file from an online source to your own computer
18 binary data that represents an image or display
19 a computer on a network that manages network resources

memory tricks. For example, what is the difference between *uploading* and *downloading* a file? Since these
words are all very new, be sure to use a very current
dictionary or look at an online technology dictionary,
such as www.webopedia.com, when you hear or read
new technology words.

application   ('a·plə·kā·shən)
(*noun*)
a software program that lets you complete a task on
your computer, such as word processing,
listening to music, or viewing a Web page.
The computer _____ I use for word processing
is really easy to learn.

bandwidth   ('band·with)
(*noun*)
the amount of information that one can send
through a connection, usually measured in bits
per second
At work I can download files from the Internet a lot
faster because I have more _____.

bitmap   ('bit·map)
(*noun*)
the representation in rows and columns of dots of an
image in computer memory
I downloaded the _____ so I could keep the
picture on my computer.

cache   ('kash)
(*noun*)
a high-speed storage mechanism that allows a
computer to store frequently accessed
information locally
I had to download the Web page again because it
wasn't saved in my computer's _____.

cookie   ('kù·kē)
(*noun*)
a message given to a Web browser by a Web server
that is stored in the browser and sent back to
the server every time the browser contacts the
server for a Web page.
A _____ enables a Web page to recognize your
computer when you log on to it so the page
may say something like, "Welcome back,
Jessie!"

cursor   ('kər·sər)
(*noun*)
a symbol, usually a blinking line that shows where
the next letter will be typed on a computer
screen.
To type in a different part of the computer screen,
you must move the _____ using your
mouse.

database   ('dā·tə·bās)
(*noun*)
information stored and organized so that a computer
can quickly retrieve selected pieces of
information
At work, we have a _____ that includes all of
our products so we can easily check to see how
many of each item we have in stock.

download   ('daùn·lōd)
(*verb*)
the process of copying a document or file from an
online source to your own computer
I went to the national parks' website to _____ a
map of the park so we knew where to hike.

encryption   (in·ˈkrip·shən)

(*noun*)

the translation of information into a secret code

_____ is an effective way to keep information
    secure.

Ethernet   (ˈē·thər·net)

(*noun*)

a common method of enabling computers in the
    same Local Area Network (LAN— see
    Vocabulary List 12: Acronyms) to communicate
    with each other

In my office, we have 20 computers that
    communicate via _____.

firewall   (fīr·ˈwȯl)

(*noun*)

a system (using either hardware or software) that
    prevents unauthorized access to and from a
    private network

The _____ at my office protects our system
    from people who may try to hack in and ruin
    our website.

information technology (IT)   (in·fər·ˈmā·shən
                            tek·ˈnä·lō·jē)

(*noun*)

the broad subject of anything concerning processing
    or managing information, especially in a large
    company

The _____ group at my company handles all of
    the computer problems that the employees
    encounter.

keyword   (ˈkē·wərd)

(*noun*)

a word that specifies a particular record, file; in
    programming a specific command

I used the _____ *legal* to search for articles on
    the website about legal issues.

motherboard   (mə·thər·bōrd)

(*noun*)

the main circuit board of a computer

She opened the computer and showed me the
    _____; a thin piece of plastic with many
    different wires running through it.

network   (ˈnet·wərk)

(*noun*)

a group of two or more computers linked together

At work we have 20 computers on our _____.

plug-in   (ˈpləg·in)

(*noun*)

a piece of hardware or software that adds a specific
    feature to a larger, already existing system

Once I downloaded the _____, I was able to see
    and listen to movie clips on my computer.

search engine   (ˈsərch·ˈen·jən)

(*noun*)

a program that searches documents, websites, and
    databases for a keyword and then provides a list
    of those documents

When I'm looking for information about my car, I
    usually type in the model and year into an
    online _____ and I find many websites
    devoted to cars like mine.

server   (ˈsər·vər)

(*noun*)

a computer on a network that manages network
    resources

When the _____ is down, we can't access any of
    our files at work.

upload (əp·ˈlōd)

(*verb*)

the opposite of download; to transmit documents from your computer to an online source

When I built my Web page, I had to _____ the final page to our network to add it to the website.

workstation (ˈwərk·stā·shən)

(*noun*)

a type of computer that has enough power to run applications used in work environments, such as graphic design programs and software design programs; also refers to any computer connected to a LAN, whether a personal computer or workstation

At home I have a personal computer, but at work I have a much faster _____ because I use it to develop video games.

WORDS IN CONTEXT

The following exercise will help you figure out the meaning of some words from Vocabulary List 7 by looking at context clues. After you have read and understood the paragraph, explain the context clues that helped you with the meaning of the vocabulary word. Check the answer section at the end of this chapter for an example.

> On Tom's first day of work as a computer programmer, he had to set up his *workstation*. He was really excited because his computer was really fast and many of the *applications* he would use for work were already installed. First he connected his *workstation* to the *network* by using the *Ethernet* cord at his desk. Now he would be able to communicate with all of the other computers in the office. Once he was con-
> nected to the *network,* he opened up his Internet program and went immediately to his favorite *search engine.* He wanted to see how his favorite baseball team did in their game so he typed in "baseball" as the *keyword* in the search engine, and it gave him a list of several baseball-related websites. He quickly checked the score of the game and then got back to work.

SENTENCE COMPLETION

Insert the correct word from Vocabulary List 7 into the following sentences.

1. At work, I can communicate with the other computers in the office as long as they are connected to on our _____.

2. The _____ prevents people without authorization from accessing our system or potentially damaging it.

3. When the _____ goes down, we cannot access the Internet, save files, or communicate with other computers on the network.

4. I was so surprised that the Web page said, "Welcome back, Margaret!" But then my friend explained how _____ work.

5. The clerk said that they were out of the sofa we wanted to buy, but said she would check the _____ to see if one of their other stores had it in stock.

6. In my computer class, I learned how to use several different graphic design _____(s).

7. When I first open my Internet program, the last Web page I went to appears in my browser window because it is saved in my computer's _____.

8. My friend e-mailed me a funny animated cartoon, but I couldn't watch it because I didn't have the right _____.

9. I wanted to do some research on the medication my doctor prescribed, so I used the name of the medication as the _____ in my search.

10. I would like to work in the _____ group at a company because I like to work with computers and help people use them more effectively.

11. When you press return on your keyboard, the _____ moves to the next line.

12. It took me a long time to download the file because I didn't have enough _____.

13. I opened the _____ in a graphic design program so I could edit the image.

14. At work, our network is connected via _____.

15. He studied _____, the translation of information into a secret code.

16. Before I left for my camping trip, I used a _____ to search for information about the campsite.

17. I like to _____ songs from the Internet so that I can listen to them on my computer.

18. I _____(ed) my resume from my computer to an online job board.

19. My _____ has a lot more memory than my computer at home.

20. I thought it would be really hard to add more memory to my computer, but I followed the directions and all I had to do was put it in the slot located on the _____ of my computer.

TRUE/FALSE

In the space provided, write a *T* if the word from List 7 is true and an *F* if the sentence is false. If the sentence is false, cross out the false word and write the correct word from Vocabulary List 7 above it.

21. __ When I see pictures on the Web that I like, I *download* the images from the Web to my computer.

22. __ A *cookie* is a high-speed storage mechanism that allows my computer to store information I frequently use.

23. __ I used the *server* to do research on my new car by typing in the model and year and then it gave me a list of websites relating to my car.

24. __ I just installed this new *application* on my computer that enables me to balance my checkbook and keep track of my expenses on my computer.

25. __ Our office recently added five more computers to our *network*.

26. __ Our computers are all connected via *encryption* so my computer can communicate with all of the other computers in the office.

27. __ When you *upload* a file, you transmit it from your computer to an online bulletin board or network.

28. __ The *database* is the main circuit board of the computer.

29. ___ At work I can download files from the Internet much faster than at home because I have more *bitmap.*

30. ___ A *firewall* is used to protect a private network from unauthorized access.

CHOOSING THE RIGHT WORD

Circle the word in bold that best completes the sentence.

31. At work I have a(n) (**application, workstation**), which is much faster than my computer at home.

32. I saved the image I created in my design program on my computer as a (**bitmap, cookie**) so I could open it again in a different program.

33. When my mother first used a computer, she had difficulty seeing the (**cache, cursor**) but now that she is used to it, she knows to look for a blinking line.

34. He studied (**encryption, information technology**) and became an expert at deciphering secret codes used to protect hidden information.

35. When doing research, it is useful to come up with several (**keywords, plug-ins**) you can use to find articles and websites about your topic.

36. I was amazed at how easy it was to use a (**network, search engine**) to find so many websites—all I had to do was type in whatever topic I wanted to learn about, and then click the search button.

37. My boss asked me to create a (**server, database**) of all of our business contacts and clients so all of the contact information would be organized and easy to retrieve.

38. My friend sent me a funny animated cartoon, but when I opened it, a window popped up on the screen that said I didn't have the right (**plug-in, cookie**) to play the cartoon, but that I could download it for free from another website.

39. My sister got a job in the (**Ethernet, information technology**) group at this company so now she helps fix computer problems in the office and helps people use their computers more effectively for their work.

40. The (**motherboard, server**) is the computer at work that manages all of our network resources, so when there is a problem with the (**server, motherboard**) we can't share files with other computers or work on the website.

MATCHING

Match the word in the first column with the corresponding definition in the second column.

41. search engine   a. process of copying files from an online source to your computer

42. motherboard   b. process of copying files from your computer to an online or network location

43. workstation   c. word used to specify particular file or record

44. application   d. a system to protect a private network from outside access

45. cache   e. main circuit board or computer

46. database   f. a group of computers linked together

47. upload   g. a representation in rows and columns of dots of an image in computer memory

48. server   h. stored and organized information that is easily retrievable

49. firewall   i. information stored in Web browser and sent to a server when the browser contacts that server

50. bandwidth   j. translation of information into a secret code

51. cursor   k. program used to search for websites or documents containing a given keyword

52. ethernet   l. a high-speed computer used in work environments

53. plug-in   m. protocol used to connect two or more computers to each other

54. network   n. a module that adds a specific feature to a larger system

55. information technology   o. subject of anything concerning processing or managing information

56. bitmap   p. the capacity of data transfer

57. cookie   q. a program that performs a certain task on a computer

58. download   r. a computer on a network that manages all of the network resources

59. encryption   s. a high-speed storage mechanism used to store frequently accessed information

60. keyword   t. blinking line on computer screen

PRACTICE ACTIVITIES

Find an article about technology in the technology section of your local newspaper or in a magazine. Add at least five new technology words to your vocabulary list and write down the definition of your new words based on the context clues in the article. Look up your new words and write down the dictionary definition. Go back and reread the article with your vocabulary list handy and note how the new words are used in the article.

Go to your local library or computer center and use a computer to search on a search engine using some of your new vocabulary words as keywords. See if you can find articles or websites that refer to your new vocabulary words. Does knowing these new vocabulary words make using a computer easier? Can you find any online dictionaries or other tools to help you develop your vocabulary?

ANSWERS

WORDS IN CONTEXT

The first word we encounter is *workstation*. Just from dissecting the word we can determine that it is a station where one does work. Tom is a computer programmer, so it must refer to the computer he will use for work. The context clues tell us that the *applications* are on his computer and are things that he will use for work, so we can conclude that *application* must mean programs on a computer. He connects to the *network* via the *Ethernet* so he can communicate with the other computers. The *network* is what he is connecting to, so *network* must mean the group of computers in the office. *Ethernet* is the type of cord he is using to connect to the network, so it must be a means of connecting several computers to each other. Finally, he uses a *search engine* to find information about baseball. The *keyword* is the word he uses to search and the *search engine* is a program that provides search results about baseball.

SENTENCE COMPLETION

1. *network*. If you got this answer wrong, refer back to the word's definition.
2. *firewall*. If you got this answer wrong, refer back to the word's definition.
3. *server*. If you got this answer wrong, refer back to the word's definition.
4. *cookies*. If you got this answer wrong, refer back to the word's definition.
5. *database*. If you got this answer wrong, refer back to the word's definition.
6. *application*. If you got this answer wrong, refer back to the word's definition.
7. *cache*. If you got this answer wrong, refer back to the word's definition.

8. *plug-in*. If you got this answer wrong, refer back to the word's definition.
9. *keyword*. If you got this answer wrong, refer back to the word's definition.
10. *information technology*. If you got this answer wrong, refer back to the word's definition.
11. *cursor*. If you got this answer wrong, refer back to the word's definition.
12. *bandwidth*. If you got this answer wrong, refer back to the word's definition.
13. *bitmap*. If you got this answer wrong, refer back to the word's definition.
14. *Ethernet*. If you got this answer wrong, refer back to the word's definition.
15. *encryption*. If you got this answer wrong, refer back to the word's definition.
16. *search engine*. If you got this answer wrong, refer back to the word's definition.
17. *download*. If you got this answer wrong, refer back to the word's definition.
18. *upload*. If you got this answer wrong, refer back to the word's definition.
19. *workstation*. If you got this answer wrong, refer back to the word's definition.
20. *motherboard*. If you got this answer wrong, refer back to the word's definition.

SYNONYMS

21. True
22. False, correct word is cache
23. False, correct word is search engine
24. True
25. True
26. False, correct word is Ethernet
27. True
28. False, correct word is motherboard

29. False, correct word is bandwidth
30. True

CHOOSING THE RIGHT WORD

31. workstation
32. bitmap
33. cursor
34. encryption
35. keywords
36. search engine
37. database
38. plug-in
39. information technology
40. server

MATCHING

41. k
42. e
43. l
44. q
45. s
46. h
47. b
48. r
49. d
50. p
51. t
52. m
53. n
54. f
55. o
56. g
57. i
58. a
59. j
60. c

Across

- 3 cache
- 7 workstation
- 9 cursor
- 10 motherboard
- 11 bandwidth
- 14 encryption
- 15 plug-in
- 16 application
- 17 database

Down

- 1 keyword
- 2 Ethernet
- 4 upload
- 5 cookie
- 6 firewall
- 8 search engine
- 12 network
- 13 download
- 18 bitmap
- 19 server

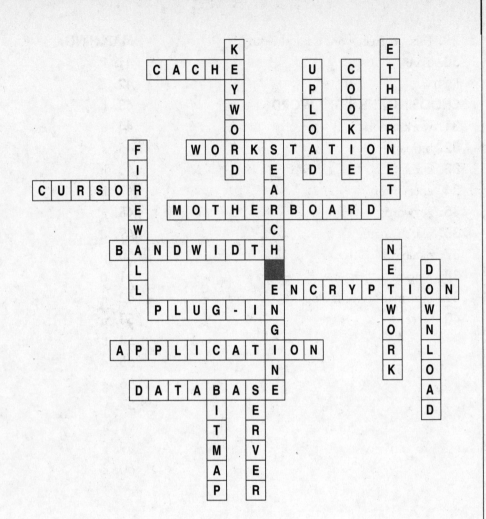

VOCABULARY LIST 8: LEGAL TERMS

CHAPTER SUMMARY

Legal terms are incredibly important to know, but often seem intimidating. The law governs every aspect of our lives, so it is very important to understand the legal documents with which we come in contact. Most likely you have already signed a legal contract if you have a credit card, rent an apartment, have bought or sold a car, or have car insurance. Legal documents are devised to protect the rights of citizens, but because many legal terms are not used in common everyday speech, legal documents can appear intimidating and confusing if you are unfamiliar with the vocabulary.

In this chapter, you will learn many legal terms commonly used in the legal profession. Read through the list and see which words are familiar to you. Where have you seen or heard them before? Look at the prefix, root, and suffix of each word and see if there are any similarities between these new words and other words you already know which may serve as useful memory tricks. Once you are comfortable with these words, continue to build your legal vocabulary by reading articles and stories about courtroom cases, adding new legal terms to your vocabulary.

Choose the word from the Vocabulary List that best fits into the crossword puzzle. You can check your answers at the end of the chapter following the answers to the questions.

Vocabulary List 8:
Legal Terms

abrogate
adjudicate
appellate
affidavit
bequest
contraband
deposition
exhume
extradite
intestate
ipso facto
larceny
lien
litigious
jurisprudence
malfeasance
perjury
plagiarism
sanction
tort

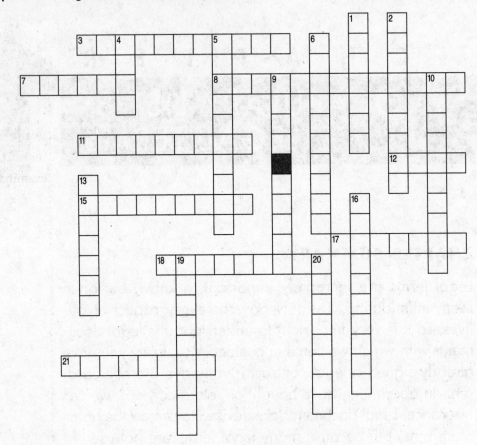

Down

1 the act of giving or leaving by will
2 having the power to review the judgment of another court
4 a charge upon real or personal property for the satisfaction of some debt
5 to act as a judge
6 testimony taken down in writing under oath
9 by that very fact or act
10 prohibited by law
13 the voluntary violation of an oath; false swearing
16 the act of stealing and passing off the ideas or words of another as one's own
19 having made no valid will
20 to approve or authorize

Across

3 wrongdoing or misconduct especially by a public official
7 to dig up, to unbury
8 the science or philosophy of law
11 a sworn statement in writing made under oath
12 a wrongful act for which you can get damages or an injunction
15 to surrender an alleged criminal to the state or country in which he or she can be tried
17 theft, purloining
18 contentious, argumentative
21 to abolish

abrogate ('a·brə·gāt)

(*verb*)

to abolish by authoritative action

During the United States Civil War, the North fought the South and wanted the American government to _____ slavery.

adjudicate (ə·'jü·di·kāt)

(*verb*)

to act as a judge, to settle judicially

"You are not going to _____ this case, I am," the judge said to the attorney.

appellate (ə·'pe·lət)

(*adj.*)

having the power to review the judgment of another court

When a case is appealed, it is tried in an _____ court.

affidavit (a·fə·'dā·vət)

(*noun*)

a sworn statement in writing made under oath

He was not asked to testify; instead the attorney asked him to sign a written _____ that described what he knew about the case.

bequest (bi·'kwest)

(*noun*)

the act of bequeathing, the act of leaving someone something in a will, something that is bequeathed

When my grandmother died, she gave me her house as a _____.

contraband ('kän·trə·band)

(*noun*)

illegal or prohibited exporting or importing of goods

Cuban cigars are _____ in this country; it is against the law to import them into the U.S.

deposition (de·pə·'zi·shən)

(*noun*)

testimony under oath, taken down in writing

In his _____, he said that he saw a gun, but under cross-examination in court, he said that he didn't remember seeing a gun.

exhume (ig·'züm)

(*verb*)

to remove from a grave; to bring back from neglect or obscurity

When archeologists excavate ancient tombs, they frequently _____ the remains of the people who are buried there.

extradite ('ek·strə·dīt)

(*verb*)

to surrender an alleged criminal to the state or country in which he or she can be tried

After ten years of hiding, he was _____ to the U.S. to stand trial for the murder of his girlfriend.

intestate (in·'tes·tāt)

(*adj.*)

one who dies without a will

My grandfather died _____, so we didn't know who in the family should inherit his piano.

ipso facto   (ˈip·sō·ˈfak·tō)

(*adverb*)

by the very fact or act, an inevitable act

In bankruptcy, an _____ provision is a
    provision which automatically comes into play
    when a company files for bankruptcy.

larceny   (ˈlärs·nē)

(*noun*)

the unlawful taking of someone else's property with
    the intention of not giving it back

He was accused of _____ when he was found
    driving the stolen car.

lien   (ˈlēn)

(*noun*)

a charge against real or personal property for the
    satisfaction of a debt or duty originally arising
    from the law

Before the bank would lend me the money, I had to
    prove that there were no previous _____
    (s) on my property.

litigious   (lə·ˈti·jəs)

(*adj.*)

contentious situation, prone to litigation

When my landlord did not give us our security
    deposit back after we moved out, it turned into
    a _____ situation.

jurisprudence   (jur·əs·ˈprü·dən(t)s)

(*noun*)

a system of laws, the science or philosophy of the law

At law school, people study _____.

malfeasance   (mal·ˈfē·zən(t)s)

(*noun*)

wrongdoing or misconduct especially by a public
    official

When a government official embezzles money, it is
    an act of _____.

perjury   (pər·jə·rē)

(*noun*)

lying or intentionally omitting information under
    oath

When she lied under oath, she committed

    _____.

plagiarism   (ˈplā·jə·ri·zəm)

(*noun*)

the act of passing off someone else's work as your
    own

In college, you can be expelled if you engage in

    _____.

sanction   (ˈsan(k)·shən)

(*noun*)

authoritative permission or approval that makes a
    course of action valid, a law or decree

(*verb*)

to give permission or approval, to encourage or
    tolerate by indicating approval

The ruling was a _____; it made it clear that the
    court approved of the defendant's behavior.

When the judge gave his ruling, he turned to the
    defendant and said, "I find you guilty as
    charged. This court does not _____ your
    behavior."

tort   (ˈtȯrt)

(*noun*)

wrongdoing for which damages can be claimed; an
    unintentional violation of someone's rights,
    which can result in civil action but not criminal
    proceedings

A _____ is an unintentional violation of
    another person's rights.

WORDS IN CONTEXT

The following exercise will help you figure out the meaning of some words from Vocabulary List 8 by looking at context clues. After you have read and understood the paragraph, explain the context clues that helped you with the meaning of the vocabulary word. Check the answer section at the end of this chapter for an example.

The attorney explained that if I gave a *deposition* then I probably would not have to testify in court. I would still be under oath, but my testimony would be given and transcribed into written form before the trial actually began. I was glad I didn't have to testify because the case seemed pretty ridiculous to me. My Aunt Sally died *intestate* and without children, so the family did not know what she wanted us to do with her possessions. I was sure that she meant her house to be a *bequest* for my mother who is her sister; yet my aunt's ex-husband, Tom, said the house should be his. He said he had a signed *affidavit* stating that my aunt told him she would leave him the house. Initially, my mom and I thought we could keep this from becoming a *litigious* matter, but Tom wasn't willing to discuss the matter with us and come to a compromise. He wanted a third party to *adjudicate* this dispute, so he hired an attorney and we were forced to do the same.

SENTENCE COMPLETION

Insert the correct word from Vocabulary List 8 into the following sentences.

1. The president issued a _____ stating that the administration approved the federal budget.

2. When the attorney lost the case, she swore she would take it to _____ court for appeal.

3. As a witness to the crime, I was asked to give a _____; the attorney asked me many questions under oath, while a stenographer wrote everything I said down.

4. Drugs are _____, but many people still try to smuggle them in across the border.

5. I am leaving my estate as a _____ to my daughter.

6. When I sold my land, I was asked to sign an owner's _____ stating that I knew the property was in good shape and free of debt.

7. Many people have lobbied for the government to _____ nuclear weapons.

8. In small claims court, a judge and not a jury _____(s) the dispute.

9. In the past, many states did not let family members sue each other over _____(s) because they were concerned that it would ruin the family, but now it is believed that if someone has violated another's rights, there probably already has been a breakdown of the family.

10. When she stole the car, she was charged with _____.

11. A(n) _____ clause is a statement that says a contract or agreement will automatically terminate on the expiration date of the agreement unless otherwise amended.

12. I do not want to die _____, so I plan to draft a will that clearly states who should inherit my possessions.

13. When public officials engage in _____, many citizens feel betrayed.

14. Committing _____ while under oath is a very serious offense.

15. The teacher accused the student of _____ when she handed in a paper she found on the Internet.

16. _____, the philosophy of the law, is an interesting but complicated topic.

17. When the criminal escaped to Mexico, we hoped Mexico would _____ him so we could make him stand trial in the US for his crime.

18. We have a _____ on our house, because we were not able to pay off our debt, so now the bank from which we borrowed the money may take our house to satisfy the loan.

19. The body was _____(ed) from the crypt.

20. When the attorney called, I knew that the matter had become _____ and we were no longer going to try and settle our disagreement out of court.

TRUE/FALSE QUESTIONS

In the space provided, write a *T* if the sentence is true or an *F* if it is false. If the sentence is false, cross out the incorrect word and write the correct word from Vocabulary List 8 above it.

21. ___When the Mayor embezzled money from the city it was an act of **jurisprudence**.

22. ___Cases are appealed in **appellate** court.

23. ___In a court of law, the judge is the person who will **abrogate** the case.

24. ___Lying under oath is an act of **plagiarism**.

25. ___When the cops found him with the stolen diamond ring, they charged him with **larceny**.

26. ___When the witness gave her **affidavit**, she was asked many questions under oath while a stenographer wrote down both the questions and her responses.

27. ___When I went through customs at the airport, they asked me if I was carrying any **contraband** items.

28. ___After her death, her family realized that she had died **intestate** so they were not sure what to do with her estate.

29. ___If you run to another country after committing a crime, there is a very good chance that the country will **exhume** you to your homeland to be prosecuted.

30. ___A **litigious** matter is a contentious matter and one that will most likely be dealt with through the justice system.

CHOOSING THE RIGHT WORD QUESTIONS

Circle the word in bold that best completes the sentence.

31. Her father died (**ipso facto, intestate**) so she and her siblings had some difficulty figuring out how to deal with his estate.

32. Before we could close the deal, the borrower had to provide evidence to the lender that there were no (**liens, larcenies**) against the borrower's property.

33. In our town, our water was contaminated because a local factory was not disposing of dangerous chemicals properly, so we brought a (**sanction, tort**) claim against them and won.

34. I am very interested in studying (**jurisprudence, malfeasance**) because I am fascinated by the different systems of law and the philosophical tenets on which they are based.

35. In our country child labor was (**extradited, abrogated**) a long time ago; however, in some countries, people are still fighting to end it.

36. When my grandfather died, he left me his piano as a(n) (**contraband, bequest**) which touched me deeply because he taught me how to play.

37. After they found the tomb, the explorers wanted to (**extradite, exhume**) the remains to see if they could determine the date of the tomb.

38. The contract stated that the parties must give written notification of intent to extend the contract, otherwise the contract (**ipso facto, adjudicate**) terminated on the expiration.

39. Before the bank would give us our loan, the attorney prepared a(n) (**deposition, affidavit**) which stated that our property was debt-free and environmentally-sound and asked me to sign it under oath.

40. In most schools, it is a violation of the honor code to engage in an act of (**perjury, plagiarism**) because it is unethical to hand in someone else's work and pretend it is your own.

MATCHING

Match the word in the first column with the corresponding definition in the second column.

41. lien   **a.** the very fact

42. extradite   **b.** testimony under oath

43. adjudicate   **c.** the act of passing someone else's writing off as your own

44. bequest   **d.** to abolish

45. contraband   **e.** a violation of someone's rights

46. perjury   **f.** one who dies without a will

47. jurisprudence   **g.** the act of bequeathing

48. ipso facto   **h.** charge against real property to satisfy a debt

49. exhume   **i.** to act as judge

50. abrogate   **j.** contentious

51. appellate   **k.** misconduct especially of a public official

52. larceny   **l.** to surrender a criminal to country where s/he can be tried

53. tort   **m.** lying under oath

54. sanction   **n.** to remove from a grave

55. affidavit   **o.** stealing

56. litigious   **p.** sworn written statement

57. malfeasance   **q.** illegal import or export of goods

58. plagiarism   **r.** authoritative approval

59. intestate   **s.** the philosophy of the law

60. deposition   **t.** having the power to review the judgment of another court

PRACTICE ACTIVITIES

Read an article about a current or historical court case and see how many of the vocabulary words from this chapter appear in the article. Write down any additional words you see in the article and their definitions based on the context clues. Be sure to look up each word in your dictionary and to write down its definition as well.

Find a legal document such as the lease for your apartment, the back of a credit card application, a letter from a lawyer, the agreement with your car insurance company, or any other contract you can find. Read through the document, add any new words to your vocabulary list, and look them up. As you read, think about the following questions: How is the document written? Is it easy to understand, why or why not? How are legal words used in the document?

ANSWERS

WORDS IN CONTEXT

The first word we encounter is *deposition*. The context tells us that it is an alternative to testifying in court, but you are still under oath. We can conclude that it means a written testimony under oath prior to a trial. Sally died *intestate*, leaving the family unsure of how she wanted them to split up her belongings, so *intestate* must mean without a will. The narrator says he thinks Sally meant the house to be a *bequest*, or meant the narrator's mother to inherit the house. So *bequest* must mean something that is left to someone in a will. Tom has a signed *affidavit*, so an *affidavit* must mean a written statement. The narrator didn't want this to become *litigious* but it has, so we can conclude that *litigious* must mean contentious and prone to litigation. Finally, Tom wants someone else to *adjudicate*, or settle this dispute. So *adjudicate* must mean to act as judge or to settle judicially.

SENTENCE COMPLETION

1. *sanction.* If you got this question wrong, go back and review the word's definition.
2. *appellate.* If you got this question wrong, go back and review the word's definition.
3. *deposition.* If you got this question wrong, go back and review the word's definition.
4. *contraband.* If you got this question wrong, go back and review the word's definition.
5. *bequest.* If you got this question wrong, go back and review the word's definition.
6. *affidavit.* If you got this question wrong, go back and review the word's definition.
7. *abrogate.* If you got this question wrong, go back and review the word's definition.
8. *adjudicate.* If you got this question wrong, go back and review the word's definition.

9. *tort.* If you got this question wrong, go back and review the word's definition.
10. *larceny.* If you got this question wrong, go back and review the word's definition.
11. *ipso facto.* If you got this question wrong, go back and review the word's definition.
12. *intestate.* If you got this question wrong, go back and review the word's definition.
13. *malfeasance.* If you got this question wrong, go back and review the word's definition.
14. *perjury.* If you got this question wrong, go back and review the word's definition.
15. *plagiarism.* If you got this question wrong, go back and review the word's definition.
16. *jurisprudence.* If you got this question wrong, go back and review the word's definition.
17. *extradite.* If you got this question wrong, go back and review the word's definition.
18. *lien.* If you got this question wrong, go back and review the word's definition.
19. *exhume.* If you got this question wrong, go back and review the word's definition.
20. *litigious.* If you got this question wrong, go back and review the word's definition.

TRUE/FALSE

21. False, correct word is malfeasance
22. True
23. False, correct word is adjudicate
24. False, correct word is perjury
25. True
26. False, correct word is deposition
27. True
28. True
29. False, correct word is extradite
30. True

CHOOSING THE RIGHT WORD

31. intestate

32. liens

33. tort

34. jurisprudence

35. abrogated

36. bequest

37. exhume

38. ipso facto

39. affidavit

40. plagiarism

MATCHING

41. h

42. l

43. i

44. g

45. q

46. m

47. s

48. a

49. n

50. d

51. t

52. o

53. e

54. r

55. p

56. j

57. k

58. c

59. f

60. b

Across

3 malfeasance
7 exhume
8 jurisprudence
11 affidavit
12 tort
15 extradite
17 larceny
18 litigious
21 abrogate

Down

1 bequest
2 appellate
4 lien
5 adjudicate
6 deposition
9 ipso facto
10 contraband
13 perjury
16 plagiarism
19 intestate
20 sanction

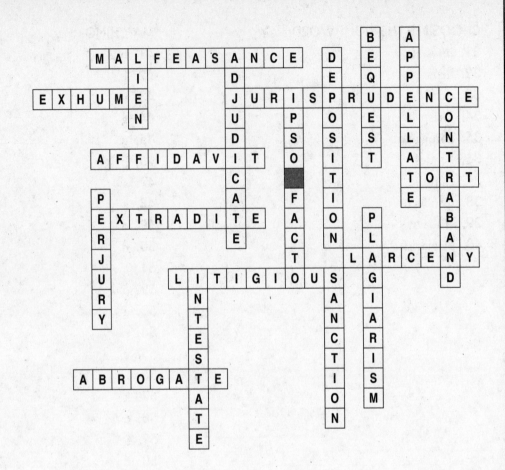

C·H·A·P·T·E·R

VOCABULARY LIST 9: TERMS RELATING TO LANGUAGE AND LITERATURE

CHAPTER SUMMARY

This chapter will introduce you to a number of widely used literary terms or, words used to talk about language and literature. When we say *literary terms* we mean ideas that are useful when discussing or analyzing a piece of literature such as a novel, short story, or poem. Yet, literary terms are also applicable when we may wish to describe elements of text encountered in every day life.

That is, it is not only in the context of an English class or a seemingly sophisticated conversation about the fine points of literature that we employ such terminology. For example, we encounter *irony* not only in Joseph Heller's famous novel, *Catch-22,* but when the math teacher unexpectedly, considering her supposed expertise, makes more computation errors than all her students combined!

Try to consider the following vocabulary words both in terms of how they may appear in literary texts as well as in the more general fabric of our lives.

Choose the word from the Vocabulary List that best fits into the crossword puzzle. You can check your answers at the end of the chapter following the answers to the questions.

Vocabulary List 9:
Terms Relating to Language
and Literature

anecdote
anthropomorphism
archetype
aphorism
construe
deduce
epigram
etymology
infer
irony
onomatopoeia
personification
perspective
protagonist
prose
pun
rhetoric
satire
soliloquy
trite

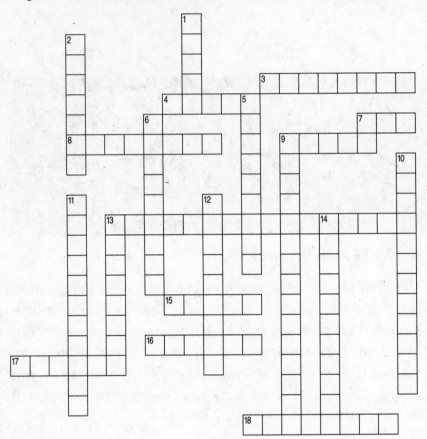

Across

3 using language effectively and persuasively
4 banal, ordinary, common
7 play on words
8 maxim, adage
9 ordinary writing
13 humanization
15 incongruity, or expressing something other than, or opposite to, the literal meaning
16 infer
17 the use of ridicule, usually to criticize
18 explain, interpret

Down

1 deduce, judge
2 a poem or paragraph dealing with a single thought
5 word origins
6 model, exemplar
9 embodiment
10 using words whose sounds suggest the meaning
11 outlook, point of view
12 talking to oneself, usually in drama, to reveal thoughts without actually addressing the listener
13 short tale relating an incident
14 main character

anecdote   ('a·nik·dōt)

(noun)

a short account of an interesting or humorous
    incident

In order to capture classroom life for the visiting
    parents at "Back to School Night," the teacher
    shared a number of comical _____(s)
    about her kindergarten students.

anthropomorphism   (an(t)·thrə·pə·'mȯr·fi·zəm)

(noun)

attribution of human motivation, characteristics, or
    behavior to inanimate objects, animals, or
    natural phenomena

The Native American legend evidenced _____
    as it was a bear who emotionally narrated the
    tale of loss on the reservation.

archetype   ('är·ki·tīp)

(noun)

an original model or type after which other similar
    things are patterned; an ideal example of a type

Shakespeare's dramas provide a literary _____
    that has influenced many subsequent authors
    who follow the pattern his work provides.

aphorism   ('a·fə·ri·zəm)

(noun)

a brief statement of a truth or opinion; a saying or an
    adage

The old _____, "Good things come to those
    who wait," proved true when after many years
    the patient boy got his wish.

construe   (kən·'strü)

(verb)

to explain the meaning of; interpret; to analyze the
    grammatical structure of (a sentence)

The hopeful son _____(d) his mother's silence
    as granting him permission to go to the party.

deduce   (di·'düs)

(verb)

to reach a conclusion by reasoning; to infer from a
    general principle; to trace the origin of

Are you able to _____ the meaning of a word
    once you are given ample context clues?

epigram   ('e·pə·gram)

(noun)

a short, witty poem expressing a single thought or
    observation; a concise, clever, often paradoxical
    statement or saying

The novelist began her text with a short _____
    on the first page that truly captured the
    complexity of the story that followed.

etymology   (e·tə·'mä·lə·jē)

(noun)

the origin and historical development of a word's
    forms, meanings and usages

Students were asked to trace the _____ of the
    word, looking in particular for its earliest usage.

infer   ('in·fər)

(verb)

to conclude or reason from evidence, premises, or
    circumstance; to hint or imply

Given the circumstances, we may _____ that
    the young mother's motive in putting her baby
    up for adoption was indeed honorable.

irony   ('ī·rə·nē)

(noun)

the use of words to express something different from,
    and often opposite to, their literal meaning; a
    literary style employing such contrasts for witty
    effect; incongruity between what might be
    expected and what actually occurs

The _____ of his name, "Mr. Short," became
    apparent when I saw the seven-foot tall man for
    the first time.

onomatopoeia (ä·nə·mä·tə·ˈpē·ə)
(noun)
the formation or use of words such that imitate the
    sounds associated with the objects or actions to
    which they refer
I admire the poem's use of _____ as it truly
    brings the various sounds of a developing
    storm—*buzz, murmur, crash*—to life!

personification (pər·sä·nə·fə·ˈkā·shən)
(noun)
a person or thing typifying a certain quality or idea;
    an embodiment or exemplification; a figure of
    speech in which inanimate objects or
    abstractions are endowed with human qualities
    or are represented as possessing human form
Peter was a true _____ of joy as he danced
    around in utter bliss.

perspective (pər·ˈspek·tiv)
(noun)
a mental view or outlook; a point of view; the ability
    to perceive things in their actual interrelations
    or comparative importance
A careful look at the child's past afforded the counselor
    important _____ on the present situation.

protagonist (prō·ˈta·gə·nist)
(noun)
the main character in a drama or other literary work
Holden Caufield, the _____ of J.D. Salinger's
    Catcher in the Rye, is of central interest to
    young readers who relate to his rebellious voice.

prose (ˈprōz)
(noun)
ordinary speech or writing, without metrical
    structure (as in poetry)
The improved quality of the students' _____
    was evidenced in the journals they kept over
    the course of the year.

pun (ˈpən)
(noun)
play on words
We laughed at the _____ when the frazzled
    doctor exclaimed that he had no more patience.

rhetoric (ˈre·tə·rik)
(noun)
the art or study of using language effectively and
    persuasively
The politician's speech was particularly effective not
    so much because of its actual content, but
    because of his persuasive _____ that
    captivated the audience.

satire (ˈsa·tīr)
(noun)
a literary work in which human vice or folly is
    attacked through irony or wit
The political cartoon was a _____ of the
    presidential election process as it exposed its
    ridiculous nature.

soliloquy (sə·ˈli·lə·kwē)
(noun)
a dramatic or literary form of discourse in which a
    character talks to himself or herself or reveals
    his or her thoughts without addressing a listener
The audience becomes privy to Hamlet's inner
    struggles as Shakespeare's protagonist begins
    his well-known _____ with, "To be or not
    to be."

trite (ˈtrīt)
(adj.)
lacking power to evoke interest through overuse or
    repetition; hackneyed
Sue was unmoved by her lover's valentine that read,
    "Roses are red, violets are blue, sugar is sweet
    and so are you," calling it _____ and
    overused.

WORDS IN CONTEXT

The following exercise will help you figure out the meaning of some words from Vocabulary List 9 by looking at context clues. After you have read and understood the paragraph, explain the context clues that helped you with the meaning of the vocabulary word. Check the answer section at the end of this chapter for an example.

When asked why the *prose* of the new novelist, Jane Jackson, appealed to me, I immediately thought of what makes any good novel. Considering the standard *archetype,* the successful novel should include mastery of a range of literary elements. In Jackson's case, she indeed effectively employs the device of *anthropomorphism,* in particular, when she writes in her latest work of the Angry Storm waiting to take her revenge. It is as if the storm itself is the novel's *protagonist:* its central and most dynamic character. An *anecdote* I would like to share regarding the popularity of Jackson's writing takes place on the NYC subway. I noticed a young woman reading Jackson's latest novel: a *satire* that exposes and makes fun of the divorce rate in the United States. When I, instinctively as a literary critic, approached the reader to ask her opinion, I realized it was Jackson herself! The *irony* of the situation was that the novelist still wished to critique the text she had authored; she was her own worst critic!

SENTENCE COMPLETION

Insert the correct word from Vocabulary List 9 into the following sentences.

1. When one tells a short, comical story, she is sharing a(n) _____.

2. The _____ of a word reveals to us its source and various usages.

3. To explain something through analysis or interpretation is to _____ its meaning.

4. A short witty poem or saying called an _____ sometimes begins a larger work in order to set the tone.

5. _____ is when an inanimate object assumes human features or characteristics.

6. When something or someone typifies or embodies a given idea, it is a _____ of that concept.

7. An ideal example of a given type is known as a standard or a(n) _____.

8. A _____ is a play on words.

9. _____ is the art of effective language use.

10. When a character or performer reveals her thoughts without addressing a listener, she is issuing a _____.

11. A brief statement of truth or opinion is known as a(n) _____ or a saying.

12. One is often able to _____, or to reach a conclusion by reasoning or inference.

13. The complex device, _____, is when words are used to express something different from and opposite to their literal meaning.

14. *Buzz* is a clear example of _____, when a word imitates the sounds associated with the actions of objects to which they refer.

15. To _____ is to understand from a hint or implication, rather than from something directly stated.

16. Putting a situation in the proper _____ often requires a certain mental outlook or point of view.

17. A novel's main character, or _____, is central to the action of the text.

18. When a saying, idea or word is so overused that it fails to evoke interest or convey meaning, we may call it _____.

19. The finest novelists have a real signature to their writing or the _____ they produce.

20. Irony and wit contribute to the makings of an effective _____ that attacks human folly.

SYNONYMS

The following exercise lists vocabulary words from this chapter. Each word is followed by five answer choices. Four of them are synonyms of the vocabulary word in bold. Your task is to choose the one that does **not** fit.

21. archetype
   a. standard
   b. statement
   c. example
   d. ideal
   e. model

22. protagonist
   a. main character
   b. principal figure
   c. fastest player
   d. first actor
   e. leader of a cause

23. perspective
   a. point of view
   b. prescription
   c. evaluation of significance
   d. outlook
   e. perceived interrelations

24. prose
   a. depressing language
   b. ordinary writing
   c. non-metrical writing
   d. commonplace expression
   e. ordinary speech

25. pun
   a. ambiguous expression
   b. play on words
   c. similar sound
   d. rhetorical joke
   e. powerful understanding

26. satire
   a. classical text
   b. ironic ridicule
   c. witty literature
   d. caricature
   e. lampoon

27. trite
   a. commonplace
   b. habitual
   c. powerful
   d. overused
   e. banal

28. aphorism

   a. saying

   b. adage

   c. statement of truth

   d. euphemism

   e. maxim

29. deduce

   a. conclude

   b. compare

   c. infer

   d. reason

   e. suppose

30. construe

   a. to go against

   b. interpret

   c. render

   d. explain the meaning of

   e. analyze the structure of

TRUE/FALSE

True/False Questions: In the space provided, write a *T* if the italicized word from Vocabulary List 9 fits correctly, and an *F* if the sentence is false. If the sentence is false, cross out the false word and write the correct word from Vocabulary List 9 above it.

31. ___In journalism class, we used the news article as an *archetype* of what quality journalism looks like.

32. ___The coach offered me an inspiring *aphorism*, "It's not whether you win or lose but how you play the game."

33. ___Based on the given evidence and circumstances, I was able to *construe* my own hypothesis.

34. ___*Irony* is when words imitate the sounds associated with the actions to which they refer.

35. ___My *perspective* on the subject shifted when the author's prose helped me step into another point of view.

36. ___Cinderella, a well-known *pun*, captivates many readers who dream of transformation.

37. ___The film was a parody or *soliloquy* of the futuristic genre as it poked fun at depictions of space travel and alien encounters.

38. ___Her *prose* was seamless and descriptive as she narrated her travels abroad for a captive audience.

39. ___Throughout the story, the lion was a *personification* of all things regal and really stood as a symbol of royalty.

40. ___A word's *epigram* can reveal a great deal about the history of its usages.

CHOOSING THE RIGHT WORD

Circle the word in bold that best completes the sentence.

41. I thought she was such a good storyteller as she shared a number of humorous (**anecdotes, archetypes**) about her beloved grandmother.

42. The valentine card included a short, witty (**etymology, epigram**) that I found quite clever.

43. The character was a (**personification, satire**) of fear as she truly embodied the emotion.

44. There was such (**irony, onomatopoeia**) in the way she unexpectedly ended up rejecting the job she had worked for all her career.

45. Sometimes two words that mean different things yet sound the same provide the opportunity for a (**prose, pun**).

46. The (**rhetoric, protagonist**) in the persuasive essay was so strong it convinced me to change my position.

47. As a reader I tend to relate to a (**soliloquy, protagonist**) whose experiences reflect mine.

48. Although the poet did have some unique talent, he employed many phrases that were overused and that I found (**trite, ironic**).

49. What was so compelling about the actor's (**soliloquy, satire**) was how the audience came to understand the inner workings of his mind, even though he never addressed them directly.

50. The way the author used flashbacks provided an interesting (**pun, perspective**) on the protagonist's life story.

PRACTICE ACTIVITIES

Rent a movie with a friend and try talking about the way the story unfolds: *how* the actors, screenplay writers, and directors give you, the viewer, your information. In your film (also a literary text) discussion, try to use, in context, a number of words from Vocabulary List 9.

Recommend a book to a friend and in explaining why it is a worthwhile read, try using some of the literary terms you learned in Vocabulary List 9. Also, read the *New York Times* book review section. You'll see that those literary critics may talk about the quality of *prose*, an author's *rhetorical* gift or style, or the *ironic* plot twist the reader encounters.

ANSWERS

WORDS IN CONTEXT

After reading this paragraph, we understand one literary critic's opinion of new novelist Jane Jackson's *prose*. We understand that *prose* refers to the novelist's writing: written text as opposed to metrical poetry (Jackson is a novelist, not a poet). We are also privy to a direct experience the critic had with the novelist herself. The critic shares this *anecdote*, or story-like episode, in order to convey the *irony*, or unlikelihood, of Jackson being more critical of her own work than any other reader. We are able to recognize *archetype* as meaning ideal or standard both because of the way the critic refers to it as a model of what "good prose" should have, and also because the word is used in conjunction with the word *standard*, a synonym for *archetype*. The three literary terms—*anthropomorphism*, *protagonist*, and *satire*—may be understood in context as the critic explains how they specifically relate to the novelist's *prose*. Jackson evidently writes about a storm that possesses human qualities *(anthropomorphism)* and in fact, this animated storm operates as the main character *(protagonist)*. The critic also describes Jackson's latest novel as a *satire*: a text that exposes and mocks, in this case, the cultural phenomenon of rampant divorce.

SENTENCE COMPLETION

1. *anecdote.* If you got this question wrong, refer back to the word's definition.
2. *etymology.* If you got this question wrong, refer back to the word's definition.
3. *construe.* If you got this question wrong, refer back to the word's definition.
4. *epigram.* If you got this question wrong, refer back to the word's definition.
5. *anthropomorphism.* If you got this question wrong, refer back to the word's definition.
6. *personification.* If you got this question wrong, refer back to the word's definition.
7. *archetype.* If you got this question wrong, refer back to the word's definition.
8. *pun.* If you got this question wrong, refer back to the word's definition.
9. *rhetoric.* If you got this question wrong, refer back to the word's definition.
10. *soliloquy.* If you got this question wrong, refer back to the word's definition.
11. *aphorism.* If you got this question wrong, refer back to the word's definition.
12. *deduce.* If you got this question wrong, refer back to the word's definition.
13. *irony.* If you got this question wrong, refer back to the word's definition.
14. *onomatopoeia.* If you got this question wrong, refer back to the word's definition.
15. *infer.* If you got this question wrong, refer back to the word's definition.
16. *perspective.* If you got this question wrong, refer back to the word's definition.
17. *protagonist.* If you got this question wrong, refer back to the word's definition.
18. *trite.* If you got this question wrong, refer back to the word's definition.
19. *prose.* If you got this question wrong, refer back to the word's definition.
20. *satire.* If you got this question wrong, refer back to the word's definition.

SYNONYMS

21. **b.** *statement.* An archetype is an original model after which other things are patterned, so *statement,* simply something that is said or put forth, would not be a synonym.

22. **c.** *fastest player.* A protagonist is the main character in a drama or other literary work. In ancient Greek drama, a protagonist is the first actor to engage in dialogue. A protagonist is also a champion or leader of a cause. Speed has little to do with a protagonist's centrality, therefore, *fastest player* would not be a synonym.

23. **b.** *prescription.* Perspective is a mental outlook, point of view or the ability to perceive things as they actually relate to one another. *Prescription* is the establishment of a claim up front: literally, written beforehand, and would not be a synonym.

24. **a.** *depressing language.* Prose is ordinary speech or writing, without metrical structure. It is also a term used to denote commonplace expression. That language may be depressing does not define it as prose. Thus, *depressing language* would not be a synonym.

25. **e.** *powerful understanding.* A pun is wordplay, sometimes on different senses of the same word and sometimes on the similar sense or sound of different words. *Powerful understanding* would not be a synonym.

26. **a.** *classical text.* A satire is a literary work in which human folly or vice is attacked through wit or irony. A text's being considered a classic does not constitute it a satire. Therefore, *classical text* would not be a synonym.

27. **c.** *powerful.* When language, for example, is trite, it lacks power to evoke interest through overuse or repetition. *Powerful* is in fact the opposite of trite and would thus not be a synonym.

28. **d.** *euphemism.* An aphorism is a brief statement of truth or opinion: adage and maxim are essentially synonymous with aphorism while a *euphemism* is a nice way of saying something that may be offensive. *Euphemism* is not a synonym for aphorism.

29. **b.** *compare.* To deduce is to reach a conclusion by reasoning or to infer from a general principle. Comparison—considering two things in terms of each other—is not a matter of deductive reasoning. Therefore, *compare* would not be a synonym.

30. **a.** *to go against.* To construe is to explain the meaning of, to interpret, or to analyze the structure of a sentence, for example. This does not mean *to go against:* not a synonym for construe.

TRUE/FALSE

31. True

32. True

33. False, the correct word is infer

34. False, the correct word is onomatopoeia

35. True

36. False, the correct word is protagonist

37. False, the correct word is satire

38. True

39. True

40. False, correct word is etymology

CHOOSING THE RIGHT WORD

41. *anecdotes.* Context clue is that she is telling stories that are humorous.

42. *epigram.* Context clue is that an epigram or short saying may be described as witty or clever.

43. *personification.* Context clue is that personification refers to a person's typifying or embodying a certain quality: in this case, fear.

44. *irony.* Context clue is that irony conveys the incongruity between what might be expected and what actually occurs.

45. *pun.* Context clue is that a pun is a play on words, such as those that may sound alike.

46. *rhetoric.* Context clue is that rhetoric is the art of using language effectively and persuasively.

47. *protagonist.* Context clue is that a protagonist is the main character of a text whose experiences provide the central action.

48. *trite.* Context clue is that trite phrases are described as overused and here, in contrast to the poet's talent.

49. *soliloquy.* Context clue is that a soliloquy is a dramatic form in which a character talks to himself, revealing his thoughts without addressing a listener.

50. *perspective.* Context clue is that perspective refers to a point of view; in this case, that particular viewpoint as achieved through the device of flashback.

Across

3 rhetoric
4 trite
7 pun
8 aphorism
9 prose
13 anthropomorphism
15 irony
16 deduce
17 satire
18 construe

Down

1 infer
2 epigram
5 etymology
6 archetype
9 personification
10 onomatopoeia
11 perspective
12 soliloquy
13 anecdote
14 protagonist

VOCABULARY LIST 10: SHORT WORDS THAT MEAN A LOT

13

CHAPTER SUMMARY

Sometimes we may falsely assume that vocabulary building means learning a host of long, multi-syllabic words. We may hope to throw around these ten-dollar words in our speech and writing in order to sound smart and articulate.

While a greater vocabulary may in fact increase our confidence as well as our comprehension and self-expression, these goals do not rest on the length of the words we come to know. After all, how often does *antidisestablishmentarianism* come up in conversation?

This chapter seeks to familiarize you with a number of short, but important words that frequently appear in a variety of contexts.

Choose the word from the Vocabulary List that best fits into the crossword puzzle. You can check your answers at the end of the chapter following the answers to the questions.

Vocabulary List 10:
Short Words that Mean a Lot

acme
awry
bane
cite
crux
dire
dupe
eke
elite
gibe
maim
mete
moot
oust
purge
roil
sham
staid
veer
vie

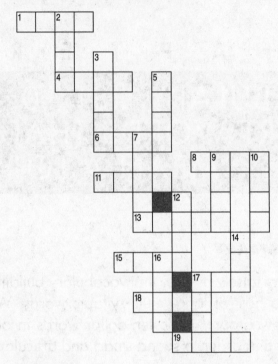

Across

1 force out
4 to allot
6 fool, chump
8 to cripple
11 askew, twisted
13 cream of the crop, upper crust
15 awful, appalling
17 to contest
18 to jeer or scoff
19 core, kernel

Down

2 a hoax, an impostor
3 serious, somber
5 source of persistent annoyance
7 to cleanse, to rid
9 pinnacle, high point
10 a case no longer of actual significance
12 to quote as an authority
14 to supplement, to make something last
16 to provoke, contaminate
17 to turn, or digress

acme   ('ak·mē)

(*noun*)

the highest point, as of achievement or development

When the singer was awarded the Lifetime Achievement Award, she know she had reached the _____ of her career.

awry   (ə·'rī)

(*adv.*)

in a position that is turned or twisted toward one side or away from the correct course; askew.

When a number of difficult variables entered into the situation, his carefully mapped plans went terribly _____.

bane   ('bān)

(*noun*)

fatal injury or ruin; a cause of harm, ruin, or death; a source of persistent annoyance or exasperation

The persistent beetles that continued to eat away at the crop of string beans in spite of all efforts at extermination became the _____ of the farmer's existence.

cite   ('sīt)

(*verb*)

to quote as an authority or example

The historian was careful to _____ a number of examples in order to back her claim that revolutions happen slowly.

crux   ('krəks)

(*noun*)

the basic or central point or feature; a puzzling or apparently insoluble problem

After hours of debate, the opponents finally arrived at the _____ of the matter and at last the central question became clear.

dire   ('dīr)

(*adj.*)

warning of, or having dreadful or terrible consequences; urgent; desperate

The poorly funded hospital was in _____ need of medical supplies given the number of neglected patients in desperate need.

dupe   ('düp)

(*noun*)

an easily deceived person

The unsuspecting young man felt like a _____ when he saw his girlfriend walk by in the arms of another man.

eke   ('ēk)

(*verb*)

to supplement or get with great effort; to make last by practicing strict economy

With careful management, the townspeople were able to _____ out three more day's use of water, although the well had virtually run dry.

elite   (ā·'lēt (i·'lēt, ē·'lēt))

(*noun*)

a group or class of persons or a member of such a group or class, enjoying superior intellectual, social, or economic status; the best or most skilled members of a group

The college's _____ students enjoyed not only their own high grades, but membership in the exclusive and esteemed honors program.

gibe   ('jīb)

(*verb*)

to make taunting, heckling, or jeering remarks

Mom made it clear that it was not acceptable to _____ our younger brother at the dinner table even though we insisted our taunting was in good fun.

maim   (ˈmām)

(*verb*)

to disable or disfigure; to make imperfect or
defective; impair

Is it possible that such a seemingly mild car accident
would _____ the driver to such
proportions, causing him to lose one of his
arms?

mete   (ˈmēt)

(*verb*)

to distribute by or as if by measure; allot

It was the captain's responsibility to carefully
_____ out the limited rations so that each
man received an equal amount.

moot   (ˈmüt)

(*noun*)

a hypothetical case argued as an exercise; a case no
longer of actual significance

Since the position was no longer available, discussing
who might better fill the spot became a
_____ point.

oust   (ˈaùst)

(*verb*)

To eject from a position or place; force out

The community hoped to _____ the
superintendent from the school district since
his policies had proved not only ineffective, but
damaging.

purge   (ˈpərj)

(*verb*)

to free from impurities; purify; to rid of sin, guilt, or
defilement; to clear a person of a charge; to get
rid of people considered undesirable

After her candid testimony that evidenced her
innocence, the woman on the stand was able to
_____ herself of all criminal charges.

roil   (ˈrȯi(ə)l)

(*verb*)

to make a liquid muddy or cloudy by stirring up
sediment; to displease or disturb; vex

My husband's disturbing refusal to help with the
housework began to _____ me.

sham   (ˈsham)

(*noun*)

something false or empty that is said to be genuine;
one who assumes a false character; an impostor

After a year of marriage, he recognized his wife as a
_____ and sadly saw that his relationship
was based on deception and lies.

staid   (ˈstād)

(*adj.*)

characterized by sedate dignity and propriety; sober.
Fixed; permanent

At her mother's funeral, Sue remained _____
and sober, demonstrating her unwavering grief.

veer   (ˈvir)

(*verb*)

to turn aside from a course, direction, or purpose;
swerve

The car's driver was able to _____ in the other
direction in order to avoid a dangerous crash
with an oncoming biker.

vie   (ˈvī)

(*verb*)

to strive for superiority; compete; rival

The two elite players would _____ for the
championship.

WORDS IN CONTEXT

The following exercise will help you figure out the meaning of some words from Vocabulary List 10 by looking at context clues. After you have read and understood the paragraph, explain the context clues that helped you with the meaning of the vocabulary word. Check the answer section at the end of this chapter for an example.

There are many examples I am able to **cite** in order to make the case that I am in fact the biggest *dupe* that ever lived. I know this sounds extreme, but when I realized what a *sham* my girlfriend is, I had to ask myself why I never saw through all her lies and deception. I guess I sensed that things began to go *awry* between us early last year, but I hoped they would straighten out and get back on course naturally before the situation became too *dire.* I was able to **eke** out the truth, but only after some pretty serious prying. She was cheating all along, and honestly, I can't even look at her face anymore; she has become the *bane* of my existence!

SENTENCE COMPLETION

Insert the correct word from Vocabulary List 10 into the following sentences.

1. When a situation goes off course, it is said to have gone _____.

2. To quote as an authority or an example is to _____.

3. The _____ of one's freedom, for example, is the cause of freedom's decay or disappearance.

4. When you reach the _____ of your career, you know you achieved the highest point possible.

5. A(n) _____ is an easily deceived person.

6. One who enjoys superior status in a given arena is considered _____.

7. To _____ out supplies is to distribute them carefully in equal amounts.

8. The _____ of an argument is its basic or central feature.

9. You may be able to _____ out an income by working multiple jobs.

10. A hypothetical case may be considered _____.

11. If your situation is urgent or desperate, you are perhaps in _____ need of assistance.

12. To _____ is to make heckling, taunting remarks.

13. A lecture can _____ off course or change direction if the speaker is not very careful.

14. To disable or disfigure a person is to _____ his or her body.

15. His _____ composure belied the inner turmoil on his mind.

16. When you disturb or vex another person, you _____ her.

17. You pretended to be genuine, but you are completely false and a total _____!

18. We wondered whether to _____, or force out, the coach after he became unprofessional with his players.

19. It became necessary to _____ his body of toxins in order to purify the system and restore health.

20. The competitive siblings felt they needed to _____ for the approval of their parents.

SYNONYMS

The following exercise lists vocabulary words from this chapter. Each word is followed by five answer choices. Four of them are synonyms of the vocabulary word in bold. Your task is to choose the one that does **not** fit.

21. acme
   a. summit
   b. apex
   c. highest point
   d. culmination
   e. average

22. cite
   a. attribute
   b. view
   c. honor
   d. reference
   e. quote

23. elite
   a. chosen
   b. lightweight
   c. nobility
   d. superiors
   e. the best

24. purge
   a. soil
   b. cleanse
   c. clear of charge
   d. eliminate
   e. evacuate

25. sham
   a. imitation
   b. false pretense
   c. impostor
   d. hero
   e. deceitful

26. veer
   a. steer
   b. swerve
   c. shift direction
   d. turn off course
   e. deviate

27. staid
   a. serious
   b. tired
   c. sedate
   d. permanent
   e. proper

28. roil
   a. displease
   b. disturb
   c. cheat
   d. vex
   e. stir up

29. bane
   a. curse
   b. killing
   c. ruin
   d. twist
   e. evil

30. awry
   a. turned
   b. elevated
   c. twisted
   d. amiss
   e. askew

ANTONYMS

Choose the word from Vocabulary List 10 that means the opposite, or most nearly the opposite, of the following groups of words.

31. nadir, bottom, lowest point, underachievement _____

32. soil, condemn, retain, keep _____

33. actual, significant, relevant, important _____

34. protect, retain, house, host _____

35. please, calm, clarify, comfort _____

36. dynamic, shifting, changing, animated _____

37. genuine, trustworthy, sincere, authentic _____

38. inferior, sub-par, subordinate, second rate _____

39. savior, relief, preserver, gift _____

40. straight, direct, right, good _____

MATCHING

Match the word in the first column with the corresponding word in the second column.

41. dire   a. easily deceived

42. sham   b. to get with great effort

43. gibe   c. to distribute by measure

44. eke   d. to turn aside from a course

45. crux   e. to disable or disfigure

46. dupe   f. having dreadful consequences

47. mete   g. to make taunting remarks

48. veer   h. basic or central feature

49. maim   i. impostor

50. awry   j. askew

PRACTICE ACTIVITIES

Now that you know these short but important words, they'll turn up everywhere! You may also find, especially if you make a deliberate effort, that ample opportunities arise for you to try these words out for yourself.

Because of their commonality, give yourself the challenge of both listening for them when you watch the news on TV, for example, and inserting them into your own common speech, on the phone for example. Confide in your friend that things have really gone *awry* in your household (we hope not) or that your mother-in-law has become the *bane* of your existence!

ANSWERS

WORDS IN CONTEXT

This frustrated individual begins to explain his situation by communicating that he is able to *cite*, or quote by way of example, reasons he sees himself as a *dupe*. We may infer that his being a *dupe* has to do with his having been unsuspectedly deceived: cheated on by his girlfriend. He refers to his girlfriend as a *sham*, having assumed the false character of a loyal partner. When he explains that he sensed his relationship was beginning to go off course, he uses the word *awry*, meaning to stray or go askew. The narrating *dupe* hoped that things would straighten out before becoming too *dire*: in context, clearly a negative term in the extreme (having dreadful consequences). Unfortunately, after *eking* out the truth—this process is said to have involved prying—he is disgusted by the emotional harm the **sham** has caused him; he refers to her as the *bane* of his existence (source of persistent annoyance).

SENTENCE COMPLETION

1. *awry.* If you got this question wrong, refer back to the word's definition.
2. *cite.* If you got this question wrong, refer back to the word's definition.
3. *bane.* If you got this question wrong, refer back to the word's definition.
4. *acme.* If you got this question wrong, refer back to the word's definition.
5. *dupe.* If you got this question wrong, refer back to the word's definition.
6. *elite.* If you got this question wrong, refer back to the word's definition.
7. *mete.* If you got this question wrong, refer back to the word's definition.
8. *crux.* If you got this question wrong, refer back to the word's definition.
9. *eke.* If you got this question wrong, refer back to the word's definition.
10. *moot.* If you got this question wrong, refer back to the word's definition.
11. *dire.* If you got this question wrong, refer back to the word's definition.
12. *gibe.* If you got this question wrong, refer back to the word's definition.
13. *veer.* If you got this question wrong, refer back to the word's definition.
14. *maim.* If you got this question wrong, refer back to the word's definition.
15. *staid.* If you got this question wrong, refer back to the word's definition.
16. *roil.* If you got this question wrong, refer back to the word's definition.
17. *sham.* If you got this question wrong, refer back to the word's definition.
18. *oust.* If you got this question wrong, refer back to the word's definition.
19. *purge.* If you got this question wrong, refer back to the word's definition.
20. *vie.* If you got this question wrong, refer back to the word's definition.

SYNONYMS

21. e. *average.* Acme is the highest point of achievement or development. It is not at all *average* but rather the best one can do. *Average* would not be a synonym.
22. b. *view.* To cite is to quote or reference as an authority or an example. While cite may sound like sight and site which do relate more closely to *view*, *view* would not be a synonym for cite.
23. b. *lightweight.* To be (an) elite is to belong to a group or class of people who enjoy superior

status. The elite are chosen, superior, or the best in a given arena. Lightweight would not be a synonym of elite.

24. **a.** *soil.* To purge is to free from impurities, to remove or to eliminate. In law, it means to clear someone of a charge. Soil means to dirty or taint and would not be a synonym of purge.

25. **d.** *hero.* A sham is something or someone false that is purported to be genuine. A *hero* generally possesses sincere, noble, and admirable qualities. *Hero* would not be a synonym for sham.

26. **b.** *steer.* To veer is to turn aside from a course, direction or purpose. Swerve and deviate also describe such derailing action. *Steer* implies guided control and would not be a synonym.

27. **b.** *tired.* Staid characterizes sedate dignity, and serious, sober propriety. It also means fixed or permanent. Fatigue is not necessarily associated being staid and so, *tired* would not be a synonym.

28. **c.** *cheat.* To roil is to disturb or displease. It also refers to making a liquid muddy by stirring up sediment. Though one may become vexed or roiled if cheated by another, *cheat* is not a synonym of roil.

29. **d.** *twist.* Bane describes fatal injury or ruin. *Twist* would not be a synonym as it is not necessarily the cause of harm, ruin, or death.

30. **b.** *elevated.* Awry describes a position that is turned or twisted toward one side. Askew and amiss also convey this sense. To *elevate* means to lift up or raise not twist or turn and so would not be a synonym.

ANTONYMS

31. *acme.* Acme means the highest point of achievement or development, the opposite of the meaning of the words in the group.

32. *purge.* Purge means to free from impurities or guilt, the opposite of soil or condemn. It also means to get rid of, the opposite of retain or keep.

33. *moot.* Moot means a hypothetical case, opposite of actual. It also means not longer of actual significance, opposite of the rest of the words listed.

34. *oust.* Oust means to eject or force out, opposite of the words listed which mean to keep and comfort in a protected space.

35. *roil.* Roil means to make cloudy or stir up, the opposite of calm or clarify. It also means to disturb or vex, the opposite of please, or comfort.

36. *staid.* Staid means sedate, sober, fixed, or permanent, the opposite of the words in the group.

37. *sham.* A sham is something or someone false or an impostor, the opposite of the words in the group.

38. *elite.* To be elite is to enjoy superior status, the opposite of the words in the group.

39. *bane.* Bane is fatal injury or the cause of ruin or death, the opposite of the positive, redemptive words in the group.

40. *awry.* Awry means turned or twisted, or off the expected or correct course, the opposite meaning of the words in the group.

MATCHING

41. f
42. i
43. g
44. b
45. h
46. a
47. c
48. d
49. e
50. j

Across

1 oust
4 mete
6 dupe
8 maim
11 awry
13 elite
15 dire
17 vie
18 gibe
19 crux

Down

2 sham
3 staid
5 bane
7 purge
9 acme
10 moot
12 cite
14 eke
16 roil
17 veer

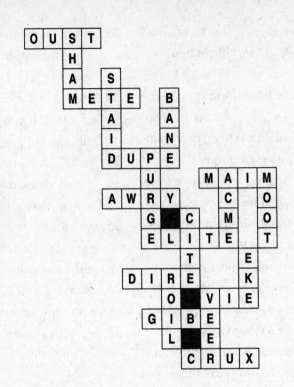

VOCABULARY LIST 11: ADJECTIVES

CHAPTER SUMMARY

Adjectives are typically understood as words used to describe nouns, that is, people, places, and things. But, beyond this textbook definition, we may begin to think about the role of adjectives in our experiences as readers, writers, speakers, and listeners.

What does careful description add to a given conversation, story, or explanation? Adjectives add color, definition, and detail to any piece of writing. They serve to qualify and clarify the subject at hand. Consider a mental image coming into focus as additional information is put forth: "There was a man; There was an old man; There was an old, dolorous man." In this way, adjectives help us account for specificity when trying to conjure up a figure, picture, mood, or situation in our minds.

Choose the word from the Vocabulary List that best fits into the crossword puzzle. You can check your answers at the end of the chapter following the answers to the questions.

Vocabulary List 11: Adjectives

audacious
churlish
demure
dolorous
epicurean
extenuating
facetious
feisty
flippant
imperious
jaunty
myriad
oblique
ornate
palpable
prodigious
prone
relevant
sardonic
vehement

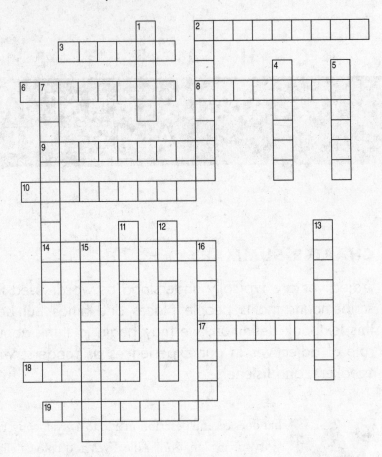

Across

2 something that's meant to be funny
3 shy, modest, reserved
6 relating to
8 touchable, perceptible
9 devoted to the pursuit of sensual pleasure, gourmet
10 bold, adventuresome, insolent
14 commanding
17 indirect, circuitous
18 innumerable
19 surly

Down

1 apt, disposed to
2 glib, lacking appropriate respectfulness
4 stylish, lively
5 spunky, showing aggressiveness, liveliness
7 tempering, moderating
11 elaborate, sumptuous
12 woeful, melancholy
13 intense, desperate
15 amazing, massive
16 cynical, scornful

audacious   (ȯ·ˈdā·shəs)

(*adj.*)

fearlessly, often recklessly daring, adventurous, and
    brave; unrestrained by convention or propriety;
    insolent

The student's _____ behavior—swearing at the
    teacher in class—resulted in detention for a
    week.

churlish   (ˈchər·lish)

(*adj.*)

boorish or vulgar; having a bad disposition; surly;
    difficult to work with; intractable

The child was immediately punished for his bad
    attitude and _____ behavior.

demure   (di·ˈmyu̇r)

(*adj.*)

modest and reserved in manner or behavior; shy

Having always been attracted to the shy and quiet
    type, James predictably fell for the _____
    woman to whom he was introduced.

dolorous   (ˈdō·lə·rəs)

(*adj.*)

exhibiting sorrow, grief, or pain

My friend's _____ expression could be
    explained by the painful divorce process in
    which she found herself.

epicurean   (e·pi·kyu̇·ˈrē·ən)

(*adj.*)

devoted to the pursuit of sensual pleasure, especially
    to good food and comfort

The _____ feast lasted for hours as those in
    attendance enjoyed fine wine, delicacies, and
    the host's beautiful home.

extenuating   (ik·sten·yə·wāt·ing)

(*adj.*)

lessened the magnitude or seriousness of, especially
    by making partial excuses

After hearing the entire story surrounding the
    supposed crime, the judge realized there existed
    _____ circumstances that put the
    situation in perspective.

facetious   (fə·sē·shəs)

(*adj.*)

playfully jocular

"Don't be _____," requested the girl's mother,
    who was tired of her daughter's refusal to take
    the situation seriously.

feisty   (ˈfī·stē)

(*adj.*)

touchy; quarrelsome; full of spirit; frisky or spunky

Our new young puppy was extremely _____,
    jumping playfully all over the apartment and
    licking our faces.

flippant   (ˈfli·pənt)

(*adj.*)

marked by disrespectful levity or casualness; pert

Her _____ remarks during the interview cost
    her the job as she failed to demonstrate the
    necessary respect for her potential co-workers.

imperious   (im·ˈpir·ē·əs)

(*adj.*)

arrogantly domineering or overbearing; dictatorial

"It is my _____, ruthless political strategy that
    will conquer all contesting factions in this city,"
    exclaimed the egocentric, overconfident mayor.

jaunty ('jȯn·tē)

(*adj.*)

having a buoyant or self-confident air; brisk; crisp and dapper in appearance

The _____ groom looked dapper in his stylish suit and hat as he confidently entered the church on his wedding day.

myriad ('mir-ē·əd)

(*adj.*)

constituting a very large, indefinite number; innumerable; composed of numerous diverse elements or facets

(*noun*)

a great number, countless

The _____ species of fish, plants, and micro-organisms populate the ocean.

oblique (ō·'blēk)

(*adj.*)

having a slanting or sloping direction, course, or position; indirect or evasive; devious, misleading, or dishonest

While the president's _____ political maneuvers were expedient, they did not earn him the trust of the general public.

ornate (ȯr·'nāt)

(*adj.*)

elaborately and often excessively ornamented; showy or flowery

The actress's _____ flashy style of dress was tastelessly overdone.

palpable ('pal·pə·bəl)

(*adj.*)

capable of being handled, touched, or felt; tangible

The tension in the room was so _____ one felt it could be cut it with a knife.

prodigious (prə·'di·jəs)

(*adj.*)

impressively great in size, force, or extent; extraordinary; marvelous

The pianist's _____ musical talent won him many honors and awards.

prone ('prōn)

(*adj.*)

lying with the front or face downward; having a tendency; inclined

One must understand that some young children are _____ to mischief and tend to get into trouble without so intending.

relevant ('re·lə·vənt)

(*adj.*)

having a bearing on or connection with the matter at hand

I realize this comment may not appear directly _____, but I believe it does bear some connection to our conversation.

sardonic (sär·'dä·nik)

(*adj.*)

scornfully or cynically mocking

Although she recognized her friend as having a _____ personality, he saw her constant mockery and cynicism as grounded in insecurity.

vehement ('vē·ə·mənt)

(*adj.*)

characterized by forcefulness of expression or intensity of emotion or conviction; fervid; intense

Your _____ refusal makes me think there is no point in trying to persuade you any longer.

WORDS IN CONTEXT

The following exercise will help you figure out the meaning of some words from Vocabulary List 11 by looking at context clues. After you have read and understood the paragraph, explain the context clues that helped you with the meaning of the vocabulary word. Check the answer section at the end of this chapter for an example.

When my young daughter, Tanya, came home one day claiming she had adopted a lost puppy, I thought this an *audacious* move. After all, we live in a small two-bedroom apartment, and further, Tanya knows her sister is *prone* to allergies, especially around hairy dogs like this pup she found. Under normal circumstances, I probably would have demanded we let the dog go. Yet, there were *extenuating* circumstances that seemed *relevant* to the decision I had to make. The playful and *feisty* puppy reminded us so very much of Jelly, the playful dog next door who, three months ago, was tragically killed by a speeding SUV. The loss had stayed with my daughters and me; our sadness was *palpable,* filling our home with gloom. And so, I agreed that the sweet stray would become a member of our family.

SENTENCE COMPLETION

Insert the correct word from Vocabulary List 11 into the following sentences.

1. Her _____ behavior was modest and quite reserved.

2. The _____ proposal was boldly and fearlessly presented.

3. One is often able to _____ the seriousness of a situation with a sense of humor.

4. I cannot work with this rude and vulgar person; she is positively _____!

5. "You don't have to get so _____," she said to her touchy, quarrelsome sister.

6. The day our father died we were _____ and grief-stricken.

7. He made a number of _____ remarks that were meant to be playful.

8. Your _____ remarks are disrespectful and not appreciated!

9. His _____ tastes led him to deeply enjoy the finest in food and drink.

10. As the game began, the crowd's excitement was _____; you could feel it in the air!

11. There are _____ job opportunities in a city to large as New York.

12. If you have pale skin you are more _____ to sunburn.

13. The students did not respond well to their teacher's _____ style as they found it too domineering.

14. His _____ answers to my questions were indirect and evasive.

15. Her upbeat, _____ air conveyed self-confidence.

16. Your _____ denial is so insistent that I no longer believe that you are responsible.

17. The room was too _____ for my taste with its gaudy, showy, elaborate décor.

18. The _____ storm was so huge and strong I thought it the most powerful weather we had experienced all year.

19. He never seemed open to new experiences; he and his _____ attitude mocked everything even remotely unfamiliar.

20. My past experiences proved _____ to the situation once I was able to make the connection.

SYNONYMS

The following exercise lists vocabulary words from this chapter. Each word is followed by five answer choices. Four of them are synonyms of the vocabulary word in bold. Your task is to choose the one that does **not** fit.

21. audacious
   a. daring
   b. defiant
   c. insolent
   d. fearless
   e. churlish

22. demure
   a. prudish
   b. graceful
   c. shy
   d. solemn
   e. modest

23. dolorous
   a. demure
   b. sorrowful
   c. unpleasant
   d. painful
   e. distressful

24. flippant
   a. careless
   b. flexible
   c. disrespectful levity
   d. rudely casual
   e. pert

25. ornate
   a. showy
   b. flowery
   c. epicurean
   d. highly decorated
   e. excessively ornamented

26. jaunty
   a. dapper
   b. buoyant
   c. self-confident
   d. athletic
   e. stylish

27. palpable
   a. substantial
   b. touchable
   c. weighable
   d. tangible
   e. sensitive

28. sardonic
   a. sarcastic
   b. prodigious
   c. cynical
   d. caustic
   e. scornfully mocking

29. vehement
   a. fervid
   b. passionate
   c. relevant
   d. zealous
   e. forceful

30. myriad
   a. plenty
   b. numerous
   c. indefinite
   d. countless
   e. oblique

ANTONYMS

31. conservative, restrained, reserved, timid _____

32. polite, poised, tractable, malleable _____

33. joyful, blissful, happy, mirthful _____

34. respectful, mindful, serious, courteous _____

35. finite, numerical, limited, homogenous _____

36. clear, straight, honest, direct _____

37. plain, unadorned, modest, simple _____

38. intangible, imperceptible, subtle, untouchable _____

39. irrelevant, disconnected, moot, unrelated _____

40. ordinary, weak, unimpressive, pedestrian _____

CHOOSING THE RIGHT WORD

Circle the word in bold that best completes the sentence.

41. I found your casual, (**flippant, feisty**) attitude during the formal ceremony very disrespectful.

42. "Might makes right!" declared the (**facetious, imperious**) dictator.

43. It's difficult to know whether you are serious when you are so (**facetious, jaunty**) with me.

44. It was very (**audacious, churlish**) to stand up before the crowd and recklessly begin speaking without having prepared at all.

45. I can't work with you in this professional environment when you are so (**extenuating, churlish**).

46. How can you afford your (**epicurean, extenuating**) tastes; they are so lavish and luxurious!

47. Can't you forgive me considering the (**extenuating, feisty**) circumstances?

48. Did you notice how (**dolorous, feisty**) she became when the touchy subject came up and she was suddenly so argumentative?

49. His (**oblique, jaunty**) answers to my simple questions left me at a loss for understanding.

50. She became (**prodigious, prone**) to illness when her immune system began to fail her.

PRACTICE ACTIVITIES

Go to your favorite magazine and while reading an article, story, or any considerably lengthy feature, circle all the adjectives (words that describe or qualify nouns) you encounter. Take note of the nouns (people, places, things) they describe or qualify, and then ask yourself how the presence of adjectives contributes to the piece in specific cases, and also as a whole.

The next time you write an e-mail or an old-fashioned letter to a friend, see what happens to the quality and character of your prose when you make a point of including carefully selected adjectives including those you learned in Vocabulary List 11.

ANSWERS

WORDS IN CONTEXT

Tanya's move of bringing home the puppy was seen as *audacious*, or bold and even reckless, considering both the size of her family's apartment and the fact that her sister is *prone*, or susceptible to allergies. Yet, Tanya's reasonable mother is willing to consider the *relevant* (having bearing on the matter at hand) *extenuating* circumstances, which allow her to make an exception or an excuse that, all things considered, (namely her family's *palpable*, or tangible gloom when the neighbor's dog died) it wouldn't be such a huge deal for this *feisty* puppy—so obviously playful and full of spirit— to stay.

COMPLETING THE SENTENCE

1. *demure*. If you got this question wrong, refer back to the word's definition.
2. *audacious*. If you got this question wrong, refer back to the word's definition.
3. *extenuate*. If you got this question wrong, refer back to the word's definition.
4. *churlish*. If you got this question wrong, refer back to the word's definition.
5. *feisty*. If you got this question wrong, refer back to the word's definition.
6. *dolorous*. If you got this question wrong, refer back to the word's definition.
7. *facetious*. If you got this question wrong, refer back to the word's definition.
8. *flippant*. If you got this question wrong, refer back to the word's definition.
9. *epicurean*. If you got this question wrong, refer back to the word's definition.
10. *palpable*. If you got this question wrong, refer back to the word's definition.

11. *myriad*. If you got this question wrong, refer back to the word's definition.
12. *prone*. If you got this question wrong, refer back to the word's definition.
13. *imperious*. If you got this question wrong, refer back to the word's definition.
14. *oblique*. If you got this question wrong, refer back to the word's definition.
15. *jaunty*. If you got this question wrong, refer back to the word's definition.
16. *vehement*. If you got this question wrong, refer back to the word's definition.
17. *ornate*. If you got this question wrong, refer back to the word's definition.
18. *prodigious*. If you got this question wrong, refer back to the word's definition.
19. *sardonic*. If you got this question wrong, refer back to the word's definition.
20. *relevant*. If you got this question wrong, refer back to the word's definition.

SYNONYMS

21. e. *churlish*. Audacious means fearlessly or recklessly daring. Defiant and insolent convey similar meaning, whereas *churlish* means vulgar and would therefore not be a synonym of audacious.
22. b. *graceful*. Demure describes modest and reserved behavior. *Graceful* describes pleasing attractive movement and though one may find modesty graceful, would not be a synonym for demure.
23. a. *demure*. Dolorous means exhibiting pain, grief or sorrow. *Demure* means mild-mannered or shy and would not be a synonym.
24. b. *flexible*. Flippant means marked by disrespectful levity. Being overly casual in a disrespectful

manner or being pert or careless would also describe this attitude. *Flexible* means able to bend, change, or move, and would not be a synonym.

25. c. *epicurean.* Ornate means elaborately and excessively ornamented. Something ornate may also be considered showy or flowery. *Epicurean* means devoted to the pursuit of sensual pleasures and thus would not be a synonym.

26. d. *athletic.* Jaunty means having a buoyant or self-confident air. It also means having a crisp, dapper, stylish appearance. *Athletic,* meaning good at sports, would not be considered a synonym.

27. e. *sensitive.* Palpable means capable of being handled, touched or felt. All the words in the group except *sensitive* denote this characteristic of being touchable. *Sensitive* means highly receptive to senses (including, but not exclusively to touch) and is not a synonym.

28. b. *prodigious.* Sardonic means scornfully or cynically mocking. All the words and groups of words above suggest this disposition except for *prodigious. Prodigious* means extraordinary or impressively great in size or force and would not be a synonym.

29. c. *relevant.* Vehement means characterized by forcefulness or intensity. The word choices are all useful vocabulary terms that have similar meanings to vehement except for *relevant,* which means having a connection with the matter at hand. *Relevant* would not be a synonym.

30. e. *oblique.* Myriad means constituting a very large or indefinite number. *Oblique* would not be considered a synonym as it means indirect or evasive.

ANTONYMS

31. *audacious.* Audacious means bold, the opposite of the meaning of the words in the group.

32. *churlish.* Churlish means vulgar or difficult to work with, the opposite of the meaning of the words in the group.

33. *flippant.* Flippant means marked by disrespectful levity or casualness, the opposite of the meaning of the words in the group.

34. *dolorous.* Dolorous means marked by sorrow, the opposite of the meaning of the words in the group.

35. *myriad.* Myriad means indefinite, the opposite of the meaning of the words in the group.

36. *oblique.* Oblique means slanting or misleading, the opposite of the meaning of the words in the group.

37. *ornate.* Ornate means elaborately ornamented, the opposite of the meaning of the words in the group.

38. *relevant.* Relevant means having a bearing on or a connection with the matter at hand, the opposite of the meaning of the words in the group.

39. *palpable.* Palpable means capable of being touched or felt, the opposite of the meaning of the words in the group.

40. *prodigious.* Prodigious means impressively great or extraordinary, the opposite of the meaning of the words in the group.

CHOOSING THE RIGHT WORD

41. *flippant.* Context clue is that flippant means marked by disrespectful casualness. Though being overly feisty may also be considered disrespectful, considering the context clues, flippant is the stronger choice.

42. *imperious.* Context clue is that imperious means dictatorial and domineering.

43. *facetious.* Context clue is that facetious means playfully jocular; when one is facetious, it may sometimes be difficult to determine whether one is joking or not!

44. *audacious.* Context clue is that audacious means recklessly daring.

45. *churlish.* Context clue is that churlish means difficult to work with, specifically on the grounds of vulgarity (that would be problematic in the mentioned "professional" environment).

46. *epicurean.* Context clue is that epicurean means devotes to the pursuit of sensual pleasure, especially fine food.

47. *extenuating.* Context clue is that extenuating means lessened the magnitude or seriousness of (in this case, whatever the speaker did for which she asks forgiveness).

48. *feisty.* Context clue is that feisty means touchy or quarrelsome (argumentative being a synonym thereof).

49. *oblique.* Context clue is that oblique means indirect or evasive; such responses would not yield clarity or understanding.

50. *prone.* Context clue is that prone means susceptible or inclined towards.

Across

2 facetious
3 demure
6 relevant
8 palpable
9 epicurean
10 audacious
14 imperious
17 oblique
18 myriad
19 churlish

Down

1 prone
2 flippant
4 jaunty
5 feisty
7 extenuating
11 ornate
12 dolorous
13 vehement
15 prodigious
16 sardonic

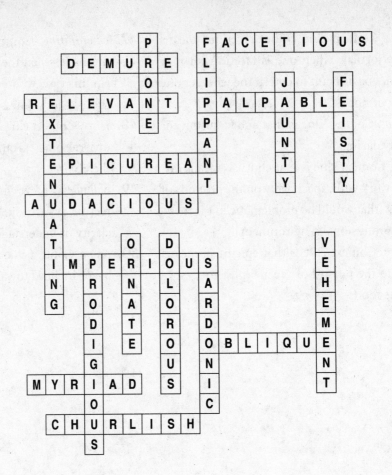

C·H·A·P·T·E·R

VOCABULARY LIST 12: ACRONYMS

15

CHAPTER SUMMARY

What is an acronym? While this term may in itself be a new vocabulary word for you, you are probably more familiar with a number of acronyms than you may think. Have you ever written RSVP at the bottom of an invitation? Have you wondered about the amount of RAM on your latest computer?

An acronym is a word formed from the initial letter or letters of each of the successive parts (or major parts) of a compound term. The routes *acr* or *acro* mean (among other related things including end, tip, top, and peak) *beginning*, thus, the adoption of the *first* letters in each word in a given complex term work together to made a single new word: an acronym.

In a way, understanding acronyms is like breaking down a code. Each of the letters, or initials in the acronym represent an entire other word. For example, the letters in *scuba* may be expanded and stand for Self Contained Underwater Breathing Apparatus. And, it makes sense: that's really what scuba diving is all about, right?

Choose the word from the Vocabulary List that best fits into the crossword puzzle. You will use 19 words from the vocabulary list to solve this puzzle. You can check your answers at the end of the chapter following the answers to the questions.

Vocabulary List 12: Acronyms

ASAP
CAT scan
CD-ROM
dinks
DOS
ESL
FAQ
ISP
laser
LAN
HTML
modem
moped
RAM
radar
REM
snafu
scuba
URL
yuppie

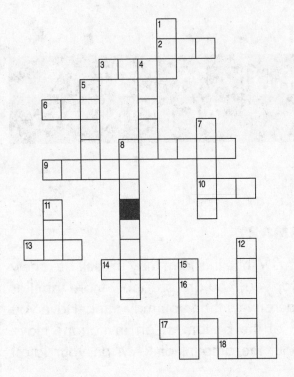

Across

2 a type of computer access memory that can be accessed randomly
3 the coding on many Web page documents
6 local area network
8 a compact disc that contains data a computer can read
9 self-contained underwater breathing device
10 English as a second language
13 a company that provides access to the Internet
14 a device that generates electromagnetic radiation
16 as soon as possible
17 frequently asked questions
18 rapid eye movement

Down

1 the address of documents and resources on the Web
4 a motor-powered bike that can also be pedaled
5 a mix up
7 a device that converts signals from digital to analog to transmit over phone lines
8 a 3D image of a body structure
11 disk operating system
12 a young, professional adult who works and lives in or near a city
15 radio detecting and ranging

ASAP   (ā·s·ā·p)
(*adv.*)
an abbreviation for As Soon As Possible
Please don't waste any time; I need you to complete
    this assignment _____.

CAT scan   ('kat·'skan)
(*noun*)
Computerized Axial Tomography scan—a three-
    dimensional image of a body structure made
    from a series of cross-sectional images and put
    together by a computer
John had to check into the hospital after his car
    accident for a routine _____ just to make
    sure he did not have a concussion.

CD-ROM   (sē·dē·'räm)
(*noun*)
Compact Disk-Read Only Memory—a compact disk
    that contains data a computer can read
That SAT study guide comes with a _____ you
    can put in your computer to practice test
    questions.

dink (a subset of yuppies)   ('diŋk)
(*noun*)
double income couple, no kids
I confess, we are sometimes a bit envious of the
    thirty-something _____ next door, though
    we would never trade in the time we have with
    our children for all their wealth and career
    power.

DOS   ('däs)
(*noun*)
the Disk Operating System used on personal
    computers (PCs)
When you are having a technical problem with your
    personal computer, it is often a good idea to
    return to _____, the opening screen, to see
    what may be wrong.

ESL   (ē·es·el)
(*noun*)
English as a Second Language
It is critical that we have _____ programs in our
    schools so that the immigrant youth
    population may improve their English and not
    be at a disadvantage in the classroom setting.

FAQ   (ef·ā·kyü)
(*noun*)
an abbreviation for Frequently Asked Question
Before you raise your hand, please note that in the
    back of the Driver's Ed manual you will find an
    _____ section and perhaps your own
    question will be included there.

ISP   (ī·es·pē)
(*noun*)
Internet Service Provider—a company that provides
    internet access to consumers
It may be difficult to select an _____ when there
    are so many comparable ones—Compuserve,
    AOL, Earthlink—from which to choose.

laser   ('lā·zər)
(*noun*)
light amplification by stimulated emission of
    radiation—a device that generates electro-
    magnetic radiation
It is now possible to remove your tattoos by way of
    _____ surgery where no needles are
    involved: only light and radiation.

LAN   (el·ā·en)

(*noun*)

Local Area Network—a network of directly connected machines that are close together and
provide high-speed communication over, for
example, fiber optics or coaxial cable (like for
phone service or cable TV)

I've been satisfied with my _____ as I never
have any trouble making local calls, and the
customer service is excellent if I have any
questions about my phone service or my
monthly bills.

HTML   (āch·tē·em·′el)

(*noun*)

Hyper Text Markup Language—a system of tagging
documents to define a document's structure
and appearance on a Web page

Each Web page on our website must be coded in
_____ before it gets posted on the
Internet.

modem   (′mō·dəm)

(*noun*)

modulator/demodulator—a device used to convert
digital signals into analog signals—and vice-
versa—for transmissions over phone lines

This old _____ on my computer is so slow; it
connects to the Internet at only 14,400k. The
newer models connect at up to 56,000k.

moped   (′mō·ped)

(*noun*)

motor pedal—a small, light, motor-powered bike
that can also be pedaled

While I have never ridden a _____, I imagine it
is just like riding a bike, only motorized!

radar   (′rā·där)

(*noun*)

radio detecting and ranging—a device that sends out
radio waves and processes them for display;
usually used for locating objects or surface
features of an object (such as a planet)

What's amazing is how I was able to pick up your
signal on my _____ even though you were
out of sight.

RAM   (′ram)

(*noun*)

Random Access Memory (on a computer)—a type of
computer memory that can be accessed
randomly

With so many programs installed on your home
computer, it's no wonder you no longer have
enough _____ available for new files.

REM   (′rem)

(*noun*)

Rapid Eye Movement (in sleep)—a rapid movement
of the eyes associated with REM sleep and
dreaming.

I guessed you were dreaming in your deep sleep
when I saw your eyes twitching under their lids
in _____.

scuba   (′skü·bə)

(*noun*)

self-contained underwater breathing apparatus—
equipment that is used for breathing
underwater

Jim packed up all his _____ gear including his
flippers, goggles, and tank before he left for his
trip to the Caribbean where there would be
excellent diving.

snafu   (sna·ʹfü)
(*noun*)
situation normal, all fouled up
As it turns out we ran into a major _____ and
  we need your help!

URL   (ū·ar·el)
(*noun*)
Uniform Resource Locator—the address of
  documents and resources on the Internet
Our auto company's _____ is not too original,
  but it is sure easy to remember: www.cars.com.

yuppie   (ʹyə·pē)
(*noun*)
young urban professional—a young, college-
  educated adult who works and lives in or near a
  large city
Since when have you become such a _____,
  with your upscale clothes and cars, and at such
  a young age!

WORDS IN CONTEXT

The following exercise will help you figure out the
meaning of some words from Vocabulary List 12 by
looking at context clues. After you have read and understood the paragraph, explain the context clues that
helped you with the meaning of the vocabulary word.
Check the answer section at the end of this chapter for
an example.

> I finally took it upon myself to become
> more knowledgeable when it comes to us-
> ing my home computer. My resolution set
> in when I was trying to attach a simple text
> file to an e-mail document, and ran into a
> frustrating little *snafu*. Everything froze and
> I thought my PC had crashed. Quickly
> turning to the *FAQ* section in my user's

manual, I realized that the problem was really with my *modem*. That's why my e-mail
wasn't going through. I called my *ISP* to verify my diagnosis of the problem. The customer service agent on the phone said he
had to check on it, but that he would call me
back *ASAP*. Though he said that it would
only take a second, I found myself waiting
for hours. Born of my own impatience,
my goal to become more independently
computer-savvy was born!

COMPLETING THE SENTENCE

Insert the correct word from Vocabulary List 12 into
the following sentences.

1. I took my _____ out for a drive.

2. I felt incompetent when I ran into a(n)
   _____.

3. Please come see me _____; it's really
   important.

4. The ship's _____ was able to detect
   signals indicating it was not alone in that area
   of the sea.

5. When I came to the United States I was
   considered a(n) _____ student since
   Spanish was my first language.

6. The doctors could not detect the problem
   using a regular X-ray so they ordered a
   _____.

7. A young successful professional working in the
   city may be called a(n) _____.

8. Questions that come up a lot are considered
   _____.

9. I saw some marvelous underwater life the first time I went _____ diving.

10. An organization's _____ on the Internet usually ends in the letters "org."

11. I bought a _____ that had the entire world atlas on a single disk!

12. I took a class in _____ coding so that I would know how to build a web page.

13. There was no incision involved when I had _____ surgery on my eyes, only light amplification from radiation.

14. We know a couple of _____ who have so much money to spend; they have no children to support and both his and her jobs are quite lucrative.

15. Your _____ made me know you were in deep sleep.

16. My _____ is offering a deal now so you may want to switch and have them be your service provider since you rely so much on Internet access.

17. I think your disk may not be working due to a malfunction in _____.

18. The _____ was busy putting in new phone lines in our area after the storm did so much damage.

19. You can't connect to the Internet on that old laptop computer because it doesn't have a _____.

20. When I bought my new computer I increased the amount of _____ so that it would have ample memory to handle all these programs.

MATCHING

Match the acronym in the first column with the corresponding definition in the second column.

21. dinks   a. self-contained underwater breathing apparatus

22. ISP   b. rapid eye movement

23. FAQ   c. young urban professional

24. laser   d. as soon as possible

25. CD-ROM   e. double income couple, no kids

26. ASAP   f. compact disk read only memory

27. RAM   g. light amplification by stimulated emission of radiation

28. moped   h. Internet service provider

29. HTML   i. English as a second language

30. radar   j. hyper text markup language

31. scuba   k. modulator/demodulator

32. LAN   l. random access memory

33. REM   m. situation normal, all fouled up

34. yuppie   n. radio detecting and ranging

35. URL   o. motor pedal

36. CAT scan   p. local area network

37. DOS   q. computerized axial tomography scan

38. ESL   r. disk operating system

39. FAQ   s. frequently asked questions

40. snafu   t. uniform resource locator (World Wide Web address)

TRUE/FALSE QUESTIONS

In the space provided, write a *T* if the italicized word from Vocabulary List 12 is correctly used, and an *F* if the sentence is false. If the sentence is false, cross out the misused word and write the correct word from Vocabulary List 12 above it.

41. ___The operating system used in IBM compatible computers is called *DOS*.

42. ___The computerized axial tomography scan one might receive to check for internal injury is a *CD-ROM*.

43. ___Double income couples without any children are sometimes referred to as *dinks*.

44. ___Before I left for my diving adventure in Indonesia, I purchased some state of the art *radar* gear.

45. ___If you want something done quickly, you may ask for it *ASAP*.

46. ___At the new planetarium I saw an amazing *laser* light show amplified on the ceiling!

47. ___Since she newly immigrated to the United States, she is considered a *FAQ* student.

48. ___The *LAN* section of a user's manual may be of tremendous use if you have questions and are struggling to put something together—a bicycle, for example.

49. ___My computer is overloaded with so many programs; I probably have to upgrade my *HTML*.

50. ___Having the correct *URL* enabled me to get to the website with ease.

PRACTICE ACTIVITIES

It is *relatively* easy (though no piece of cake) to remember the so-called definitions of acronyms because the letters that make up the acronym serve as clues in that they are also initials of the words that make up the extended definition. For example, when completing the matching section, you may have quickly associated the acronym ISP with its definition—Internet Service Provider—since the corresponding letters I-S-P probably jump out at you. The next step in committing these acronyms to your vocabulary repertoire is *really* understanding what they mean. Try to go beyond simply relying on the mnemonic initials and substituting a longer name that doesn't necessarily make clear sense. Make sense?

A suggestion is to check out either a website or a trade magazine relating to the subject of the acronym. Often, acronyms exist as abbreviations for complex, technical terms that "one doesn't really need to get." But that's not so! Just because I will *never* scuba dive doesn't mean my vocabulary and literacy won't benefit from my visiting a scuba website to see and understand that all the gear really is a self-contained underwater breathing apparatus. Flipping through *Wired* magazine or the Science section of the *New York Times* on Tuesdays might allow us to more deeply, in context, read explications and applications of some of the acronyms relating to science and technology.

ANSWERS

WORDS IN CONTEXT

When this computer novice's computer freezes, it may be understood as a *snafu*: a normal situation of trying to attach a file becomes fouled up! For guidance, he turns to the *FAQ* section of the user's manual thinking that perhaps others have had similar problems and asked similar questions. The fact that his e-mail was not going through indicates that perhaps the *modem* was the source of the problem as a modem allows for the necessary connection to the Internet. The logical company to contact at that point would be one's *ISP*: the Internet Service Provider. The customer service representative explains that he will get back to the customer momentarily: as soon as he is able, or, *ASAP*. As the customer impatiently waits, he resolves to learn to rectify such *snafus* on his own.

SENTENCE COMPLETION

1. *moped.* If you got this question wrong, refer back to the word's definition.
2. *snafu.* If you got this question wrong, refer back to the word's definition.
3. *ASAP.* If you got this question wrong, refer back to the word's definition.
4. *radar.* If you got this question wrong, refer back to the word's definition.
5. *ESL.* If you got this question wrong, refer back to the word's definition.
6. *CAT scan.* If you got this question wrong, refer back to the word's definition.
7. *yuppie.* If you got this question wrong, refer back to the word's definition.
8. *FAQs.* If you got this question wrong, refer back to the word's definition.
9. *scuba.* If you got this question wrong, refer back to the word's definition.

10. *URL.* If you got this question wrong, refer back to the word's definition.
11. *CD-ROM.* If you got this question wrong, refer back to the word's definition.
12. *HTML.* If you got this question wrong, refer back to the word's definition.
13. *laser.* If you got this question wrong, refer back to the word's definition.
14. *dinks.* If you got this question wrong, refer back to the word's definition.
15. *REM.* If you got this question wrong, refer back to the word's definition.
16. *ISP.* If you got this question wrong, refer back to the word's definition.
17. *DOS.* If you got this question wrong, refer back to the word's definition.
18. *LAN.* If you got this question wrong, refer back to the word's definition.
19. *modem.* If you got this question wrong, refer back to the word's definition.
20. *RAM.* If you got this question wrong, refer back to the word's definition.

MATCHING

21. e
22. h
23. s
24. g
25. f
26. d
27. l
28. o
29. j
30. n
31. a
32. p

33. b

34. c

35. t

36. q

37. r

38. i

39. s

40. m

TRUE/FALSE

41. True

42. False, correct word is CAT scan

43. True

44. False, correct word is scuba

45. True

46. True

47. False, correct word is ESL

48. False, correct word is FAQ

49. False, correct word is RAM

50. True

Across

2 RAM
3 HTML
6 LAN
8 CD-ROM
9 scuba
10 ESL
13 ISP
14 laser
16 ASAP
17 FAQ
18 REM

Down

1 URL
4 moped
5 snafu
7 modem
8 CAT scan
11 DOS
12 yuppie
15 radar

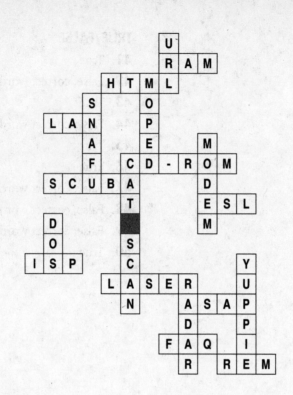

VOCABULARY LIST 13: COMMONLY TESTED WORDS

CHAPTER SUMMARY

In this chapter you will learn words that don't fit neatly into any particular category, but are used occasionally in adult-level writing and very often found on standardized tests. It can sometimes seem as if test makers have some magical list of words that they think will trip up the average test taker. Of course that is not the case, but if you had never encountered these words before you see them on a test, it can certainly be intimidating. Perhaps many of these words are somewhat familiar from your reading or studies, but they are the type of words that you quickly skip over and hope you can understand the reading passage without *really* having to know the unknown word. It is just these kinds of words that test makers know will allow them to reward the test takers who have gone that extra mile to learn some of the most difficult words. By learning and mastering the words in this chapter, you can give yourself the extra advantage you need on tests and in your reading.

Choose the word from the Vocabulary List that best fits into the crossword puzzle. You can check your answers at the end of the chapter following the answers to the questions.

Vocabulary List 13:
Commonly Tested Words

anomaly
badinage
brusque
cower
diffident
dross
extricate
fodder
garrulous
hyperbole
malapropism
pertinacity
plausible
prehensile
rancor
resolute
ruminate
simian
stolid
succor

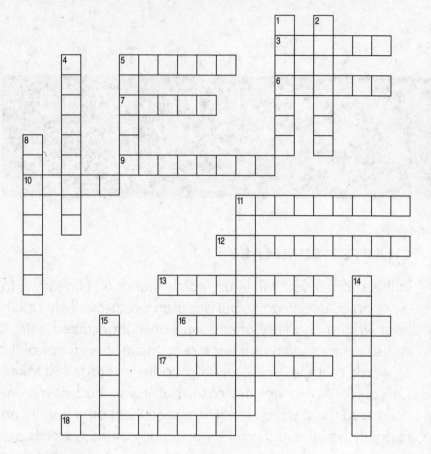

Across

3 animosity
5 apathetic, impassive
6 related to, or resembling an ape
7 to cringe
9 ponder, muse
10 waste
11 possible
12 adapted for wrapping around, grabbing
13 bashful
16 misuse
17 to set free, disentangle
18 wordy

Down

1 blunt, brief
2 deviation from the norm
4 exaggeration
5 aid, assistance
8 banter
11 obstinance
14 determined
15 coarse food for cows and horses

anomaly   (ə·′nä·mə·lē)

(*noun*)

abnormality; irregularity; deviation from the norm
or usual

The one year the company did not break even was
just an _____ .

badinage   (ba·dən·′äzh)

(*noun*)

playful and joking conversation or banter

The two men never met without beginning a little
_____ that entertained us all.

brusque   (′brəsk)

(*adj.*)

abrupt, blunt, or short in manner or speech

His _____ manner was often mistaken for
rudeness by people who did not know him
better.

cower   (′kaù·(ə)r)

(*verb*)

to shrink and tremble, as from someone's anger or
threats; to cringe

It was unnerving to watch the dog _____ in the
corner when he misbehaved.

diffident   (′di·fə·dənt)

(*adj.*)

modest, shy, reserved, bashful, humble

Her _____ smile seemed to indicate that she
wanted to dance if only someone would ask
her.

dross   (′dräs)

(*noun*)

the worthless part of something that is separated
from the better part; waste; garbage

The cook trimmed the fillet and swept the
_____ away.

extricate   (′ek·strə·kāt)

(*verb*)

to set free or release; to disentangle, as from a
difficulty or embarrassment

She hung up the phone and wondered how she
would ever _____ herself from really
having to attend the luncheon.

fodder   (′fà·dər)

(*noun*)

dry, coarse food for cattle, horses, or sheep, like hay
or straw; often also used in expressions
unrelated to animals

We were waiting by the barn for the new _____
to be delivered.

garrulous   (′gar·ə·ləs)

(*adj.*)

overly talkative about unimportant things; chattering

I regretted striking up a conversation with him when
I remembered how _____ he can be.

hyperbole   (hī·′pər·bə·lē)

(*noun*)

exaggeration for effect, not to be taken literally

He often spoke with _____, as when he said he
was so hungry he could eat a horse.

malapropism   (′ma·lə·prä·pi·zəm)

(*noun*)

a ridiculous or humorous misuse of words, usually
due to a resemblance in sound

She was quite amusing with her frequent _____,
like when she excused herself from the table to
go to the laboratory.

pertinacity   (per·tən·ˈa·sə·tē)

(*noun*)

firm or unyielding adherence to some purpose; stubbornness; persistence

No matter what anyone said, there was no way to reason with his _____.

plausible   (ˈplȯ·zə·bəl)

(*adj.*)

seemingly true and acceptable, but usually used with implied disbelief; possible

The excuse seemed _____, so we had to accept their apology for not attending our dinner party.

prehensile   (prē·ˈhen(t)·səl)

(*adj.*)

adapted to grasp, seize, or hold

Chimpanzees and humans both have a _____ hand.

rancor   (ˈraŋ·kər)

(*noun*)

a continuing and bitter hatred or ill will

The negotiators worked for peace among the opposing factions, despite their obvious _____.

resolute   (ˈre·zə·lüt)

(*adj.*)

determined; firm of purpose; resolved

I would try and stop you, but I can see you are _____ in your decision.

ruminate   (rü·mə·nāt)

(*verb*)

to meditate on or ponder something; to think over

One could see him _____ over the question for a few moments before he answered.

simian   (ˈsi·mē·ən)

(*adj.*)

dealing with apes or monkeys; ape-like

The researcher was investigating several aspects of _____ behavior.

stolid   (ˈstä·ləd)

(*adj.*)

showing little or no emotion or awareness; unexcitable; expressionless

We wondered how he could remain so _____ upon hearing such awful news.

succor   (ˈsə·kər)

(*noun*)

aid; help; assistance, especially that which relieves and ends stress, need, or a difficulty

She gladly offered _____ when he had nowhere else to turn.

WORDS IN CONTEXT

The following exercise will help you figure out the meaning of some words from Vocabulary List 13 by looking at context clues. After you have read and understood the paragraph, explain the context clues that helped you with the meaning of the vocabulary word. Check the answer section at the end of this chapter for an example.

I will never forget the day I accompanied Professor Mackey into the apes' facility for the first time. He delighted in introducing me to all their interesting and individual *simian* behaviors. There were several who remained quite *diffident* during our visit, but most went about their normal behavior, and a few even came forward to greet us. One little charming fellow even offered us a piece of food with his *prehensile* hand. The professor pointed out the leader, who quietly remained a *stolid* observer of all the proceedings in the cage. Mackey explained that when the leader did move about, all the apes would become excited and several of his previous victims would *cower* in the corner. Two of the apes fought violently during our visit, but fortunately their *rancor* seemed focused solely on each other. Undoubtedly, the most fascinating resident was one of the males named Yankee. When the professor closed the cage door after he had brought them their lunch, Yankee came to the door and looked for the keyhole. I watched him *ruminate* there for a few minutes, staring intently at the door and the keys on the bench beside us. He then tried every imaginable way to *extricate* himself from the cage, and regardless of how impossible it would be without the keys, he seemed *resolute* enough to continue for hours. Indeed, the professor said he was still trying when he returned later that evening.

SENTENCE COMPLETION

Insert the correct word from Vocabulary List 13 into the following sentences.

1. He seemed so _____ when we first met him, but he really can be quite outgoing and fun.

2. I guess the forecast is _____ enough, but I am going to pack an umbrella anyway.

3. The _____ tail of the lemur allows it to hang upside down from tree branches.

4. The new waiter will have to learn to be less _____ with his customers if he wants to continue working at this restaurant.

5. When he told us he had parked his car in the parking *garbage,* we laughed at his latest _____, and went to look for it in the parking *garage.*

6. How will he ever _____ himself from this new predicament?

7. The refugees turned to us for _____, but we already had taken in too many others.

8. I think we have had too much _____ spoken around here; this is not a *disaster.*

9. We noticed a/an _____ in the charts that indicated a problem.

10. We will just add the leftovers in with the _____ we were going to feed the horses.

11. If she is that _____, I think she will get the job done.

12. The movie was nearly ruined for me by the _____ couple seated behind us; they didn't stop talking throughout the entire movie.

13. The guard was a true professional, and stood in a _____ and upright stance despite the distracting crowds.

14. I will need to _____ over your proposal for a while, so don't expect an answer immediately.

15. The dog showed unusual _____ when it was attempting to reach the dinner on the counter.

16. We kept the few minerals we found in the sample and just brushed the _____ away.

17. His stooped posture, long arms, and wild hair cast an almost _____ aspect to his appearance.

18. Nothing pleases me more than a little _____ with someone who has a quick wit.

19. The _____ between them had existed for years, and it was rumored to have begun from some long forgotten argument.

20. The booming thunder made the two children _____ under the covers and reach out an arm to hold onto one another.

SYNONYMS

The following exercise lists vocabulary words from this chapter. Each word is followed by five answer choices. Four of them are synonyms of the vocabulary word in bold. Your task is to choose the one that does **not** fit.

21. pertinacity
  a. persistence
  b. stubbornness
  c. loudness
  d. determination

22. ruminate
  a. ponder
  b. think over
  c. meditate about
  d. clean

23. brusque
  a. courteous
  b. brief
  c. abrupt
  d. blunt

24. rancor
  a. hatred
  b. fondness
  c. dislike
  d. contempt

25. cower
  a. cringe
  b. tremble
  c. rip
  d. shrink away

26. succor
  a. aid
  b. assistance
  c. help
  d. stress

27. plausible
  a. deceitful
  b. true
  c. believable
  d. possible

28. diffident
  a. shy
  b. reserved
  c. furious
  d. bashful

29. anomaly
  a. irregularity
  b. abnormality
  c. deviation
  d. average

30. simian
  a. ape-like
  b. concerning apes
  c. having to do with animals
  d. having to do with monkeys

ANTONYMS

Choose the word from Vocabulary List 13 that means the opposite, or most nearly the opposite, of the following groups of words.

31. treasure, valuables, prize   _____

32. fact, literal truth, exactness   _____

33. debate, discourse, argument   _____

34. excited, enthusiastic, upset   _____

35. love, friendship, affection   _____

36. quiet, solemn, serious   _____

37. cuisine, delicacy, feast   _____

38. careless, indecisive, uncertain   _____

39. catch, imprison, confine   _____

40. impossible, unlikely, false   _____

CHOOSING THE RIGHT WORD

Circle the word in bold that best completes the sentence.

41. It is a very interesting offer, but I will need to (**extricate, ruminate**) on it a bit before I give you my answer.

42. The lecturer explained the tremendous advantages that our earliest ancestors had over other species—the evolution of a (**stolid, prehensile**) hand.

43. She showed amazing (**pertinacity, hyperbole**) at the meeting and eventually succeeded in persuading the entire room.

44. He acted very (**simian, diffident**) when we approached, and we wondered if our forwardness made him uncomfortable.

45. The employee was warned about being so (**dross, garrulous**) on the phone, and was advised to be more professional and direct.

46. The pitcher who made the all-star team was not just a (an) (**anomaly, malapropism**); he was the cream of the crop.

47. The press was delighted when he came out of the building, but he was (**brusque, badinage**) with them and rushed out of there a moment later.

48. I believe your theory is (**prehensile, plausible**), but I still think we should do a little more research.

49. The neighbor was shocked at the boy's strange (**diffident, simian**) behavior and vowed to notify his parents later that day.

50. All they could do was (**cower, succor**) in fear as the bears approached them; they were so afraid that they couldn't even run away.

PRACTICE ACTIVITIES

Write a letter to a friend, teacher, or coworker using at least 5–7 of the words from the Vocabulary List. Perhaps your letter could be a description of an unusual visit (like this chapter's visit to the apes), or a problem you have noticed somewhere. Look back over the list and try to see a few connections between the words.

When an idea comes to you, go with it. The most important thing is to try and use as many new words as possible in the correct manner.

Try to discover as many alternate forms of the words from the word list as you can. For example, *diffident* is an adjective used to describe someone who is shy or reserved, and *diffidence* is the noun form that identifies that shyness or modesty. Jot down as many alternate form of the words as you can guess, and then check yourself with a good dictionary. Can you use each of the forms of the words in a sentence?

ANSWERS

WORDS IN CONTEXT

The paragraph is a recollection of a visit to see the apes and the behaviors noticed by the narrator; thus we should certainly conclude that *simian* means ape-like or concerning apes. When we read that some apes remained *diffident* but others came forward to greet the visitors, we can understand that *diffident* could mean shy or reserved. The friendly ape that offers food in his *prehensile* hand must surely have a hand that is capable of holding something. Since the leader of the apes quietly remains a *stolid* observer, we can know that he is showing no emotion or expression, because he is juxtaposed to his fellow apes who get excited. The other apes that have been victim to his anger before *cower* in the corner when he does move about, so we can understand that they are cringing and trembling in fear of him. The two apes that fight during the visit apparently have *rancor* only for each other, so we should know that *rancor* means hatred or ill will. The ape Yankee seems to be staring at the door and trying to figure out a means of escape, so we can conclude that *ruminate* means to think over or ponder. Yankee's attempts to *extricate* himself from the cage, despite it being impossible without the keys, indicate that *extricate* must mean free or release. Finally, since we are told Yankee is *resolute* enough to continue his attempt for hours, we can understand that *resolute* must mean determined and firm of purpose.

SENTENCE COMPLETION

1. *diffident.* If you got this question wrong, refer back to the word's definition.
2. *plausible.* If you got this question wrong, refer back to the word's definition.
3. *prehensile.* If you got this question wrong, refer back to the word's definition.
4. *brusque.* If you got this question wrong, refer back to the word's definition.
5. *malapropism.* If you got this question wrong, refer back to the word's definition.
6. *extricate.* If you got this question wrong, refer back to the word's definition.
7. *succor.* If you got this question wrong, refer back to the word's definition.
8. *hyperbole.* If you got this question wrong, refer back to the word's definition.
9. *anomaly.* If you got this question wrong, refer back to the word's definition.
10. *fodder.* If you got this question wrong, refer back to the word's definition.
11. *resolute.* If you got this question wrong, refer back to the word's definition.
12. *garrulous.* If you got this question wrong, refer back to the word's definition.
13. *stolid.* If you got this question wrong, refer back to the word's definition.
14. *ruminate.* If you got this question wrong, refer back to the word's definition.
15. *pertinacity.* If you got this question wrong, refer back to the word's definition.
16. *dross.* If you got this question wrong, refer back to the word's definition.
17. *simian.* If you got this question wrong, refer back to the word's definition.
18. *badinage.* If you got this question wrong, refer back to the word's definition.
19. *rancor.* If you got this question wrong, refer back to the word's definition.
20. *cower.* If you got this question wrong, refer back to the word's definition.

SYNONYMS

21. **c.** *loudness. Pertinacity* means firm or unyielding adherence to some purpose. Since *loudness* means the audible volume of something, it is not a synonym.

22. **d.** *clean. Ruminate* means to think something over. Since *clean* means to wash or make neat, it is not a synonym.

23. **a.** *courteous. Brusque* means being short or abrupt in manner or speech. Since *courteous* means polite and gracious, it is not a synonym.

24. **b.** *fondness. Rancor* means continuing hatred or ill will. Since *fondness* means warm affection, it is not a synonym.

25. **c.** *rip. Cower* means to cringe or tremble in fear. Since *rip* means to tear or shred something, it is not a synonym.

26. **d.** *stress. Succor* means aid or assistance in a time of need. Since *stress* means tension or pressure, it is not a synonym.

27. **a.** *deceitful. Plausible* means seemingly true and acceptable. Since *deceitful* means dishonest and fraudulent, it is not a synonym.

28. **c.** *furious. Diffident* means shy and reserved. Since *furious* means violently angry and raging, it is not a synonym.

29. **d.** *average. Anomaly* means an irregularity or abnormality. Since *average* means usual or commonplace, it is not a synonym.

30. **c.** *having to do with animals. Simian* means apelike or having to do with apes or monkeys. Since *having to do with animals* is too broad a definition, it is not a synonym.

ANTONYMS

31. *Dross* means the waste or worthless part of something, the opposite of the words listed.

32. *Hyperbole* means an exaggeration for effect, not to be taken literally, the opposite of the words listed.

33. *Badinage* means playful conversation or banter, the opposite of the words listed.

34. *Stolid* means showing little emotion or awareness, the opposite of the words listed.

35. *Rancor* means continuing hatred or ill will, the opposite of the words listed.

36. *Garrulous* means overly talkative about unimportant things or chattering, the opposite of the words listed.

37. *Fodder* means dry, coarse food for cattle, horses, or sheep, the opposite of the words listed.

38. *Resolute* means determined and firm of purpose, the opposite of the words listed.

39. *Extricate* means to set free or release, the opposite of the words listed.

40. *Plausible* means seemingly true and possible, the opposite of the words listed.

CHOOSING THE RIGHT WORD

41. *ruminate. Extricate* means free or release, so surely the person will have to think over or *ruminate* on the offer.

42. *prehensile.* Context clues indicate that the hand evolved to be an advantage, so it is logical that is capable of holding something, or *prehensile*.

43. *pertinacity. Pertinacity* means persistence or stubbornness, so undoubtedly this quality is what helped her persist and eventually persuade the entire room.

44. *diffident. Diffident* means shy and reserved, so it is logical that he would act that way if the others made him feel uncomfortable when they meet, but he would not act *simian* or ape-like.

45. *garrulous. Garrulous* means overly talkative and chattering, which would be something an employee might be warned against. *Dross* means the unusable part of something, or waste.

46. *anomaly.* Since the one good player stands out on the team, he or she must be an *anomaly,* or an abnormality or deviation from the norm. A *malapropism* is a humorous misuse of words that sound alike.

47. *brusque. Brusque* means abrupt, blunt or short in manner or speech. *Badinage* is playful or joking banter.

48. *plausible. Plausible* means seemingly true and possible, so it would apply to a theory that the speaker believes but still wants to research further. *Prehensile* means adapted to seize or hold something.

49. *simian. Simian* means ape-like, so if the boy was acting that way, it may be an exaggeration, but the neighbor might easily be shocked and want to notify the parents. *Diffident* means shy and reserved, so that would not be shocking.

50. *cower. Cower* means tremble or cringe in fear, which could be an appropriate response to approaching bears. *Succor* is aid or assistance in a time of need.

Across

3 rancor
5 stolid
6 simian
7 cower
9 ruminate
10 dross
11 plausible
12 prehensile
13 diffident
16 malapropism
17 extricate
18 garrulous

Down

1 brusque
2 anomaly
4 hyperbole
5 succor
8 badinage
11 pertinacity
14 resolute
15 fodder

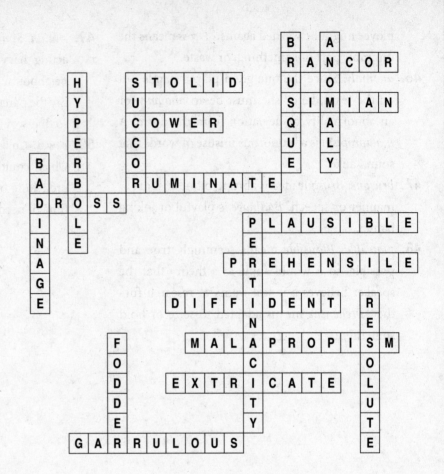

VOCABULARY LIST 14: MORE COMMONLY TESTED WORDS

CHAPTER SUMMARY

Here is another group of words that are commonly found on standardized tests. No doubt you have encountered some of them before in your reading, but you may be seeing many of the words on this list for the first time. Be sure to say the words aloud to yourself as you read over the word list. Perhaps you have heard some of these words used before in common phrases but have never seen them in print before.

Choose the word from the Vocabulary List that best fits into the crossword puzzle. You can check your answers at the end of the chapter following the answers to the questions.

Vocabulary List 14:
More Common Tested Words

addle
ambivalent
bevy
disconsolate
guffaw
genteel
guttural
inert
insouciance
mutable
obtuse
omniscient
pallor
partisan
purloin
resonant
rubric
smidgen
sycophant
wallow

Across

2 indulge
5 group of women
7 small amount
9 a person who tries to get ahead by flattering people of wealth or power
10 a category
12 having conflicting or divided feelings
14 all-knowing
16 throaty
18 confuse or fluster
20 carefree, easy-going

Down

1 steal
3 dull or dense
4 vibrant, full, resounding
6 paleness, wanness, pastiness
8 melancholy
11 strongly in favor of one side or political party
13 hearty chuckle
15 stationary, inactive
17 refined, polite
19 changeable

addle   ('a·dəl)

(*verb*)

to confuse, fluster, or muddle

Before the lecture I thought I understood the topic, but during the lecture, the professor did nothing but _____ me.

ambivalent   (am·'bi·və·lənt)

(*adj.*)

having at the same time two conflicting feelings or emotions toward another person or thing, such as love and hate; having divided feelings about something or someone; equivocal; uncertain

Invite her if you want her to come; I am _____ about her.

bevy   ('be·vē)

(*noun*)

a group of girls or women; or a flock of birds

The young men were delighted to see a _____ of beauties at the party.

disconsolate   (dis·'kän(t)'sə'lət)

(*adj.*)

hopeless, sad, melancholy, dejected

The widow was _____ for many years after her husband's death.

genteel   (jen·'tē(ə)l)

(*adj.*)

refined, polite, elegant, gentlemanly, or ladylike

Though he was dressed poorly, we were quite impressed with his _____ manners.

guffaw   (gə·'fȯ)

(*noun*)

a loud, rough burst of laughter

After Marty's joke, his _____ shattered the silence of the room, and everyone turned to look at who had made such a noise.

guttural   ('gə·tə·rəl)

(*adj.*)

throaty; used to describe sounds that originate in the throat, like the *k* in *kite*

He made a few _____ noises as he was trying to clear his throat.

inert   (i·'nərt)

(*adj.*)

inactive, sluggish, without power to move

The hot days of summer make me so _____ I have no motivation to do any work.

insouciance   (in·'sü·sē·ən(t)s)

(*noun*)

the attitude and manner of being carefree, easy-going, and happy-go-lucky

Because the rest of the class was nervously trying to cram in their studying right up until the last minute, they were astonished at her _____ the night before the exam.

mutable   ('myü·tə·bəl)

(*adj.*)

changeable, unstable, variable

He knew the plan was confirmed, but because of his unpredictable schedule, he made sure it was _____ when difficulties arose.

obtuse   (äb·'tüs)

(*adj.*)

dull, not sharp or acute; when used to describe a person, it means slow to understand or notice, or insensitive

We thought the new manager would be more understanding of our needs, but he turned out to be just as _____ as the last one.

omniscient   (äm·'ni·shənt)

(*adj.*)

all knowing; having universal knowledge of all things

The Judeo-Christian God is believed to be

_____.

pallor   ('pa·lər)

(*noun*)

lack of color; unnatural paleness, often used to

describe a face

She was struck by the eerie _____ of the strange

man who always peered out from the windows

of his dark house.

partisan   ('pär·tə·zən)

(*adj.*)

strongly in favor of one side or political party;

blindly or unreasonably devoted to a party

The senator knew he would not be able to persuade

his _____ peers.

purloin   (pər·'lȯin)

(*verb*)

to steal

Where did you _____ that new coat you're

wearing? You can't afford one like that.

resonant   ('re·zən·ənt)

(*adj.*)

used to describe sounds, it usually means vibrant,

full, ringing, intensified, resounding, rich

Everyone loved to hear his _____, bass voice fill

the concert hall.

rubric   ('rü·brik)

(*noun*)

a formal way to say *name* or *title,* or a category of

something; an established rule or tradition

We found what we were looking for under the

general _____ of *respiratory diseases.*

smidgen   ('smi·jən)

(*noun*)

a very small particle; an insignificant piece or

amount

I am not sure what it does, but my aunt always adds

a _____ of dill to the dish.

sycophant   ('si·kə·fənt)

(*noun*)

a person who tries to get ahead by flattering people

of wealth or power

Only a shameless _____ could tell the boss that

he likes his horribly ugly, orange tie.

wallow   ('wä·lō)

(*verb*)

to roll about pleasantly in water or mud; can also be

used to mean to overindulge in something

pleasurable

We watched the pigs _____ in the mud and

listened to their squeals of delight.

WORDS IN CONTEXT

The following exercise will help you figure out the
meaning of some words from Vocabulary List 14 by
looking at context clues. After you have read and understood the paragraph, explain the context clues that
helped you with the meaning of the vocabulary word.
Check the answer section at the end of this chapter for
an example.

As we rang the doorbell, Joe was combing
his hair for the third or fourth time. Someone let us in, and we immediately turned on
our most *genteel* manners. We mingled a
little with the adults and some of the other
kids there, and no one seemed to guess that
we were crashing the party. Our plan was
working smoothly, when Pete suddenly

erupted with a loud *guffaw* after Joe whispered a wisecrack in his ear. Pete's *insouciance* is one of the things we love about him, but sometimes such a happy-go-lucky attitude can be a problem, and he can be absolutely *obtuse* about when and where he ought to restrain himself. When those around us quieted and cast disapproving stares in our direction, we wandered off in search of a *bevy* of young ladies to entertain. We found a few in the large dining room. Pete approached one with an oddly attractive *pallor* to her face, which was accentuated by her beautiful dark eyes and gorgeous black hair. He made them all laugh within a few moments, and then Pete introduced us to the pale girl's two friends and we asked the three of them to dance. Two said yes, but the third seemed to want to remain *inert,* so I stayed to talk to her. She was *disconsolate.* I soon learned she had recently broken up with the boy she had been dating and had come to the party only at her friends' request. She had been making a few attempts to enjoy herself, but she was *ambivalent* about meeting anyone or trying to have a good time. Knowing that a good remedy for an aching heart can be two moving feet, I pulled her out onto the dance floor. By the end of the party, she was laughing and singing, and on the way out all three girls thanked the hostess for inviting such charming young gentlemen to dance with. She laughed and said it was her pleasure, but as we exited past the woman's puzzled, smiling face, I could see her confusion. Of course, when Pete said this party had been better than her last and gave the woman a goodbye kiss, it did nothing but **addle** her further.

SENTENCE COMPLETION

Insert the correct word from Vocabulary List 14 into the following sentences.

1. I hate to be such a _____, but it seems the only way to get the boss to notice the hard work I am doing is to make her feel like she is the genius who came up with the idea in the first place.

2. We suspected that the suspicious looking man in the dark sunglasses was attempting to _____ the valuable sculpture.

3. His _____ manners were a pleasant, new side to him we had not seen before.

4. The cord was unplugged and I knew the blades were _____, so I thought it was safe to try and repair the fan.

5. The manager told all the new housekeepers that he did not want to see even a _____ of dirt or dust anywhere in the hotel.

6. If a story is written from an _____ point of view, the reader can learn what all of the characters are thinking.

7. Joe felt _____ about hearing his best friend had been accepted at the university because it was so far from home.

8. Because the clay was still _____, she was able to alter the nose of the statue to make it a better likeness.

9. The mother warned her children to avoid the mud, but she knew if they passed the big

puddle in back they would _____ in it until they were filthy.

10. Even in the brightly lit laboratory, the un-natural _____ of the corpse unnerved us.

11. Once it was clear that no rescue party would be coming, several of the survivors grew completely _____, and it seemed nothing could ease their minds.

12. When the girls posed for the picture, everyone could see what a wonderful _____ of beauties they were.

13. If she can put aside her _____ beliefs for the sake of the public good, I think she will make an excellent governor.

14. I am working well on the project, but if I answer the phone it will just _____ me and make me lose my whole train of thought.

15. I wish I had my brother's _____ and could not worry so much about finding a job this summer.

16. I think that goes under the general _____ of "things that will get you fired in under an hour."

17. Jill's new guitar has such a beautiful _____ tone.

18. I heard a _____ from across the room, and I knew my comical uncle must have been telling some of his jokes again.

19. The pain in my side was not _____; I felt sharp stabs of pain every time my torso twisted even just a bit.

20. Some strange _____ sound rose from the sleeping patient's mouth.

SYNONYMS

The following exercise lists vocabulary words from this chapter. Each word is followed by five answer choices. Four of them are synonyms of the vocabulary word in bold. Your task is to choose the one that does **not** fit.

21. inert
    a. inactive
    b. sluggish
    c. boisterous
    d. incapable of moving

22. genteel
    a. polite
    b. soft
    c. refined
    d. well-mannered

23. sycophant
    a. one who is rude to the boss
    b. one who flatters the boss
    c. one who always showers compliments on the boss
    d. one who offers to pick up the dry cleaning for the boss

24. wallow
    a. roll around in
    b. bask
    c. indulge
    d. avoid

25. insouciance
    a. a carefree attitude
    b. anxiety
    c. lightheartedness
    d. unconcern

26. resonant
    a. vibrant
    b. ringing
    c. resounding
    d. weak

27. smidgen
    a. crumb
    b. particle
    c. plenty
    d. drop

28. guffaw
    a. frown
    b. laugh
    c. giggle
    d. chuckle

29. bevy
    a. group
    b. crowd
    c. bunch
    d. example

30. rubric
    a. name
    b. crimson
    c. title
    d. category

ANTONYMS

Choose the word from Vocabulary List 14 that means the opposite, or most nearly the opposite, of the following groups of words.

31. sharp, acute, sensitive   _____

32. explain, teach, illustrate   _____

33. fixed, permanent, stable   _____

34. impartial, unbiased, unprejudiced   _____

35. certain, decided, sure   _____

36. ignorant, naïve, limited in knowledge   _____

37. joyful, happy, glad   _____

38. rude, impolite, discourteous   _____

39. color, brightness, tint   _____

40. give, present, donate   _____

MATCHING

Match the word in the first column with the corresponding word in the second column.

41. inert   **a.** changeable

42. smidgen   **b.** throaty

43. addle   **c.** group

44. guttural   **d.** inactive

45. obtuse   **e.** resounding

46. purloin   **f.** dull

47. mutable   **g.** small particle

48. resonant   **h.** sad

49. bevy   **i.** confuse

50. disconsolate   **j.** steal

PRACTICE ACTIVITIES

Many of the words in this chapter's vocabulary list have several synonyms. Find a good thesaurus and find the synonyms for each word. Try to list five synonyms for each word. If you have difficulty finding the word in the thesaurus, use an alternate form of the word (like resonate for resonant). Your synonyms may be one word long or you may choose to write a few words in a phrase that makes the meaning clear.

To practice your spelling skills, as well as your understanding of the meanings of the words from this chapter's vocabulary list, construct another crossword puzzle. Choose one of the longer words to start with, and write it down in the middle of a page. Then find a word that you can connect to this word because they both share a letter, and write the second word going down through this word. Then try and connect a word to that word, and continue doing this until you have connected every word on the list. Draw boxes around all the letters (or just use graph paper), and place a number in the box with the first letter in each word. Finally, make a list of clues for your crossword puzzle for both the Across and the Down words. Can any of your friends solve your puzzle?

ANSWERS

WORDS IN CONTEXT

Because the boys in this passage are trying their best to blend in at a fancy party they were not invited to, we can guess that when they put on their best *genteel* manners upon arriving, that they are trying to be polite, refined, and gentlemanly. Pete's loud *guffaw* that disrupts the room after Joe whispered a joke in his ear helps us understand that *guffaw* means a loud, rough burst of laughter. The next sentence helps us identify Pete's lovable *insouciance* as his troublesome happy-go-lucky attitude, and since the narrator feels Pete can be *obtuse* about noticing when to restrain himself, we can conclude that *obtuse* can mean insensitive, or slow to understand or notice. Since the boys search for and find a *bevy* of young ladies, we must assume that *bevy* is a group of some kind. The pale girl's dark eyes and hair accentuate her *pallor*, making it possible for us to guess that *pallor* means lack of color or unnatural paleness. The third girl chooses not to dance and remain *inert*, so we can read *inert* as inactive or incapable of moving. The reason she won't dance is because she is heartbroken, which helps us understand the word *disconsolate* means sad, hopeless, or dejected. Since she seems to have mixed feelings about being at the party and trying to meet new people and enjoying herself, we should assume that *ambivalent* means divided and uncertain feelings, or feeling two opposite feelings at the same time. Finally, Pete's humorous attempts to add to the hostess's confusion at not recognizing the party crashers helps us conclude that *addle* must mean confuse, fluster, or muddle.

SENTENCE COMPLETION

1. *sycophant*. If you got this question wrong, refer back to the word's definition.

2. *purloin*. If you got this question wrong, refer back to the word's definition.

3. *genteel*. If you got this question wrong, refer back to the word's definition.

4. *inert*. If you got this question wrong, refer back to the word's definition.

5. *smidgen*. If you got this question wrong, refer back to the word's definition.

6. *omniscient*. If you got this question wrong, refer back to the word's definition.

7. *ambivalent*. If you got this question wrong, refer back to the word's definition.

8. *mutable*. If you got this question wrong, refer back to the word's definition.

9. *wallow*. If you got this question wrong, refer back to the word's definition.

10. *pallor*. If you got this question wrong, refer back to the word's definition.

11. *disconsolate*. If you got this question wrong, refer back to the word's definition.

12. *bevy*. If you got this question wrong, refer back to the word's definition.

13. *partisan*. If you got this question wrong, refer back to the word's definition.

14. *addle*. If you got this question wrong, refer back to the word's definition.

15. *insouciance*. If you got this question wrong, refer back to the word's definition.

16. *rubric*. If you got this question wrong, refer back to the word's definition.

17. *resonant*. If you got this question wrong, refer back to the word's definition.

18. *guffaw*. If you got this question wrong, refer back to the word's definition.

19. *obtuse*. If you got this question wrong, refer back to the word's definition.

20. *guttural.* If you got this question wrong, refer back to the word's definition.

SYNONYMS

21. c. *boisterous. Inert* means not moving or not able to move, and *deceased* means dead and no longer living, which is not a synonym.

22. b. *soft. Genteel* means polite, refined, and gentlemanly or ladylike. You may have confused *soft* and its synonym *gentle* with *genteel.*

23. a. *one who is rude to the boss.* A *sycophant* is one who tries to get ahead by flattery. Choice **a** is the only choice that is not appropriate.

24. d. *avoid. Wallow* means to overindulge in something, making a spectacle of oneself, like the way a pig will roll about in the mud. *Avoid* means to steer clear of, so it is not a synonym.

25. b. *anxiety. Insouciance* is an easy-going and happy-go-lucky attitude. Since *anxiety* means painful uneasiness of the mind, or worry, so it is not a synonym.

26. d. *weak. Resonant* is used to describe sounds and means vibrant, full, and resounding. *Weak* would not be a synonym because *resonant* sounds are strong, loud sounds.

27. c. *plenty.* A *smidgen* is a very small particle or amount. Since *plenty* means an abundance or full supply of something, it is not a synonym.

28. a. *frown.* A *guffaw* is a loud burst of laughter. Since a *frown* is a look of displeasure or disapproval, it is not a synonym.

29. d. *example.* A *bevy* is a group or flock. Since an *example* is a model or specimen of something, it is not a synonym.

30. b. *crimson.* A *rubric* is a formal word for name or category. *Crimson* is a deep red color.

ANTONYMS

31. *Obtuse* means dull and not sharp, or slow to notice, the opposite of the words listed.

32. *Addle* means to confuse, fluster, or muddle, the opposite of the words listed.

33. *Mutable* means changeable or variable, the opposite of the words listed.

34. *Partisan* means strongly devoted to one side in a conflict or a political party.

35. *Ambivalent* means having conflicting feelings about something, the opposite of the words listed.

36. *Omniscient* means all knowing, the opposite of the words listed.

37. *Disconsolate* means sad, dejected, and hopeless, the opposite of the words listed.

38. *Genteel* means refined, polite, and elegant, the opposite of the words listed.

39. *Pallor* means a lack of color, or an unnatural paleness, the opposite of the words listed.

40. *Purloin* means to steal, the opposite of the words listed.

MATCHING

41. d
42. g
43. i
44. b
45. f
46. j
47. a
48. e
49. c
50. h

Across

2 wallow
5 bevy
7 smidgen
9 sycophant
10 rubric
12 ambivalent
14 omniscient
16 guttural
18 addle
20 insouciance

Down

1 purloin
3 obtuse
4 resonant
6 pallor
8 disconsolate
11 partisan
13 guffaw
15 inert
17 genteel
19 mutable

VOCABULARY LIST 15: PHILOSOPHICAL TERMS

CHAPTER SUMMARY

Some of the most influential work done over the last few thousand years has been done not by any person who built a famous building, won a great battle, or discovered a new land, but by some men and women who have sat around and thought. They have investigated the nature of the world, explored the meanings of concepts like truth, honor, and love, and tried to determine the ultimate purpose of life. These people were philosophers, and their work and study is called philosophy. Everyone is a bit of a philosopher in his or her own right, because each of us must decide what values we will live by and what our life's purpose will be. Some people may think about these matters occasionally or very briefly, while others will spend their lives endlessly searching for answers.

I n this chapter you will study some new words that are commonly used to discuss concepts and ideas in various fields such as philosophy, politics, religion, and so on. Many of the words are also used every day in the newspaper or on television. Perhaps once you have mastered the words in this chapter, you too will begin to use them in your writing and speech, and someone will wonder if you yourself are a philosopher.

Choose the word from the Vocabulary List that best fits into the crossword puzzle. You can check your answers at the end of the chapter following the answers to the questions.

Vocabulary List 15:
Philosophical Terms

abstraction
altruism
antithesis
banal
dichotomy
dogma
empiric
erudite
hedonism
ideology
logic
paradigm
paradox
pragmatism
semantic
syllogism
tautology
teleology
tenet
utopia

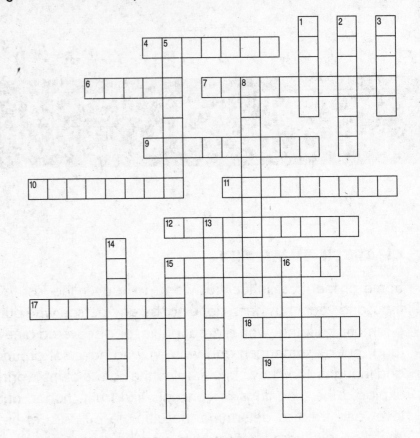

Across

4 a statement that seems to contradict itself
6 a belief that is asserted to be true
7 a practical or realistic attitude
9 division of a subject into two opposite classes or aspects
10 the belief in a pleasure-seeking lifestyle
11 redundancy
12 the exact opposite
15 logical reasoning that leads to a conclusion
17 an example or model
18 paradise
19 the science of reasoning

Down

1 worn out by overuse, trite
2 a quack
3 official beliefs or teachings of particular politics, philosophy, or religion
5 unselfish concern for others
8 theoretical idea or concept
13 "all natural processes occur for a reason"
14 scholarly, learned
15 subtle differences between word meanings
16 doctrines

abstraction   (ab·'strak·shən)

(*noun*)

something that is not concrete or tangible, but is more of a theoretical idea or concept, like truth or beauty

We were discussing our relationships when Franklin reminded us that love itself could be looked at as just an _____.

altruism   ('al·trù·i·zəm)

(*noun*)

unselfish concern for the welfare of others

The couple's _____ had an immeasurable positive effect on the entire community center.

antithesis   (an·'ti·thə·səs)

(*noun*)

the exact opposite of something, or an extreme contrast

I was really hoping for a promotion but I received its _____, a demotion to another office.

banal   (bə·'nal)

(*adj.*)

trivial, worn out by overuse, or used so commonly as to have lost all interest and novelty

Long after people had stopped saying "far out," Tim continued to use the _____ expression.

dichotomy   (dī·'kä·tə·mē)

(*noun*)

the division of a subject into two opposite classes or aspects, such as internal and external

We were intrigued by all the interesting possibilities that the _____ of the experience presented: are ghosts real or illusions?

dogma   ('dog·mə)

(*noun*)

the official beliefs, principles, or teachings, such as those of a religion, political party, or philosophy, used most often with the added implication that these beliefs or teachings should be strictly adhered to

He lived faithfully by the _____ of his religion.

empiric   (im·'pir·ik)

(*noun*)

someone who begins a practice such as law or medicine without the proper professional education and experience; a popular slang term for this is a *quack*; or one who is ignorant of the scientific principles and relies completely on practical experience

Bethany recommended I see her friend for the pain in my back, but I had met him and was sure he was just an _____.

erudite   ('er·ə·dīt)

(*adj.*)

scholarly, learned, well read, having extensive knowledge

Her _____ opinion quickly impressed the instructor and persuaded us all to agree with her.

hedonism   (hē·dən·i·zəm)

(*noun*)

the belief that everything in life should be done to bring pleasure; a pleasure-seeking lifestyle

The _____ we practiced in our youth brought us as many problems as it did pleasures.

ideology   (ī·dē·ˈä·lə·ˈjē)

(*noun*)

the doctrines, beliefs, or opinions of a person, group, or school of thought

He explained his _____ to us and then we better understood the way he chose to live.

logic   (ˈlä·jik)

(*noun*)

the science of correct reasoning used to discover truths, or any method of reasoning, whether it reveals true and valid statements or not

If we use some _____, I am sure we can figure out this riddle.

paradigm   (ˈpar·ə·dīm)

(*noun*)

a pattern, example, or model

After hours of fruitless discussion about the project, the director presented us with a new _____ that made our goal much clearer.

paradox   (ˈpar·ə·däks)

(*noun*)

a statement that seems contradictory, unbelievable, or absurd but may actually be true; or something that is not fully understood because of contradictory appearances, statements, or actions

That is an interesting _____; I guess you really were lucky to be so unlucky.

pragmatism   (ˈprag·mə·ˈti·ˈzəm)

(*noun*)

a way of thinking or an attitude that stresses the value of being practical, realistic, and useful

We were all glad he showed such _____ at the meeting, and that he was not too idealistic about achieving our goal in just a few weeks.

semantic   (si·ˈman·tik)

(*adj.*)

concerning the meaning of something; usually used in discussing words and language and the subtle differences between the different meanings of similar words

The lawyers disputed the wording of part of the contract, but I did not have the patience to deal with _____ issues just then.

syllogism   (ˈsi·lə·ji·zəm)

(*noun*)

a form of logical reasoning that begins with two true statements and ends with a logical conclusion drawn from them, using deductive reasoning, which proceeds from general statements to the specific

Objects that can float in water are less dense than water, and I can float in water, so therefore I must be less dense than water. Is that a valid _____?

tautology   (tȯ·ˈtä·lə·ˈjē)

(*noun*)

needless repetition of an idea in a different word or phrase; redundancy

Can we eliminate any of this _____? We certainly know that the "requirements" are "necessary," so can we just call them "requirements?"

teleology   (te·lē·ˈä·lə·jē)

(*noun*)

the study of final causes; or the belief that all natural processes and events occur for a reason, and nature is directed by some kind of purpose

Looking at the forest fire with that _____, one can see how the fire renews and rejuvenates the forest in an essential way.

tenet (ˈte·nət)

(*noun*)

an opinion, principle, or belief that a person,
religion, or school of thought believes and
asserts to be true and important; a doctrine

He did not question the _____ itself, but only
asked that his teacher clarify the different
implications this new doctrine had for daily
life.

utopia (yu̇·ˈtō·pē·ə)

(*noun*)

a place or state of ideal perfection, usually imaginary;
a paradise

When we arrived at their camp by the river, it seemed
to be an unbelievable _____.

WORDS IN CONTEXT

The following exercise will help you figure out the
meaning of some words from Vocabulary List 15 by
looking at context clues. After you have read and understood the paragraph, explain the context clues that
helped you with the meaning of the vocabulary word.
Check the answer section at the end of this chapter for
an example.

It always inspires me to remember my old
teacher. He was one of the few people who
really believed we could make the world a
better place, and he had this wonderful vi-
sion of a future *utopia* that he was absolutely convinced was inevitable. For him,
altruism was not just some *abstraction*,
some big word that you could discuss in a
philosophy class and then forget about; it
was a way of life. It was a basic *tenet* of his
that each person should do all that they can
to help others and he certainly taught us

well enough by his own example. But his
pragmatism also kept him well grounded
and focused on real solutions to local concerns, and perhaps that is why none of his
critics could dismiss him. And he certainly
gave them reason enough to, if one did not
understand that the fabulous entertaining
he did was all part of his mission, and not
just some selfish *hedonism*. Rather, he was
motivating and rewarding his team, and
you could not leave one of his parties without understanding his unique *ideology* a little better, and resolved to commit even
more fully to a life of public service.

SENTENCE COMPLETION

Insert the correct word from Vocabulary List 15 into
the following sentences.

1. We will have to come up with a whole new
   _____ for this project and leave the older
   models behind.

2. My sister is interested in alternative medicines
   and sees a healer rather than a doctor, but I
   think he is just a (an) _____.

3. The division of interpersonal and
   intrapersonal is a popular _____ of the
   human experience that is often discussed in
   psychology.

4. I tried to read his manuscript, but it was filled
   with too much _____, and I got
   frustrated at having to read such repetitive
   phrases as "the cold ice" and "necessary
   essentials."

5. I know it sounds like a (an) _____, but I really am doing a better job by doing less work.

6. Why is this happening? War is the _____ of peace.

7. Wouldn't it be wonderful if we could turn this land into a (an) _____ where everyone had all the basic necessities of life, there was no crime, and people could really spend their lives living up to their potential?

8. His _____ was a real asset to our group and saved the rest of us, who idealistically thought we would just find a place to stay once we got there.

9. At the time, he was reading books on several religions and philosophies and developing his own _____ by which he would loosely govern his life for the next twenty years.

10. It was inspiring to see such a fine display of pure _____, and her efforts made all of us a little ashamed that we did so little to help them.

11. If people who smoke cigarettes greatly increase their chances of having serious health problems in their lifetime, and I am now resolved to quit smoking today, wouldn't it follow that I will no longer be greatly increasing my chances of developing serious health problems? Can anyone find a flaw with any piece of this _____, or is it logical the way it is presented?

12. The belief that everyone should have the opportunity to spend their own money as they see fit is a basic _____ of capitalism.

13. I wish I could abandon all my responsibilities, follow them down there on their vacation, and join them in their carefree _____.

14. It was an _____ opinion and I had to respect his thorough research, but nonetheless I still disagreed and thought the procedure should not be allowed to continue.

15. Can we use some _____ and see if there is another conclusion that we can draw from the evidence?

16. It is not just a small _____ mistake; you just introduced me as someone you work *with*, when we both know that I hired you to work *for me*.

17. In all the years I have known him, I have never known him to question the _____ of his church, so I think there must be some mistake.

18. He mocked us and told us we were foolish to spend our time discussing such a (an) _____, but we knew that few things were more important than trying to better understand just what *honor* really meant.

19. I subscribe to a similar _____, and I also believe that the activity of the ants has an important purpose that would be well worth understanding.

20. It is amusing to hear some people use so many _____ expressions that they probably have just learned from television.

SYNONYMS

The following exercise lists vocabulary words from this chapter. Each word is followed by five answer choices. Four of them are synonyms of the vocabulary word in bold. Your task is to choose the one that does **not** fit.

21. paradox
  a. mystery
  b. contradiction
  c. puzzle
  d. clue

22. antithesis
  a. an opposite
  b. a statement
  c. the reverse
  d. a contrast

23. semantic
  a. concerning the meaning of
  b. related to the different definitions of
  c. using too many words
  d. distinguishing different contexts

24. tenet
  a. prejudice
  b. belief
  c. opinion
  d. principle

25. hedonism
  a. pleasure-seeking
  b. debauchery
  c. solitude
  d. indulgence

26. teleology
  a. belief that nature is purposeful
  b. belief that natural processes occur for a reason
  c. belief that nature is haphazard
  d. belief that everything that occurs in the natural world is part of some higher plan

27. paradigm
  a. model
  b. pattern
  c. example
  d. drawing

28. ideology
  a. doctrines of a religion
  b. beliefs of a political organization
  c. behavior of a child
  d. opinions of a person

29. logic
  a. confusion
  b. reasoning
  c. figuring out
  d. analyzing the truth of something

30. erudite
  a. scholarly
  b. knowledgeable
  c. discourteous
  d. well read

ANTONYMS

Choose the word from Vocabulary List 15 that means the opposite, or most nearly the opposite, of the following groups of words.

31. unity, universality, oneness   _____

32. idealism, dreaminess, impracticality   _____

33. a professional, one who is properly trained, a qualified authority   _____

34. new, exciting, fresh   _____

35. selfishness, greediness, hostility   _____

36. concise writing, succinctness, speech that is not redundant   _____

37. a world of horrors, a "hell on Earth," future world of suffering and misery   _____

38. ignorant, uneducated, illiterate   _____

39. hard fact, physical evidence, tangible object   _____

40. random set of beliefs, heresy, unorthodox beliefs   _____

CHOOSING THE RIGHT WORD

Circle the word in bold that best completes the sentence.

41. The two men were known for their wild (**utopia, hedonism**); they had a reputation for always eating out at the best restaurants and cafes, and leaving often for spontaneous vacations to exotic locales.

42. His speech was very (**erudite, tautology**) and he received good reviews for his display of such fine research.

43. Her volunteer work at the nursing home was just another example of her admirable (**pragmatism, altruism**).

44. It is an interesting (**antithesis, tenet**) that followers of the faith often have difficulty with.

45. I don't know what to make of it; it sure seems like a (**paradox, paradigm**) to me.

46. Have you ever heard such a (**banal, semantic**) expression? I am just so tired of hearing that over and over again.

47. If you really analyze the first premise of that (**abstraction, syllogism**), you will see that the conclusion cannot possibly be valid.

48. She always closely followed the (**dichotomy, dogma**) of her religion, and often helped instruct others who had questions about it themselves.

49. Don't panic. Let's try and use a little (**logic, paradox**) and see if we can figure out what must have happened to the keys.

50. This place is like a little hidden (**utopia, empiric**) that we have been fortunate to find before anyone else ruined it.

PRACTICE ACTIVITIES

Go to the library and look up a book on philosophy. Not only will you read some interesting ideas by some of humanity's best thinkers, but you will no doubt see the words from this chapter in the text, as well as many others that you may not recognize. Find ten new words that you do not know the definitions of, and look up those words in the dictionary. Then practice using each word in a sentence.

Use an Internet search engine and look up some of the words from this chapter. Does the search engine have links for the word? Go to a few of those websites and see why they used that word. Is the word part of the name of the website, or is it just used in the text of the site. See how many words you can find from this list.

ANSWERS

WORDS IN CONTEXT

The reader can understand that the narrator's former teacher's optimistic belief in a *utopia* is a belief in a better world that lies somewhere in the future, and one gets the sense that it must be almost like a paradise, where finally there would be no one left who needed the kind of help the teacher always gives. Thus, we can understand from the context of the passage that *altruism* must be an admirable quality that means an unselfish concern for others, which would explain the teacher's commitment to doing all he can for others and living a life of public service. We can conclude that an *abstraction* is a theoretical idea like truth, mercy, or *altruism*, because we know that the professor does not consider it to be just a word one only discusses in a philosophy class and does not practice. The narrator explains the teacher's *tenet* that one must always strive to do more for others, so we can conclude that *tenet* means an opinion or belief of a person, religion, or school of thought. Since the teacher's *pragmatism* is praised for keeping him grounded and focused on practical efforts to help others, we should know that *pragmatism* is a way of thinking that emphasizes being practical, realistic, and useful. The teacher's choice to celebrate and throw parties is defended as not being selfish *hedonism*, so we can assume that *hedonism* means a pleasure-seeking lifestyle or philosophy. Finally, since the narrator states that he understands his teacher's unique *ideology* better after the celebrations, we can guess that *ideology* means those beliefs, opinions, or doctrines that he adheres to.

SENTENCE COMPLETION

1. *paradigm*. If you got this question wrong, refer back to the word's definition.

2. *empiric*. If you got this question wrong, refer back to the word's definition.

3. *dichotomy*. If you got this question wrong, refer back to the word's definition.

4. *tautology*. If you got this question wrong, refer back to the word's definition.

5. *paradox*. If you got this question wrong, refer back to the word's definition.

6. *antithesis*. If you got this question wrong, refer back to the word's definition.

7. *utopia*. If you got this question wrong, refer back to the word's definition.

8. *pragmatism*. If you got this question wrong, refer back to the word's definition.

9. *ideology*. If you got this question wrong, you may have mistakenly chosen *dogma*, a close synonym of *ideology*. However, *dogma* implies a belief system that is more strictly adhered to, and the context of this sentence indicates that the belief system was only loosely adhered to.

10. *altruism*. If you got this question wrong, refer back to the word's definition.

11. *syllogism*. If you got this question wrong, you may have mistakenly chosen *logic*. It is true that *logic* is being used in the reasoning in the example, but the form the reasoning takes is the unique form of a *syllogism*, so that is a better answer. It also would be inappropriate to use *logic* in the blank because the next phrase asks if the piece of reasoning presented is *logical*, and thus it would be somewhat repetitive to use *logic*.

12. *tenet*. If you got this question wrong, you may have mistakenly chosen *dogma or ideology*. Since *tenet* refers to a specific belief, and *dogma* and *ideology* refer to an entire set of beliefs, *tenet*

would be the best answer because this example only presents one specific belief.

13. *hedonism.* If you got this question wrong, refer back to the word's definition.

14. *erudite.* If you got this question wrong, refer back to the word's definition.

15. *logic.* If you got this question wrong, refer back to the word's definition.

16. *semantic.* If you got this question wrong, refer back to the word's definition.

17. *dogma.* Here, again, you may have chosen the closely related terms *ideology* or *tenet. Tenet* refers to one specific doctrine or teaching, and the context of this sentence tell us that for several years the man in question has not questioned his church's teachings, implying that it is the entire set of beliefs that is being discussed. *Dogma* would be a better choice than *ideology* because the man seems to strictly adhere to his church's teachings, and the connotation of *ideology* emphasizes the beliefs themselves, whereas the connotation of *dogma* stresses obedience and adherence to the teachings of the religion or group that is expected and required.

18. *abstraction.* If you got this question wrong, refer back to the word's definition.

19. *teleology.* If you got this question wrong, refer back to the word's definition.

20. *banal.* If you got this question wrong, refer back to the word's definition.

SYNONYMS

21. d. *clue. Paradox* means something that is hard to understand because it contains a contradiction. Since *clue* means a hint or slight indication toward solving some mystery, it is not a synonym.

22. b. *statement. Antithesis* means the exact opposite of something. Since a *statement* is a saying or an expression, it is not a synonym.

23. c. *using too many words. Semantic* means concerning the different meanings of closely related words. *Using too many words* is not a correct answer because it deals with the number of words involved and not the meanings of the words.

24. a. *prejudice.* A *tenet* is a belief, opinion, or principle that a person or an organized group holds to be true and important. A *prejudice* is a bias against something or a preconception prior to meeting or experiencing it, so it is not a synonym.

25. c. *solitude. Hedonism* is the belief that pleasure is the most important goal in life. *Solitude* is the state of being alone and by oneself, so it is not a synonym.

26. c. *belief that nature is haphazard. Teleology* is the belief that all natural processes and events happen for a reason, directed by some kind of purpose. *Haphazard* means accidental or careless, so choice c could not be a synonym.

27. d. *drawing. Paradigm* means a pattern or model, often used to help organize or conceptualize an idea. A *drawing* could serve the same purpose, but it always refers to a hand drawn visual presentation, so it is too specific and narrow to be a synonym.

28. c. *behavior of a child. Ideology* means the opinions or beliefs of a person, religion, or school of thought, so choices a, b, and d are appropriate synonyms, but *behavior of a child* is unrelated and not a synonym.

29. a. *confusion. Logic* is the science of using correct reasoning to discover a truth. *Confusion* is puzzlement or bewilderment, so it is not a synonym.

30. c. *discourteous. Erudite* means scholarly, learned, and having an extensive knowledge. *Discourteous* means rude and impolite, so it is not a synonym.

ANTONYMS

31. *dichotomy. Dichotomy* means the division of something into two opposite classes or aspects, usually for discussion or analysis, the opposite of the words listed.

32. *pragmatism. Pragmatism* means the believing in the value of being practical, realistic, and useful.

33. *empiric.* An *empiric* is someone who begins a practice such as medicine or law without the proper professional education and experience, the opposite of the words listed.

34. *banal. Banal* means trite, hackneyed, and worn out by overuse, the opposite of the words listed.

35. *altruism. Altruism* is the unselfish concern for the welfare of others, the opposite of the words listed.

36. *tautology. Tautology* is the needless repetition of an idea in slightly different words, the opposite of the words listed.

37. *utopia.* A *utopia* is an imaginary place of ideal perfection, the opposite of the words listed.

38. *erudite. Erudite* means scholarly, knowledgeable, and well read, the opposite of the words listed.

39. *abstraction.* An *abstraction* is a concept or idea that is theoretical or hypothetical and is not material or physical, the opposite of the words listed.

40. *dogma. Dogma* is the officially recognized beliefs, principles, or teachings of a religion, political party, or philosophy, the opposite of the words listed.

CHOOSING THE RIGHT WORD

41. *hedonism. Hedonism* can mean a pleasure-seeking lifestyle. *Utopia* means an imaginary perfect place.

42. *erudite. Erudite* means scholarly and knowledgeable. *Tautology* is the needless repetition of similar meaning words or phrases.

43. *altruism. Altruism* is the unselfish concern for the welfare of others, which volunteer work in a nursing home would be a good example of. *Pragmatism* is the attitude or belief that the practical, realistic, and useful are most important.

44. *tenet.* A *tenet* is a belief or principle of a person, religion, or school of thought. *Antithesis* is the exact opposite of something.

45. *paradox.* A *paradox* is a mystery, or something that is unclear or not fully understood because of some contradiction. A *paradigm* is a pattern, example, or model.

46. *banal. Banal* means worn out by overuse or trite. *Semantic* means concerning the slightly different meanings of similar words.

47. *syllogism.* A *syllogism* is a specific form of logical reasoning that begins with two premises and derives a conclusion from them. An *abstraction* is something that does not exist in the physical world but is rather a concept or theoretical idea.

48. *dogma. Dogma* is the official set of beliefs and teachings of a religion, political party, or philosophy. *Dichotomy* means the division of a subject into two opposite classes or aspects for analysis or discussion.

49. *logic. Logic* is the science of correct reasoning used to discover truths. A *paradox* is a puzzling statement that is difficult to fully understand because it contains a contradiction.

50. *utopia. Utopia* means a place of ideal perfection. *Empiric* means someone who lacks the necessary and proper training and experience to practice a profession.

Across

4 paradox
6 tenet
7 pragmatism
9 dichotomy
10 hedonism
11 tautology
12 antithesis
15 syllogism
17 paradigm
18 utopia
19 logic

Down

1 banal
2 empiric
3 dogma
5 altruism
8 abstraction
13 teleology
14 erudite
15 semantic
16 ideology

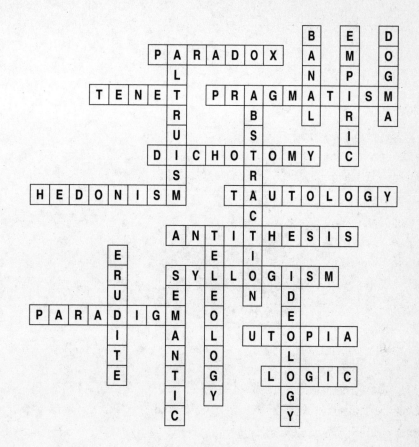

C·H·A·P·T·E·R

POST-TEST

19

Now that you've built your vocabulary and spelling skills, you're ready to test them out. Compare your score to your pretest to see how far you've come. You can go back and review any words you forgot until you know every word in this book.

SPELLING
Choose the word that is spelled correctly.

1. a. disinterrested
   b. dissinterested
   c. disinterested
   d. disintirested

2. a. belligerent
   b. belligarent
   c. belligerrent
   d. beligerent

3. a. rendezvoo
   b. rendezvous
   c. rondevous
   d. rondezvoo

4. a. contraban
   b. contriband
   c. conttraban
   d. contraband

5. a. omnishint
   b. omniscient
   c. onmscient
   d. omniscint

Choose the word that is misspelled.

6. a. euphemism
   b. transcend
   c. relentless
   d. interogate

7. a. beneficiary
   b. pergury
   c. encryption
   d. flippant

8. a. guffaw
   b. extricate
   c. anomaly
   d. idealogy

9. a. synthisis
   b. deferment
   c. bigotry
   d. larceny

10. a. biodegradable
    b. phillanthropy
    c. protracted
    d. malevolent

SENTENCE COMPLETION
Write the word from Group 1 that best fits in the blank. You can check your answers at the end of the Post-Test.

Group 1

imperious	palpable	antipathy	brusque
plausible	exhume	aphorism	purloin
prodigious	succor	guttural	dire
dogma	utopia	malaise	retrospect
parity	venerate	fluctuate	benevolent

11. We will have to _____ her body from the grave and obtain a hair sample if we hope to see if her DNA matches that of the suspect.

12. A (an) _____ came over me this winter, and I could hardly get out of bed for any reason, although I could not explain why I felt this way.

13. Have you ever heard the _____, "Pain is just weakness leaving the body"?

14. They completed a/an _____ amount of work when they stayed after hours to finish the project.

15. We received a/an _____ message from the stranded climbers saying they were giving up all hope of being rescued if no aid came before tonight.

Write the word from Group 2 that best fits in the blank. You can check your answers at the end of the Post Test

Group 2

capital	affidavit	illegible	simian
attribute	pathos	recapitulate	naïve
fiscal	cower	tenure	database
ambivalent	construe	mete	myriad
prone	verify	addle	paradox

16. The scary movie made the audience _____ in their seats.

17. The teacher could not make out who had written on the desk because the handwriting was _____.

18. The interviewer said I would hear from her after she was able to _____ my credentials.

19. He has many wonderful qualities, but the _____ I most admire in him is his honesty.

20. I still don't know if I want to go to the party or not, and I apologize for being so _____ about it for so long.

CHOOSING THE RIGHT WORD

Circle the bold word that best fits into the context of the sentence.

21. The workers' union and the board of directors finally decided to go to (**arbitration, collusion**) because their negotiations were fruitless.

22. I found the answer in the (**FAQ, ASAP**) section of the brochure.

23. I can't read this memo because it is filled with (**nepotism, jargon**) that I don't understand.

24. She is well known for her (**syllogism, pragmatism**) so I think she will be a very successful manager of the project.

25. Everything was fine until we had a little (**snafu, yuppie**) on the train.

26. I am sure I know the sound of that (**addle, guffaw**), so Joe must be here and it sounds like he is having a good time.

27. She can't sell her car because there is still a (**lien, tort**) against it.

28. The hackers tried, but they could not figure out our company's (**cache, encryption**) methods, so the files remain secure.

29. Let me tell you a very funny (**anecdote, construe**) about him.

30. The United States is hoping Spain's government will (**bequest, extradite**) the criminals who had fled there.

SYNONYMS

The following exercise lists vocabulary words from this chapter. Each word is followed by five answer choices. Four of them are synonyms of the vocabulary word in bold. Your task is to choose the one that does **not** fit.

31. protracted
  a. extended
  b. forbidden
  c. drawn out
  d. lengthy

32. rancor
   a. hatred
   b. ill will
   c. dislike
   d. ignorance

33. recapitulate
   a. summarize
   b. introduce
   c. go back over
   d. review

34. rendezvous
   a. parting
   b. meeting
   c. engagement
   d. appointment

35. flippant
   a. too casual
   b. rude
   c. tired
   d. disrespectful

36. puerile
   a. childish
   b. silly
   c. immature
   d. cautious

37. archetype
   a. model
   b. replication
   c. example
   d. standard

38. relentless
   a. occasional
   b. unstoppable
   c. harsh
   d. continuing

39. purge
   a. cleanse
   b. eliminate
   c. ruin
   d. empty

40. cryptic
   a. hidden
   b. secret
   c. ambiguous
   d. ancient

ANTONYMS

Write the word in the blank that is the most nearly opposite of the words listed.

41. clear, unmistakable, easily read   _____

42. give, restore, buy   _____

43. exact words, literal meaning, unexaggerated speech   _____

44. hidden, secret, possible to miss or pass by   _____

45. sluggish, lethargic, inactive   _____

46. fair hiring, promotions given to those most deserving, merit-based
personnel decisions   _____

47. remain constant, resist change, stay the same always   _____

48. worldly, experienced, wise   _____

49. selfishness, greediness, lack of concern for others   _____

50. unfaithfulness, disloyalty, untrustworthiness   _____

WORD PAIRS

Write *S* if the words are synonyms, or *A* if the words
are antonyms.

51. vehement, blasé ___

52. stolid, staid ___

53. genteel, urbane ___

54. avant-garde, banal ___

55. altruism, hedonism ___

56. relentless, tenacious ___

57. evident, conspicuous ___

58. laudable, churlish ___

59. gregarious, diffident ___

60. benevolent, malevolent ___

DENOTATION/CONNOTATION

The following words are all synonyms with the same
denotation, but with different connotations. Write
POS in the blank if the word carries a positive connotation, an *NEG* in the blank if the word carries a
negative connotation, and an *N* if the word carries
a neutral connotation.

Example

> **1.** _____ Project _____ Enterprise
> _____ Scheme

Answer

> **1.** *Project* carries a neutral connotation—the
> reader doesn't have any idea who or what
> might be creating or working on the project. In
> contrast, enterprise carries a positive
> connotation—*enterprise* is often associated
> with a business ventures or a new and exciting
> project, thus giving the word a positive
> connotation. In contrast, *scheme* carries a
> negative connotation—criminals and
> lawlessness are often associated with schemes.

61. _____ exorbitant _____ copious

62. _____ puerile _____ naïve
_____ facetious

63. _____ loquacious _____ garrulous

64. _____ gregarious _____ jaunty

65. _____ collusion _____ consortium

66. _____ resolute _____ tenacious
_____ relentless

67. _____ entrepreneur _____ empiric

68. _____ furtive _____ cryptic
_____ incognito

69. _____ audible _____ resonant

70. _____ aficionado _____ partisan

71. _____ provocative _____ litigious

72. _____ bane _____ antipathy

73. _____ audacious _____ flippant

74. _____ feisty _____ vivacious

75. _____ relevant _____ tangential
_____ non sequitur

ANSWERS

SPELLING

1. **c.** disinterested
2. **a.** belligerent
3. **b.** rendezvous
4. **d.** contraband
5. **b.** omniscient
6. **d.** *interogate* should be spelled *interrogate*.
7. **b.** *pergury* should be spelled *perjury*.
8. **d.** *idealolgy* should be spelled *ideology*.
9. **a.** *synthisis* should be spelled *synthesis*.
10. **b.** *phillanthropy* should be spelled *philanthropy*.

SENTENCE COMPLETION

11. *exhume. Exhume* means remove from a grave.
12. *malaise.* A *malaise* is a vague feeling of illness.
13. *aphorism.* An *aphorism* is a general statement of truth or opinion.
14. *prodigious. Prodigious* means a very large or numerous.
15. *dire. Dire* means urgent or threatening.
16. *cower. Cower* means tremble in fear.
17. *illegible. Illegible* means not able to be easily read.
18. *verify. Verify* means to establish the truth of something.
19. *attribute.* An *attribute* is a special quality or characteristic.
20. *ambivalent. Ambivalent* means having divided feelings, or having conflicting opinions about something.

CHOOSING THE RIGHT WORD

21. *arbitration. Arbitration* is the process by which disputes are settled by a third party, which would be an improvement to fruitless negotiations.

22. *FAQ. FAQ* means Frequently Asked Questions, which is where one would find the answer one sought. *ASAP* is as soon as possible.
23. *jargon. Jargon* is the specialized vocabulary of an industry or interest group.
24. *pragmatism. Pragmatism* is the belief in and emphasis on the practical, possible, and useful.
25. *snafu. Snafu* means "situation normal, all fouled up."
26. *guffaw.* A *guffaw* is a loud burst of laughter.
27. *lien.* A *lien* is a charge against property for the satisfaction of a debt imposed by the courts.
28. *encryption. Encryption* refers to the technology term for translating information into secret code.
29. *anecdote.* An *anecdote* is a short account of an interesting or humorous incident.
30. *extradite. Extradite* means to surrender an alleged criminal to the state or country he or she can be tried in.

SYNONYMS

31. **b.** *forbidden. Protracted* means extended, lengthy, or drawn out.
32. **d.** *ignorance. Rancor* is hatred, ill will, or dislike of something or someone.
33. **b.** *introduce. Recapitulate* means to summarize, go back over, or review.
34. **a.** *parting. Rendezvous* means a meeting, engagement, or appointment.
35. **c.** *tired. Flippant* means too casual, rude, and disrespectful.
36. **d.** *cautious. Puerile* means childish, silly, and immature.
37. **b.** *replication. Archetype* means model, example, or standard.

38. a. *occasional. Relentless* means unstoppable, harsh, or continuing.

39. c. *ruin. Purge* means to cleanse, eliminate, or empty.

40. d. *ancient. Cryptic* means hidden, secret, or ambiguous.

ANTONYMS

41. *illegible. Illegible* means not easily read, the opposite of the words listed.

42. *purloin. Purloin* means to steal, the opposite of the words listed.

43. *hyperbole. Hyperbole* means exaggerated speech or writing, the opposite of the words listed.

44. *conspicuous. Conspicuous* means highly visible, the opposite of the words listed.

45. *vivacious. Vivacious* means full of spirit and lively, the opposite of the words listed.

46. *nepotism. Nepotism* is the hiring and promoting of friends or family members, the opposite of the words listed.

47. *fluctuate. Fluctuate* means to change or vary, the opposite of the words listed.

48. *naïve. Naïve* means innocent, simple, and lacking knowledge of the world, the opposite of the words listed.

49. *altruism. Altruism* is the unselfish concern for the welfare of others, the opposite of the words listed.

50. *fidelity. Fidelity* means loyalty and trustworthiness, the opposite of the words listed.

WORD PAIRS

51. A
52. S
53. S
54. A
55. A
56. S
57. S
58. A
59. A
60. A

DENOTATION AND CONNOTATION

61. *Exorbitant* carries a negative connotation, inferring the person responsible for going beyond what is reasonable was excessive, and *exorbitant* is often associated with showy and ostentatious displays of wealth. *Copious* carries a positive connotation, since it means abundant and plentiful and is often associated with generosity.

62. *Puerile* carries a negative connotation, and is often used to condemn or criticize. *Naïve* usually carries a neutral connotation, and it can be used to objectively describe someone or an idea, or it can be used with a negative connotation to criticize someone who was expected to have known something they did not know. *Facetious* carries a positive connotation, and it is used to describe playful joking behavior, or to excuse an offensive remark, as in "I was just being *facetious*."

63. *Loquacious* carries a neutral connotation, as it means talkative, an attribute that could be either positive or negative depending perhaps on the speaker's own subjective view. *Garrulous,* however, carries a negative connotation, as it means overly talkative and chattering about unimportant things.

64. Both of these words carry positive connotations. *Gregarious* means sociable, and *jaunty* means confident and presenting a sharp appearance.

65. *Collusion* carries a negative connotation, and is used to identify fraudulent or deceitful business conspiracies. *Consortium* carries a neutral connotation, as it simply means a coming together of two or more businesses for a specific purpose, and there is no implication that their purpose is either honest or deceitful.

66. *Resolute* carries a neutral connotation, and does not indicate whether the firmness of purpose indicated is directed towards a positive or negative end. *Tenacious* carries a slightly negative connotation and is often used to criticize negative stubbornness. *Relentless* also usually carries a negative connotation and is used to describe persistent efforts or assaults that are unwelcome.

67. *Entrepreneur* carries a positive connotation, and identifies someone who takes on the challenge and risk of starting his or her own business. **Empiric** has a negative connotation because it identifies someone who, though he or she also shows initiative, begins a practice such as law or medicine without the proper training and experience, assuming they will learn on the job.

68. *Furtive* has a negative connotation, as it means done in a sly, stealthy, underhanded manner. *Cryptic* has a neutral connotation, and means secret or hidden, but with no implied ill will. *Incognito* has a positive connotation, because although it means disguised, it is rarely used to describe negative characters and often carries a connotation of good hearted mischief or adventure.

69. *Audible* carries a neutral connotation, and simply means able to be heard. *Resonant* carries a positive connotation, as it describes sounds that are rich, full, and vibrant.

70. *Aficionado* carries a positive connotation, as it means a person who likes, knows about, and is devoted to a particular activity or thing. It is rarely used with any negative connotations, but rather most often it is used with a complimentary or boastful connotation. *Partisan* has a negative connotation because it means strongly in favor of one view or political party, usually with the connotation of blindly following the party line, and not considering an issue by oneself or the bigger picture.

71. *Provocative* carries a negative connotation, like its root word provoke. *Provocative* means exciting emotion in a negative way and likely to stir up action or cause a riot. *Litigious* carries a negative connotation also, and is used to describe something that is disputed and needs to be settled in court. The negative connotation arises from most people's dislike of going to court, and the hassle and expense involved.

72. Both of these words have strong negative connotations. *Bane* means the source of continued annoyance or exasperation, or the cause of ruin or death. *Antipathy* means a revulsion or strong dislike of something.

73. *Audacious* carries a negative connotation. Though it means fearless, adventurous, and daring, it usually means recklessly so. *Flippant* also carries a negative connotation, as it is used to describe disrespectful levity or casualness.

74. *Feisty* carries a negative connotation, as it means full of spirit, but in a quarrelsome way. *Vivacious* carries a positive connotation because it means lively and full of spirit and is used as a compliment.

75. *Relevant* carries a positive connotation. It means related to or concerning the subject at hand, and implies that there is other material that is not relevant and therefore does not matter. *Tangential* carries a neutral or negative connotation, and describes something that is slightly related to the subject at hand. *Non sequitur* carries a negative connotation because a *non sequitur* is a statement that has no bearing with the one before it and therefore not good conversation or argument.

A · P · P · E · N · D · I · X

STUDYING FOR SUCCESS

A

How successful you are at studying has less to do with how much time you put into it than with how you do it. That's because some ways of studying are much more effective than others, and some environments are much more conducive to studying than others. Another reason is that not everyone retains information in the same way. On the following pages, you will discover how to adapt your studying strategies to the ways you learn best. You will probably pick up some new techniques to help you prepare for your test.

LEARNING STYLES

Think for a minute about what you know about how you learn. You've lived long enough to have a good feel for how you learn what you need to learn. For example, if you need directions to a new restaurant would you:

- Ask to see a map showing how to get there?
- Ask someone to tell you how to get there?
- Copy someone's written directions?

Most people learn in a variety of ways: seeing, touching, hearing, and experiencing the world around them. Many people find, however, that they are more likely to absorb information from one learning source than from others. The source that works best for you is called your dominant learning method.

There are three basic learning methods: visual, the auditory, and kinesthetic (also known as tactile).

- Visual learners understand and retain information best when they can **see** the map, the picture, the text, the word, or the math example.
- Auditory learners learn best when they can **hear** the directions, the poem, the math theorem, or the spelling of a word.
- Kinesthetic learners need to **do**—they must write the directions, draw the diagram, or copy down the phone number.

VISUAL LEARNERS

If you are a visual learner, you learn best by seeing. Pay special attention to illustrations and graphic material when you study. If you color code your notes with colorful inks or highlighters, you may find that you absorb information better. Visual learners can learn to map or diagram information later in this chapter.

AUDITORY LEARNERS

If you are an auditory learner, you learn best by listening. Read material aloud to yourself, or talk about what you are learning with a study partner or a study group. Hearing the information will help you to remember it. Some people like to tape-record notes and play them back on the tape player. If you commute to work or school by car or listen to a personal tape player, you can gain extra preparation time by playing the notes to yourself on tape.

KINESTHETIC LEARNERS

If you are a kinesthetic learner, you learn best by doing. Interact a lot with your print material by underlining and making margin notes in your textbooks and handouts. Rewrite your notes onto index cards. Recopying material helps you to remember it.

HOW TO STUDY MOST EFFECTIVELY

If studying efficiently is second nature to you, you're very lucky. Most people have to work at it. Try some of these helpful study methods to make studying easier and more effective for you.

MAKE AN OUTLINE

After collecting all the materials you need to review or prepare for the test, the first step for studying any subject is to reduce a large body of information into smaller, more manageable units. One approach to studying this way is to make an outline of text information, handout material, and class notes.

The important information in print material is often surrounded by lots of extra words and ideas. If you can highlight just the important information, or at least the information you need to know for your test, you can help yourself narrow your focus so that you can study more effectively. There are several ways to make an outline of print material. They include annotating, outlining, and mapping. The point of all three of these strategies is that they allow you to pull out just the important information that you need to prepare for the test.

Annotating

Annotations help you pull out main ideas from the surrounding text to make them more visible and accessible to you. Annotation means that you underline or highlight important information that appears in print material. It also involves responding to the material by engaging yourself with the writer by making margin notes. Margin notes are phrases or sentences in the margins of print material that summarize the content of those passages. Your margin notes leave footprints for you to follow as you review the text.

Here is an example of a passage that has been annotated and underlined.

LOCATION, LOCATION, LOCATION

<u>Find a quiet spot, have a good reading light, and turn the radio off.</u>

Find Quiet Places

Different quiet places at different times

For many adult test takers, it's difficult to find a quiet spot in their busy lives. Many adults don't even have a bedroom corner that isn't shared with someone else. <u>Your quiet spot may be in a different place at different times of the day.</u>

For example, it could be the kitchen table early in the morning before breakfast, your workplace area when everyone else is at lunch, or a corner of the sofa late at night. If you know you'll have to move around when you study, <u>make sure your study material is portable.</u>

Portable study material

Keep your notes, practice tests, pencils, and other supplies together in a folder or bag. Then you can easily carry your study material with you and study in whatever quiet spot presents itself.

<u>If quiet study areas are non-existent in your home or work environment, you may need to find a space elsewhere. The public library is the most obvious choice.</u> Some test takers find it helpful to assign themselves study hours at the library in the same way that they schedule dentist appointments, class hours, household tasks, or other necessary uses of daily or weekly time. Studying away from home or job also minimizes the distractions of other people and other demands when you are preparing for a test.

Library!

Lights

Need good light

Libraries also provide good reading lights. For some people this may seem like a trivial matter, but the eyestrain that can come from working for long periods in <u>poor light can be very tiring—a cause of fatigue you can't afford when you're studying hard.</u>

At home, the bedside lamp, the semi-darkness of a room dominated by the television, or the bright sunlight of the back porch will be of little help to tired eyes.

Outlining

You are probably familiar with the basic format of the traditional outline:

I. Main idea 1
   A. Major detail
   B. Major detail
      1. Minor detail
      2. Minor detail
II. Main idea 2
   A. Major detail
   B. Major detail

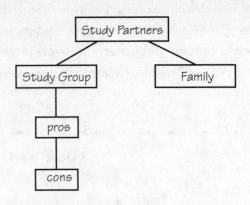

You may have used an outline in school to help you organize a writing assignment or take notes. When you outline print material, you're looking for the basic ideas that make up the framework of the text. When you are taking out the important information for a test, then you are looking for the basic ideas that the author wants to convey to you.

Mapping

Mapping is a more visual kind of outline. Instead of a making a linear outline of the main ideas of a text, when you map, you make a diagram of the main points in the text that you want to remember. The following diagrams show the same information in a map form.

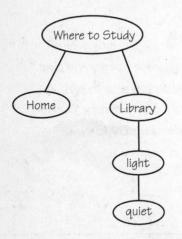

MAKE STUDY NOTES

The next step after you have pulled out all the key ideas is to make notes from which you will study. You will use these notes for the intensive and ongoing study you'll do over the period of time before the test. They're the specific items that you targeted as important to know for the test. Your notes should help you understand the information you need to know and, in many cases, commit it to memory. You should be sure to include:

- the main ideas you underlined or highlighted in the text
- the main ideas and important details you outlined or mapped from the text
- specific terms, words, dates, formulas, names, facts, or procedures that you need to memorize

How Do You Make Study Notes?

Some people like to write study notes in the back pages of their notebooks or on paper folded lengthwise so that it can be tucked between the pages of a text or review book. This format is good to use for notes that can be written as questions and answers, cause and effect, or definition and examples. You can also make notes on index cards.

Using Index Cards

It can be very helpful to write your study notes—especially those that contain material to be memorized—on index cards. Vocabulary words are significantly easier to learn using index cards.

The advantages of making notes on index cards are:

- The information on each card is visually separated from other information. Therefore it's easier to concentrate on just that one item, separate from the surrounding text. You remember the look of a vocabulary word or a math equation more clearly when it is set off by itself.
- Cards are small and portable. They can be carried in a purse or a pocket and pulled out at any time during the day for review.
- Study cards can help you with the necessary task of memorizing. If you write the key word or topic you are trying to learn on one side, and the information you must know on the other side, you have an easy wasy to quiz yourself on the material. This method is especially good for kinesthetic learners, who learn by doing.

MAKING MEMORIZING EASIER

There are many ways to take the drudgery out of memorizing information.

TAKE SMALL BITES OF TIME

Most people memorize information best when they study in small periods over a long period of time.

Memorizing facts from index cards that can be carried with you and pulled out for a few ten-minute sessions each day will yield better results than sitting down with a textbook for an hour straight. Index card notes can be pulled out in odd moments: while you are sitting in the car waiting to pick up your friend, the quiet fifteen minutes you spend on the bus in the morning, while you wait to be picked up from school or work, and so on.

You'll find that these short but regular practices will greatly aid your recall of lots of information. They're a great way to add more study time to your schedule.

BREAK IT UP

When you have a list to memorize, break the list into groups of seven or any other odd number. People seem to remember best when they divide long lists into shorter ones—and, for some reason, shorter ones that have an odd number of items in them. So instead of trying to memorize ten vocabulary or spelling words, split your list into smaller lists of seven and three, or five and five, to help you remember them.

CREATE VISUAL AIDS

Give yourself visual assistance in memorizing. If there's a tricky combination of letters in a word you need to spell, for example, circle or underline it in red or highlight it in the text. Your eye will recall what the word looks like. With some information, you can even draw a map or picture to help you remember.

DO IT OUT LOUD

Give yourself auditory assistance in memorizing. Many people learn best if they *hear* the information. Sit by yourself in a quiet room and say aloud what you need to learn. Or, give your notes to someone else and let that person ask you or quiz you on the material.

USE MNEMONICS

Mnemonics, or memory tricks, are things that help you remember what you need to know.

The most common type of mnemonic is the acronym. One acronym you may already know is HOMES, for the names of the Great Lakes (Huron, Ontario, Michigan, Erie, and Superior). ROY G. BIV reminds people of the colors in the spectrum (Red, Orange, Yellow, Green, Blue, Indigo, and Violet).

You can make a mnemonic out of anything. In a psychology course, for example, you might memorize the stages in death and dying by the nonsense word DABDA (denial, anger, bargaining, depression, and acceptance.) Another kind of mnemonic is a silly sentence made out of words that each begin with the letter or letters that start each item in a series. You may remember "Please Excuse My Dear Aunt Sally" as a device for remembering the order of operations in math (parentheses, exponents, multiply, divide, add, and subtract).

SLEEP ON IT

When you study right before sleep and don't allow any interference—such as conversation, radio, television, or music—to come between study and sleep, you remember material better. This is especially true if you review first thing after waking as well. A rested and relaxed brain seems to hang on to information better than a tired and stressed-out brain.

On the following pages, try out some of the learning strategies you discovered in this lesson. Then, check your answers.

Below is a passage from this text to underline and annotate. Make margin summaries of the key points in each paragraph. Then make a mnemonic based on your margin notes.

Take Small Bites of Time

Most people memorize information best when they study in small periods over a long period of time.

Memorizing facts from index cards that can be carried with you and pulled out for a few ten-minute sessions each day will yield better results than sitting down with a textbook for an hour straight. You'll find that these short but regular practices will greatly aid your recall of lots of information. They're a great way to add more study time to your schedule.

Break It Up

When you have a list to memorize, break the list into groups of seven or any other odd number. People seem to remember best when they divide long lists into shorter ones—and, for some reason, shorter ones that have an odd number of items in them. So instead of trying to memorize ten vocabulary or spelling words, split your list into smaller lists of seven and three, or five and five, to help you remember them.

Create Visual Aids

Give yourself visual assistance in memorizing. If there's a tricky combination of letters in a word you need to spell, for example, circle or underline it in red or highlight it in the text. Your eye will recall what the word looks like.

Do It Out Loud

Give yourself auditory assistance in memorizing. Many people learn best if they hear the information. Sit by yourself in a quiet room and say aloud what you need to learn. Or, give your notes to someone else and let that person quiz you on the material.

Use Mnemonics

Mnemonics, or memory tricks, are things that help you remember what you need to know. The most common type of mnemonic is the acronym. One acronym you may already know is **HOMES**, for the names of the Great Lakes (**H**uron, **O**ntario, **M**ichigan, **E**rie, and **S**uperior). **ROY G. BIV** reminds people of the colors in the spectrum (**R**ed, **O**range, **Y**ellow, **G**reen, **B**lue, **I**ndigo, and **V**iolet).

Note Cards

Make note cards with definitions for each kind of learning modality:

- visual
- auditory
- kinesthetic

Mapping

Below is an outline of the learning strategies covered in this chapter. Using the same information, make a map or diagram of the same material.

    I.   How to study most effectively

        A.   Annotating

        B.   Outlining

        C.   Mapping

    II.   How to make study notes

        A.   Notebook pages

        B.   Index cards

            1.   Reasons for using index cards

   III. Memory methods

COMPLETED SAMPLE
ANNOTATION

Take Small Bites of Time

Distributed practice

Most people memorize information best when they study in <u>small periods over a long period of time.</u>

Memorizing facts from portable index cards that can be carried with you and pulled out for a few ten-minute sessions each day will yield better results than sitting down with a textbook for an hour straight. You'll find that these short but regular practices will greatly aid your recall of lots of information. They're a great way to add more study time to your schedule.

Break It Up

Divide lists

When you have a list to memorize, <u>break the list into groups of seven or any other odd number.</u> People seem to remember best when they divide long lists into shorter ones—and, for some reason, shorter ones that have an odd number of items in them. So instead of trying to memorize ten vocabulary or spelling words, split your list into smaller lists of seven and three, or five and five, to help you remember them.

Create Visual Aids

Visual Aids

<u>Give yourself visual assistance in memorizing.</u> If there's a tricky combination of letters in a word you need to spell, for example, circle or underline it in red or highlight it in the text. Your eye will recall what the word looks like.

Do It Out Loud

Auditory

<u>Give yourself auditory assistance in memorizing.</u> Many people learn best if they hear the information. Sit by yourself in a quiet room and say aloud what you need to learn. Or, give your notes to someone else and let that person ask you questions and quiz you on the material.

Use Mnemonics

<u>Mnemonics</u>, or memory tricks, are things that help you remember what you need to know.

Acronym

The most common type of mnemonic is the <u>acronym</u>. One acronym you may already know is **HOMES**, for the names of the Great Lakes (**H**uron, **O**ntario, **M**ichigan, **E**rie, and **S**uperior). **ROY G. BIV** reminds people of the colors in the spectrum (**R**ed, **O**range, **Y**ellow, **G**reen, **B**lue, **I**ndigo, and **V**iolet).

Sample Mnemonic
DDVAA

Note Cards
Here are samples of how your note cards might look:

FRONT OF CARD

Visual Modality	Auditory Modality	Kinesthetic Modality

BACK OF CARD

learning by seeing	learning by listening	learning by doing

Mapping
Here is an example of how your map or diagram might look:

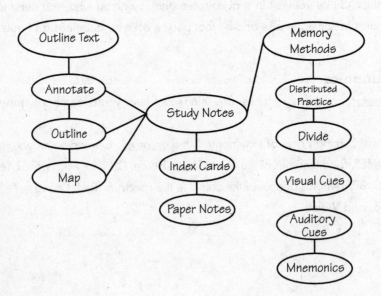

ADDITIONAL RESOURCES

The following resources will help you build your vocabulary beyond the words in this book. In this list, you will find print material to help you on your way to further word study. Before you look at any of the books listed below, you should get a good dictionary. For general reference at home, a collegiate or college dictionary should work just fine. Try *Merriam-Webster's Collegiate Dictionary*, 10th Edition. (Merriam-Webster, Inc., 1999). You can also refer to an on-line dictionary, such as Merriam-Webster's online dictionary, found at www.webster.com.

RECOMMENDED BOOKS

1001 Vocabulary & Spelling Questions (NY: LearningExpress, 1999).

Bromberg, Murray, and Julius Liebb. *601 Words You Need to Know to Pass Your Exam,* Third Edition (NY: Barron's Educational Series, 1997).

Bromberg, Murray, and Melvin Gordon. *1100 Words You Need to Know, 4th Edition* (NY: Barron's Educational Series, 2000).

Contemporary Vocabulary (NY: St. Martin's Press, 1997).

Cornog, Mary Wood. *Merriam Webster's Vocabulary Builder* (Springfield, MA: Merriam-Webster Publishing, Inc., 1994).

Elster, Charles Harrinton. *Verbal Advantage: 10 Steps to an Impressive Vocabulary* (NY: Random House Reference, 2000).

Funk, Wilfred John, and Norman Lewis. *30 Days to a More Powerful Vocabulary* (NY: Pocket Books, 1993).

Keen, Dennis. *Developing Vocabulary Skills* (Boston, MA: Heinle & Heinle ITP Publishers, 1994).

Kolby, Jeff. *Vocabulary 4000: The 4000 Words Essential for an Educated Vocabulary* (Los Angeles, CA: Nova Press, 2000).

Lewis, Norman. *Word Power Made Easy* (NY: Pocket Books, 1995).

Randol, Susan. Ed. *Random House Power Vocabulary Builder* (NY: Ballantine Books, 1996).

Robinson, Adam. *Word Smart: Building an Educated Vocabulary* (Princeton, NJ: Princeton Review Series, 2001).

Schur, Norman W. *1000 Most Important Words* (NY: Ballantine Books, 1995).